Mornings with JESUS 2020

DAILY ENCOURAGEMENT *for Your* SOUL

366 DEVOTIONS

SUSANNA FOTH AUGHTMON

ELIZABETH BERNE DEGEAR

TRACY ELDRIDGE

GWEN FORD FAULKENBERRY

GRACE FOX

HEIDI GAUL

SHARON HINCK

KATIE MINTER JONES

DIANNE NEAL MATTHEWS

MARLENE LEGASPI-MUNAR

CYNTHIA RUCHTI

ALICE THOMPSON

ISABELLA YOSUICO

Guideposts

New York

Mornings with Jesus 2020

Published by Guideposts Books & Inspirational Media
39 Old Ridgebury Rd,
Danbury, Connecticut 06810
Guideposts.org

Acknowledgments

Every attempt has been made to credit the sources of copyrighted material used in this book. If any such acknowledgment has been inadvertently omitted or miscredited, receipt of such information would be appreciated.

Scripture quotations marked (AMP) are taken from *The Amplified Bible* and *The Amplified Bible, Classic Edition*. Copyright © 2015 by The Lockman Foundation, La Habra, CA 90631. All rights reserved. Copyright © 1954, 1958, 1962, 1964, 1965, 1987 by The Lockman Foundation. Used by permission. www.Lockman.org

Scripture quotations marked (ERV) are taken from *Easy-to-Read Version Bible*. Copyright © 2006 by Bible League International.

Scripture quotations marked (ESV) are taken from the *Holy Bible, English Standard Version*, copyright © 2001 by Crossway Bibles, a division of Good News Publishers. Used by permission. All rights reserved.

Scripture quotations marked (GNT) are taken from *Good News Translation*. Copyright © 1992 by American Bible Society.

Scripture quotations marked (GW) are taken from *God's Word Translation*. Copyright © 1995 by God's Word to the Nations. Used by permission of Baker Publishing Group.

Scripture quotations marked (HCSB) are taken from the *Holman Christian Standard Bible*. Copyright © 1999, 2000, 2002, 2003 by Holman Bible Publishers, Nashville, Tennessee. All rights reserved.

Scripture quotations marked (ICB) are taken from *The Holy Bible, International Children's Bible*. Copyright© 1986, 1988, 1999, 2015 by Tommy Nelson, a division of Thomas Nelson. Used by permission.

Scripture quotations marked (ISV) are taken from *The International Standard Version of the Bible*. Copyright © 1995-2014 by ISV Foundation. All rights reserved internationally. Used by permission of Davidson Press, LL.

Scripture quotations marked (KJV) are taken from *The King James Version of the Bible*.

Scripture quotations marked (MSG) are taken from *The Message*. Copyright © 1993, 1994, 1995, 1996, 2000, 2001, 2002 by Eugene H. Peterson.

Scripture quotations marked (NAS) are taken from the *New American Standard Bible*. Copyright © 1960, 1962, 1963, 1968, 1971, 1972, 1973, 1975, 1977, 1995 by the Lockman Foundation. Used by permission. www.Lockman.org

Scripture quotations marked (NCV) are taken from the *New Century Version*. Copyright © 2005 by Thomas Nelson, Inc. Used by permission. All rights reserved.

Scripture quotations marked (NIV) are taken from two editions: *The Holy Bible, New International Version, NIV*. Copyright © 1973, 1978, 1984, 2011 by Biblica. All rights reserved worldwide. *The Holy Bible, New International Version*. Copyright © 1973, 1978, 1984 International Bible Society. Used by permission of Zondervan Bible Publishers.

Scripture quotations marked (NKJV) are taken from *The Holy Bible, New King James Version*. Copyright © , 1983, 1985, 1990, 1997 by Thomas Nelson, Inc.

Scripture quotations marked (NLT) are taken from the *Holy Bible, New Living Translation*. Copyright © 1996. Used by permission of Tyndale House Publishers, Inc., Wheaton, Illinois 60189. All rights reserved.

Scripture quotations marked (NRSV) are taken from the *New Revised Standard Version Bible*. Copyright © 1989 by the Division of Christian Education of the National Council of the Churches of Christ in the U.S.A. Used by permission. All rights reserved.

Scripture quotations marked (RSV) are taken from the *Revised Standard Version of the Bible*. Copyright © 1946, 1952, and 1971 the Division of Christian Education of the National Council of the Churches of Christ in the United States of America. Used by permission. All rights reserved.

Scripture quotations marked (TLB) are taken from *The Living Bible*. Copyright © 1971 by Tyndale House Foundation. Used by permission of Tyndale House Publishers Inc., Carol Stream, Illinois 60188. All rights reserved.

Cover and interior design by Müllerhaus
Cover photo by Shutterstock
Indexed by Indexing Research
Typeset by Aptara, Inc.

Printed and bound in the United States of America
10 9 8 7 6 5 4 3 2 1

Dear Friend,

This year Guideposts celebrates our seventy-fifth anniversary! While we remain grounded in our dynamic history, we are most excited to continue to spread the message that anything is possible with hope, faith, and prayer.

Welcome to *Mornings with Jesus 2020*! Whether you are a new reader or are already familiar with this devotional, know that each reading, like the voice of a trusted friend, offers inspiration, hope, and the peace that comes from walking with Him.

This year is a leap year, so we're delighted to present 366 devotions to encourage your soul and deepen your walk with Jesus. This daily devotional was written lovingly by thirteen women of faith. As these women share their experiences of how Jesus is at work in their lives and they learn to celebrate life's milestones with joy, courage, and sometimes tears, we hope you will see yourself in their stories.

Beloved *Mornings with Jesus* writers Susanna Foth Aughtmon, Gwen Ford Faulkenberry, Heidi Gaul, Sharon Hinck, Dianne Neal Matthews, Cynthia Ruchti, and Isabella Yosuico are back in fine form, along with Grace Fox, who has *graced* us with a series of Holy Week devotions. Authors Alice Thompson, Katie Minter Jones, Tracy Eldridge, and Marlene Legaspi-Munar make their debuts this year and share their passion for Jesus.

Jesus said, "Abide in Me, and I in you. As the branch cannot bear fruit of itself, unless it abides in the vine, neither can you, unless you abide in Me." (John 15:4, NKJV) *Mornings with Jesus 2020* is a precious reminder that He is longing to spend time with you.

Mornings with Jesus 2020 will help you cherish your time with Him each day. It is our hope that you are inspired by each Scripture, encouraged by each reading, and motivated daily to take a "Faith Step" as you walk with Jesus and abide in His love.

Faithfully yours,
Editors of Guideposts

NEW YEAR'S DAY, WEDNESDAY, JANUARY 1

Whoever can be trusted with very little can also be trusted with much.
Luke 16:10 (NIV)

I USED TO MAKE A list a mile long of New Year's resolutions. I would write things like lose fifty pounds, play Rachmaninoff's Prelude in C-sharp minor, become fluent in French, run a half marathon, memorize the book of John. When it came to the end of the year, I usually felt like a failure, but then I'd start over with a new list for the new year.

Then I observed my own kids. One day, I laid my baby on her tummy. She got stronger, and soon she was sitting up. Rocking and scooting turned to crawling. And after that, pulling up. Within a year she took her first step.

I taught them music starting with middle C. Then we moved on to basic rhythms and sharps and flats. Over time, by doing a little each day, they learned to play songs. Same with reading. First the ABCs. Then the way each letter sounds. Then what happens when you put those sounds together. Voilà! Words. It's amazing.

With children, you start out with one small step. Why do I always want to start with the bigger things? Jesus tells us in Luke 16:10 that the best place to start is with one small step. Do one thing, then do the next. First a very little, then much.

Now I don't even make New Year's resolutions. I just pick three things I really want to grow in and write them down, so Jesus and I can work on them together, one day at a time. A little here, a little there, trusting He'll get me where He wants me to go. In His time.
—GWEN FORD FAULKENBERRY

FAITH STEP: *Take your first steps today in the three areas you have decided to grow. Don't try to do too much. A year of baby steps adds up to a lot of growth if you stick with it!*

THURSDAY, JANUARY 2

Trust in the LORD with all your heart and lean not on your own understanding;
in all your ways submit to him, and he will make your paths straight.
Proverbs 3:5–6 (NIV)

I DISCOVERED MY LOVE OF writing in junior high. I wrote stories about girls who wore purple eye shadow and teal mascara. (I was forbidden to wear eye makeup until high school.) I poured all my angst into those stories. Writing became my creative outlet and safe place. Jesus has an unpredictable way of bringing our dreams full circle. Here I am, decades later, teaching junior-high schoolers how to write, unleashing dreams and potential. I'm offering a space of creativity along with a side of homework. I'm pretty sure that purple eye shadow and teal mascara are a thing again. *What are the odds?*

When I started looking for a job this past year, I wasn't even thinking of teaching. I was looking into administrative work and writing content for large companies. Jesus had other ideas. He puts us in places where we have to rely on Him. Places where we know that He's in charge and that He's *the only One* who can get us through. Jesus flings open doors of opportunity that make us more than a little sweaty. He sends opportunities where fear grips the backs of our throats and sets our hearts pounding. (Opportunities like teaching vocabulary to twenty-five sixth graders!) He wants our fears to launch us toward faith. Then He grins and says, "Do you trust Me? Because together we can do this." He's asking us to let go of *our own understanding* so that He can *make our paths straight*. —SUSANNA FOTH AUGHTMON

FAITH STEP: *What is the next step that you're getting ready to take? Are you banking on your own understanding? Ask Jesus to make your path straight. Listen for His leading.*

FRIDAY, JANUARY 3

We know that we have come to know him if we keep his commands. . . .
But if anyone obeys his word, love for God is truly made complete in them.
1 John 2:3, 5 (NIV)

LAST YEAR I JOINED A gym. I'd let too much time pass by without any regular exercise. It showed, in both my tight clothing and doctor's bills. It was time to get back in shape.

I began going to the gym three mornings a week. At first it was grueling, but soon physical benefits became apparent. The various machines and weights became as familiar as old friends.

Then I fell ill and missed several weeks. When I finally was strong enough to return, the circuit seemed impossible. I gritted my teeth and forced myself to participate. My muscles screamed at me, and I was tempted to stop going altogether. But every time I went back, it became easier. The weights didn't strain my arms and legs as much. And if I had to postpone a workout, my muscles missed it.

When I first became a Christian as an adult, many of the "rules" seemed constricting, and I questioned their necessity. I prioritized myself over Jesus, letting faith take a backseat to my lifestyle. Soon I became spiritually flabby. But my soul hungered for Jesus. The more hours I spent in Scripture, the more I enjoyed it. As I increased my prayer time, my relationship with Jesus, once tenuous, blossomed.

Just as my body requires regular exercise, my soul craves Jesus. My newest goal is to be spiritually fit. I desire the faith inside me to reflect Christ's peace. When I meet others, I hope it shows. —HEIDI GAUL

FAITH STEP: *Strengthen your faith in a new way. Read a chapter of the Bible daily or pray for a specific people group. Increase your quiet time. Read a Christian leader's biography. Sing praises to Jesus. Stretch those spiritual muscles!*

SATURDAY, JANUARY 4

If the Son therefore shall make you free, ye shall be free indeed.
John 8:36 (KJV)

I READ HEALTH AND FITNESS magazines during my trips to the hair salon. One day while waiting to be served, I read an article about food addiction. The writer shared her battle with obesity and went on to say that many addictions are due to family genetics. I thought of my family and the variety of food, drug, and emotional habits that some family members have overcome by the power of grace.

The hymn "Amazing Grace" should be my family's official anthem. *Through many dangers, toils, and snares we have already come. 'Tis grace that brought us safe thus far and grace will lead us home.*

My uncle Jay is one family member who has been transparent in sharing his struggles. For five years, he was plagued by a debilitating drug addiction. My uncle found his sobriety through a rehabilitation treatment program and keeps a daily schedule that includes meeting with a Narcotics Anonymous group. Uncle Jay has remained sober for twenty years. However, when he visits my home, inevitably our conversations turn to his triumph over those dark years. Each time, I ask the same question: "How did you beat it?" "It wasn't me," my uncle replies. "Jesus set me free."

Not one negative habit or situation is too hard for Jesus to repair or remove from my life. That is what my uncle's liberation proves to me. Today he is a shining vision of healthy living. And the same healing balm in Jesus that delivered him from the tentacles of addiction is available to you and me, right now. —ALICE THOMPSON

FAITH STEP: *Do you struggle with a habit that hinders your personal advancement? Pray today for a transformed mind in this new year and ask Jesus to reveal His exit plan for your release.*

SUNDAY, JANUARY 5

And Jesus said to him, "Today salvation has come to this house, since he also is a son of Abraham. For the Son of Man came to seek and to save the lost." Luke 19:9–10 (ESV)

IN LUKE 19 WE LEARN ABOUT ZACCHAEUS, a tax collector who was so short he had to climb a tree to see Jesus as He was passing through Jericho. When Jesus looked up and saw Zacchaeus, Jesus immediately invited Himself to Zacchaeus's house! The people in the crowd didn't think Zacchaeus was worthy of Jesus's attention. In their eyes Zacchaeus was just a sinful tax collector. But it didn't matter what they thought because Jesus thought Zacchaeus *was* worthy of both His presence and salvation.

I'm so grateful that Jesus cared about me enough to save me. He willingly gave His life for mine. And it doesn't matter what anyone else thinks. Anthony Brown and Group Therapy's song "Worth" brings tears to my eyes every time I hear it because the lyrics so powerfully convey the depth of Jesus's thoughts toward us. Because Jesus sees us as worthy, He saved us, cleaned us up, and sacrificed His life for ours so we could be made whole.

Sometimes I get so discouraged about things in my life or choices I've made that I don't feel worthy of anything. But then I remember that Paul said in Philippians 1:6 that I should be confident in the knowledge that Jesus will complete the work He started in me. So I remind myself that I'm worthy because Jesus thinks I am. I rest in knowing that He'll never give up on me. It's wonderful to know that Jesus considers me worthy. —TRACY ELDRIDGE

FAITH STEP: *We all face moments when we feel unworthy. Today, meditate on Philippians 1:6 and remember that Jesus isn't finished with you! You are worthy in His eyes.*

MONDAY, JANUARY 6

And a voice from heaven said, "This is my Son, whom I love;
with him I am well pleased." Matthew 3:17 (NIV)

GLORY ABOUNDED AT JESUS'S BAPTISM. The heavens opened as the Holy Spirit of God descended like a dove upon Him. Then God spoke of our Lord, claiming Him and encouraging Him with words of love. I can't imagine a more beautiful scene of power and hope. But in the very next verse, Jesus was led by the Spirit into the desert to be tempted by the devil. It's as if a giant pendulum swung from the best times possible to a great trial.

Recently my daughter changed jobs, moving to an office where she would face challenges, at least for a while. I've been a mother for more than thirty years, and whenever I've see her heading into a trial, be it a childish quarrel at age nine or something much more involved at twentysomething, I've always reassured her. I put my own spin on the words our Father said to Jesus in Matthew 3:17: "I love you, honey. I'm proud of you. And I know you'll do great."

I'm not sure what the future holds for my daughter. But I believe she can count on the Lord to lead her safely through every rough spot, just as Jesus depended on His Father for help. No matter the temptations, my beloved daughter knows to fall back on her faith—and the Word—when times get tough.

God spoke to our Lord, and Jesus listened. Through His Father's support, He embodied faith, knowing things would be all right. I hold to that certainty. Now so does my child. —HEIDI GAUL

FAITH STEP: *Look back on times you've found yourself head-to-head with temptation. How did God reassure you before those challenges? Rest easy, knowing that as He did for Jesus, our Father will lead us through.*

TUESDAY, JANUARY 7

Then Jesus shouted, "Lazarus, come out!" And the dead man came out, his hands and feet bound in graveclothes, his face wrapped in a headcloth. Jesus told them, "Unwrap him and let him go!" John 11:43–44 (NLT)

A FRIEND OF MINE IS an image consultant. She helps clients sort their clothes, decide what to keep and what to discard, and shop for new items. Together they develop a personal wardrobe that complements the client's skin tone and body type and reflects his or her personality. Did you know the Bible mentions wardrobes? Take Lazarus's story. He was buried wearing graveclothes designed for the dead. His outfit was appropriate for the occasion, but it became outdated the moment Jesus brought him back to life. "Unwrap him," Jesus commanded. In other words, strip off the old and don the new—clothes fit for the living. As believers, we ought to pay attention to our spiritual wardrobe. Colossians 3:5–9 describes our grave clothes prior to placing our faith in Jesus: sexual sin, shameful desires, anger, rage, malicious behavior, slander, dirty language, and lies. The moment Jesus gives us new life, those grave clothes no longer reflect who we are. We're to discard them and clothe ourselves in mercy, kindness, humility, gentleness, and patience (v. 12). We're to make allowance for each other's faults and forgive those who offend us (v. 13). The most important piece of clothing we're to wear is love (v. 14). My friend meets clients who hesitate to part with old, familiar outfits. She encourages them to be ruthless and to invest in new clothes that work better for them. Let's do the same with our spiritual wardrobe. We're alive in Christ, so let's clothe ourselves in a wardrobe that reflects Him. —GRACE FOX

FAITH STEP: *Look in your closet for a piece of clothing you no longer wear. If it's in good condition, give it to someone who will enjoy it. If not, discard it. Liken it to discarding a sinful attitude or behavior.*

WEDNESDAY, JANUARY 8

If anyone would come after me, let him deny himself and take up his cross and follow me. Matthew 16:24 (ESV)

"WALK THIS WAY," THE BUTLER said. Then he proceeded to limp his way noisily across a foyer. The visitor who followed did the same, mimicking his limp/stomp/limp/stomp, hunched over, listing-to-one-side posture. A classic comedic moment. Most credit the scene's origin to the movie *Young Frankenstein,* but the comedic gesture first appeared in the 1936 movie *After the Thin Man.*

The literalism of the follower's response added the layer of humor.

How different the scene when Jesus is the one instructing, "Walk this way." He means it. Literally.

Stepping into His footprints, walking like He walked. Offering a kind word. Stooping to heal and bless. Moving among the hungry and thirsty, offering the Bread of Life and Living Water. Rising early to be alone with the Father to pray. Forgiving those who rejected, reviled, and crucified Him.

I may be required to walk stooped over, limping, stumbling, as He did on the way to Golgotha's hill. He said that following Him means taking up our crosses—however heavy—and moving forward. He walked dusty, steep, lonely paths and asked us to do likewise.

If I complain about the discomforts I face for His sake, the sacrifices I'm required to make in order to reach the people He calls me to reach, I can imagine Jesus saying, "I asked you to walk this way. And you agreed to follow. I'm right here, leading the way. Let's move." —CYNTHIA RUCHTI

FAITH STEP: *How closely does your daily walk mimic Jesus's strides? Are you leaving a trail behind you of people who are encouraged, uplifted, healed, fed, and quenched? Take a step today and follow His footprints.*

THURSDAY, JANUARY 9

Jesus turned and saw her. "Take heart, daughter," he said,
"your faith has healed you." And the woman was healed at that moment.
Matthew 9:22 (NIV)

IN THE NORTHWEST, PRECIPITATION CAN be part of the weather forecast for months at a time. When it's not raining, the skies look like a flat gray sheet of metal. Some people, myself included, are deeply affected by the lack of sunlight. The condition is called seasonal affective disorder (SAD), and symptoms can manifest as depression and anxiety, among others. Some treatments involve special lamps and vitamin D supplements. I've tried them with little success. I've found myself crying often over nothing at all.

One day, a friend said, "Look up. There's a little spot of blue, right there." I lifted my gaze to the dreary sky, and indeed, there was a speck of blue. I felt like I'd been thrown a lifeline. I stared at the tiny break in the clouds and couldn't tear my eyes free.

Sometimes no amount of treatments or therapies can help us as much as the promise of heaven and the hope we receive through Jesus. A whole world of light and life awaits us, beyond what we can see. When earthly forms of medicine fail, I can turn to the Great Physician for help. He'll never leave or disappoint me.

I only need to trust in Jesus and be patient. He'll either lift my mood or stay by my side as I wait for spring. Whatever trials I encounter, I try to remember there are blue skies and sunshine just out of sight. I only need to keep searching the skies. And have faith to hold on and wait. —HEIDI GAUL

FAITH STEP: *Sometimes Jesus heals by removing the pain and sometimes by staying with us as we wait it out. Pray for Him to carry you through a trial or an illness you're enduring.*

FRIDAY, JANUARY 10

For in Him we live and move and exist [that is, in Him we actually have our being]. Acts 17:28 (AMP)

OUR SEVENTY-EIGHT-YEAR-OLD DAD WAS EXPERIENCING shortness of breath, and we rushed him to the hospital. A 2-D echo test was ordered, and in the examination room I saw a sonogram of the heart for the first time. I was struck with awe as I saw the images of my father's heart and heard it beat as it pumped rhythmically.

A line from Francis Chan's book *Crazy Love* came to mind: "The majority of us take for granted our kidneys, liver, lungs, and other internal organs that we're dependent upon to continue living." How very true. It's not until we experience a sharp pain or have difficulty breathing that we become concerned. We forget that our lives are a vapor, and we can die at any moment.

My father was treated and discharged from the hospital, but this incident reminded me that I only live and move and exist because of Jesus. Not only does He give me life, but according to Galatians 2:20, Jesus lives in *me*. The way to live while still here on earth is by trusting, moment by moment, the Son of God who loved me and gave Himself for me. As long as Jesus allows my heart to keep beating, then I will let His love fill me to the brim, so I can love Him back and extend that love to others. —MARLENE LEGASPI-MUNAR

FAITH STEP: *Thank God that you are alive! Remember that "in Him you live and move." If you are able, do doctor-approved cardiovascular exercises that are appropriate for you. Encourage those closest to you to take care of their hearts too.*

SATURDAY, JANUARY 11

And He said to them, "Follow Me [as My disciples, accepting Me as your Master and Teacher and walking the same path of life that I walk], and I will make you fishers of men." Matthew 4:19 (AMP)

GRANNY'S MEATBALL RECIPE IS A family favorite. I tried to duplicate it today and got close. But I've never quite mastered her flavors. Years ago, I sat at her kitchen table with my notepad and pen. "How much milk? How much bread?" I asked her.

She shrugged and answered, "Until it feels right." Then as she made the roux, she said, "Add butter until it's a good thickness." She didn't measure, but she had a relationship with the ingredients. Her experience and her interaction with the food—the way it looked, felt, sounded, smelled, and tasted—produced amazing meals.

As a follower of Jesus, I'd prefer a quick recipe for living my life with Him. Mix a third of a cup of service with a third of a cup of worship, stir, and simmer with exactly two ounces of love. Instead, Jesus asks me to have a relationship with Him—much more nuanced and complicated. Following in His steps doesn't involve a checklist. True discipleship requires interacting with Him constantly: remembering His teaching, listening for His direction, opening our eyes to where He is at work in our home and community.

Just as Granny adapted her recipes each time, Jesus helps us adjust our activities, change course when necessary, and bring out the best flavors in our lives. The basic ingredients don't change—scriptural truth is constant. But as Jesus meets us where we are, He shows us new ways to apply those truths as we follow Him. —SHARON HINCK

FAITH STEP: *As you prepare your next meal, think about ways Jesus may be inviting you to adjust your life recipe.*

SUNDAY, JANUARY 12

*Instead of being motivated by selfish ambition or vanity,
each of you should, in humility, be moved to treat one another
as more important than yourself. Philippians 2:3 (NET)*

CONVERSATIONS WITH MY GRANDCHILDREN ARE always filled with
life lessons. While I was sharing lunch with my oldest granddaughter
one Sunday, our server approached our table apologetically. A walking cast kept her from hurrying our order to us.

My granddaughter—normally introverted and admittedly uncomfortable making conversation with strangers—piped up. "No need
to apologize," she said. "Feel better soon."

"Thank you," the server said, a smile replacing her frown.

I commended my granddaughter for her kindness to the server.

My granddaughter replied, "It's not that hard to be a decent person. You just have to think of someone else instead of yourself."

That line has stayed with me. *It's not that hard to be a decent
person*—her version of what Jesus taught. His scribes worded it
this way: "Be kind to one another, tenderhearted, forgiving one
another" (Ephesians 4:32, ESV). "Regard others as more important than yourselves" (Philippians 2:3, AMP). "Love one another"
(John 13:34, NIV).

In a culture where public unkindness has become an unpleasant
and destructive trend, it blessed me to hear a young person standing firm on a Jesus principle, acknowledging that His millennia-
old idea is workable, doable, and the only smart way to live.
—CYNTHIA RUCHTI

FAITH STEP: *Jesus is alive, and so is His kindness—and it lives through you.
Show someone today that it's not hard to be a decent person.*

MONDAY, JANUARY 13

My heart has heard you say, "Come and talk with me."
And my heart responds, "LORD, I am coming." Psalm 27:8 (NLT)

BEING A MILITARY FAMILY, OUR daughter, son-in-law, and grand-children lived in three different states in 2017. In November, my husband and I helped them move across the country. During a FaceTime call a few weeks later, Lilah, our three-year-old grand-daughter, begged us to come visit again. "Nana and Paw Paw, can you come *home*?"

I almost cried at Lilah's invitation, partly because it was so sweet but also because the word *home* stirs up mixed feelings. When asked where I'm from, I often say I'm not really sure. Is home where I spent the first thirty years of my life? Or the state where we raised three children and lived for another thirty years? Since then, my husband and I have lived in three other states. So where exactly is home?

A child like Lilah instinctively knows the answer: home is where you're with people who love you. So it's good to remember that wherever I move, the One who loves me most is always with me. Sometimes I can hear Jesus asking a question similar to Lilah's: "My child, will you come home?" Every day He invites me to spend time with Him. Opening His Word and letting His Spirit teach me. Talking to Him about my burdens. Soaking up His goodness and unconditional love.

Deep down I know that earth is not my true home. One day Jesus will lead me to my forever home. Until then, I'm learning the joy of being in His presence. That's where I feel most at home.
—DIANNE NEAL MATTHEWS

FAITH STEP: *The next time you feel unsettled, go to Jesus in prayer. Ask Him to help you feel at home in Him.*

TUESDAY, JANUARY 14

You belong to your father, the devil, and you want to carry out your father's desires. He was a murderer from the beginning, not holding to the truth, for there is no truth in him. When he lies, he speaks his native language, for he is a liar and the father of lies. John 8:44 (NIV)

UNTIL RECENTLY, FEAR HAD BEEN the Achilles' heel the enemy used to hinder me. In my spiritual battle against fear, one acronym is a handy weapon: False Evidence Appearing Real (FEAR).

A subtle foe, fear sometimes shows up as rational caution, common sense, or legitimate concern. Apart from truly legitimate fears, like fleeing a burning house or falling off a cliff, many of our fears are hidden in half-truths or unknowns. But if you give fear an inch, it'll take a yard or more.

I've noticed a common thread when fear crops up: some smidgen of fact—a phone call, letter, doctor's report, or some other seemingly concrete evidence—will promptly lead to a sense of foreboding. I used to give myself over to dread and worry, assuming the worst. But I've discovered that almost always the reality is more benign. Sometimes nothing at all happens, and my fretting was fruitless.

Now whatever pops up, whether "good" or "bad," I pause, praise, and pray. I attend to whatever it is without projecting or jumping to conclusions, knowing Jesus goes with me wherever I go. I admit it sometimes feels risky to not immediately brace for the worst, but the peace I've gained through this practice is priceless.
—ISABELLA YOSUICO

FAITH STEP: *Whatever you face today, bring it to Jesus, who is the Truth!*

WEDNESDAY, JANUARY 15

So I say to you: Ask and it will be given to you; seek and you will find; knock and the door will be opened to you. Luke 11:9 *(NIV)*

THE OTHER DAY, I WAS reminded of how much times are changing. I was talking with a wise and elderly friend of mine, a nun by the name of Sister Mary Kay. Last year, her community had to sell their retirement home, so now, instead of the older generation of nuns living together next door to their younger sisters, Mary Kay and the other elders are dispersed in a number of nursing homes run by strangers.

Mary Kay, ever the optimist, is making the best of the situation and sees it as an opportunity to expand her sense of community. But she said the hardest part is that the fire code mandates that her door remain closed. After living life with an open-door policy in an environment where companionship flowed abundantly, Mary Kay is finding a new policy in a new environment to be creating isolation for her.

My heart hurts whenever I picture those closed doors. I think of Jesus letting us know that if we knock, He will always open the door to us. I guess I've always imagined us knocking to get *in* and Jesus opening the door to welcome us *inside*. But as I pray for Mary Kay and the other nuns, I now realize that sometimes when we knock, we're the ones who are inside, and we need Jesus to free us to come out and to let others pour in.

Following Jesus can mean opening doors—literal and metaphorical—that create isolation between ourselves and others. —ELIZABETH BERNE DEGEAR

FAITH STEP: *Who in your life may be experiencing isolation right now? Picture that isolation as a door and ask Jesus to open it. Imagine love and laughter crossing that doorway, back and forth, until isolation dissolves into joyful community.*

THURSDAY, JANUARY 16

Fear not, for I have redeemed you; I have called you by your name;
You are Mine. Isaiah 43:1 (NKJV)

EVERY TIME I READ THIS Scripture I get excited: Jesus knows my name! I am important to Him! One day, I decided to look up the meaning of my name. According to several websites, Tracy means *brave*, *fighter*, or *warrior*, but my mom wasn't thinking of any of those meanings when she named me. As she tells it, the story went something like this: "Sammy Davis Jr.'s daughter's name was Tracy. I'd never heard the name before, and I liked it." So there was nothing deep about how I got my name.

Although there may be no truth to the claims of baby name origins, I have decided to declare that I am a brave fighter-warrior. Fear was my constant companion so many times in my life, and I allowed it to rule me and render me a coward. I no longer run away from painful situations or avoid confronting problems head-on because walking with Jesus has given me a new foundation on which to stand. Paul said in 2 Corinthians 5:17 (NIV) that if I am in Christ, I am a "new creation." Jesus gave me the power to step on "all the power of the enemy" without being hurt (Luke 10:19, KJV), but the bigger victory is that my name is written in heaven.

There are still times that irrational fear tries to take over my thought process, but I remember that my name is brave, so I fight back and tell fear to take a hike. Jesus called me by my name. He redeemed me and I am His, so I have no reason to fear. —TRACY ELDRIDGE

FAITH STEP: *Google your name just for fun. Is the meaning a reflection of you? Whatever you find, take heart that Jesus knows your name and you are His new creation. He will help you overcome your fears.*

FRIDAY, JANUARY 17

As Jesus was going down the road, he saw Matthew sitting at his tax collector's booth. "Follow me and be my disciple," Jesus said to him. So Matthew got up and followed him. Matthew 9:9 (NLT)

THE FAITH COMMUNITY IN WHICH I grew up focused on following religious rules. Card games were banned, as were movies and dancing. I was pulled from gym class when the teacher introduced square dancing.

After high school graduation, I attended a Bible college with a strict adherence to rules. Contemporary worship music was forbidden, as were earrings and makeup. Speaking to a student of the opposite sex without permission almost guaranteed a visit to the dean's office.

For years I equated being a good rule follower with being a good Christian. Over time, Jesus revealed the error in my thinking. When He extended an invitation to someone, He never said, "Come, follow a long list of rules designed to make you a better Christian." He said, "Come, be My disciple. Follow Me."

Following religious rules doesn't make us mature believers. It makes us fearful of the consequences for breaking them and judgmental toward those who don't adhere to them. In contrast, following Jesus places the emphasis on a relationship with Him. When that friendship becomes our focus, everything else falls into place.

Here's the irony: being Jesus's disciple means we follow rules designed to make us better Christians. But His rules are different than man's. Man-made rules lead to fear and legalism. Christ's rules develop our spiritual maturity and lead to intimacy with Him.
—GRACE FOX

FAITH STEP: *Identify one man-made rule you think makes you more godly. Ask Jesus to free you and teach you how to follow Him.*

SATURDAY, JANUARY 18

And we know that in all things God works for the good of those who love him, who have been called according to his purpose. Romans 8:28 (NIV)

MY FIRST YEAR OF TEACHING has been pretty stressful. My coworker Crystal likes to remind me that most teachers don't make it to their second year. I can believe it. Middle school is no joke. The funny thing is that I feel a kinship with my middle schoolers. I want to tell them, "I feel exactly as you feel right now! Weird. Uncertain. And a little scared." But I also want to encourage them: "Middle school is a cuckoo-crazy season of life, but you are going to be okay. You may not feel great about yourself. You may be longing for a different life. But the good stuff is coming. Just give it a couple years. I know. I've been there!"

Their story is still in the process of being written. And so is yours. And mine. We need to hear the same truth. *Life is stressful... but we are going to be okay. The good stuff is coming. All the joy and hope and peace we need? It's right around the corner.* Jesus promised us that He works everything together for our good. The good, the bad, the bright, the dark, the beautiful, and the ugly. He is weaving our lives together into a story of hope. The stresses of today will be the testimonies of tomorrow. His goodness will always come through. He will use the difficult chapters of our lives to bring us closer to Him, shaping our character, reminding us of His faithfulness. In the midst of our struggles is a good time to remember that Jesus's stories always have the best endings. —SUSANNA FOTH AUGHTMON

FAITH STEP: *What chapter of your life are you in right now? Remind yourself that you are midstory. Jesus is weaving together the story of your life for His glory.*

SUNDAY, JANUARY 19

When the priests withdrew from the Holy Place, the cloud filled the temple of the LORD. And the priests could not perform their service because of the cloud, for the glory of the LORD filled his temple. 1 Kings 8:10–11 (NIV)

I GLANCED AT MY WATCH from my perch on the organ bench. Fifteen minutes until the church service would begin. I checked the organ stops, adjusted the bench, and rearranged my music. I'd prepared a challenging prelude and was nervous about a few of the hymn arrangements. The pews were filling. Murmured conversations floated in from the lobby, and the pastor settled his sermon notes on the pulpit.

The worship service flew by, and I held the last chord of the postlude, releasing it with a flourish of satisfaction. Until it hit me. I'd spent the past hour preoccupied with the tasks involved in a church service and hadn't even acknowledged the holy presence of Jesus. I was busy in my service to Him yet missed out because my focus was on those details. I lost sight of Him.

I wonder how the priests felt when Solomon dedicated the temple. Like me, they probably took their responsibilities seriously and were focused intently on their tasks of offering sacrifices. Yet the Lord's presence fell with so much glory, they had to stop what they were doing.

Serving Jesus is a wonderful thing: church committees, soup kitchens, ministries that we support with a passion, mission trips, rehearsing with the praise team, teaching a Bible study. Like the priests of old, He's called us each to serve in some way. But let's focus beyond those tangible tasks. Let's leave room for Jesus to interrupt and stop us in our tracks. The glorious presence of the Lord is waiting to fill the temple of our hearts. —SHARON HINCK

FAITH STEP: *Pause in the middle of a task that you are doing for Jesus, and ask Him to make you more aware of His presence.*

MONDAY, JANUARY 20

For where your treasure is, there your heart will be also. Matthew 6:21 (NIV)

I'M A DREAMER. I INHERITED this questionable "gift" from my father, a child at heart. Whenever his eyes took on that faraway look, I knew he was somewhere wonderful, a million miles away. Now I know this because I go there too.

Long ago, a myriad of ideas danced inside my head. I wanted my own inn. The next year I wished for a vintage car. Like soap bubbles floating free in the breeze, all those dreams drifted off and disappeared. And the goals I did achieve left me no happier than before.

Like the saying "Life happens," it did. Boy, did it! After a few setbacks and a lot of time, I gained a deeper understanding of contentment. I learned the difference between a want, a need—and a wish. Which means I don't dream smaller, I dream differently.

I use a mental checklist now, one geared toward an abundant life, not an empty existence of constantly reaching for more. I ask myself, *Are these material desires and experiences self-centered, or motivated to please the Lord? Could Jesus fill this void better than what I've chosen? Will the takeaway be temporary or eternal?*

If the answers to these questions don't jibe, I need to find a better way to spend my time and money. Joyce Meyer said, "If selfishness is the key to being miserable, then selflessness must be the key to being happy!" There's nothing wrong with dreaming and having goals. The problem lies in thinking possessions or excitement will fulfill my needs.

I still dream, but now my eyes are open. My "dream come true" is Jesus. What more could I want? —HEIDI GAUL

FAITH STEP: *Create a new type of bucket list. Number it and write at the top, "To Give Jesus Glory I'll . . ." Think of ways to honor Him. Develop a taste for these lasting treasures. Dream big!*

TUESDAY, JANUARY 21

See, God has come to save me. I will trust in him and not be afraid.
The LORD GOD is my strength and my song; he has given me victory.
Isaiah 12:2 (NLT)

I HADN'T RECOGNIZED MY LOVE for and dependence upon a predictable, daily routine until I lost it. For two years prior, I'd habitually risen at 5:00 a.m., spent an hour at the gym, returned home to enjoy my quiet time with Jesus, and then started work in my office. My husband and I ate our day's larger meal together at noon, and then I returned to my office for several hours.

Our move to the boat, immediately followed by a five-week trip overseas and then four weekends of traveling for speaking engagements, erased the word *routine* from my vocabulary. I yearned for the familiar and craved the security I felt it offered me.

One morning I caught myself thinking, *If only I could return to my old schedule, then everything would be okay.* That's when I sensed Jesus challenge me to align my thoughts with the truth.

Do not make an idol of your daily rituals, Jesus said. *They aren't the source of your strength and joy and peace; I am.* He was right! I hated to admit it, but I'd unconsciously credited my routine rather than Christ's presence and promises with the ability to satisfy my heart's needs. I would've never used the word *idol*, but that's exactly what my routines had become because I'd placed my faith in them rather than in Jesus to save me during the turmoil of transition.

Jesus graciously reminded me to return my focus to Him. In doing so, I discovered that I didn't need my old routine for everything to be okay. I had Jesus, and He was enough. —GRACE FOX

FAITH STEP: *Fill in the blank: "If only I could (have) _____, then every-thing would be okay." How does your answer align with the truth that Jesus is enough?*

TUESDAY, JANUARY 22

A leper came to him begging him, and kneeling he said to him,
"If you choose, you can make me clean." Moved with pity,
Jesus stretched out his hand and touched him, and said to him,
"I do choose. Be made clean!" Mark 1:40–41 (NRSV)

SOMEONE TOLD ME, "SHOW ME your calendar and I'll show you who you are." That's stuck with me, and convicted me. I think of myself as a person who spends time wisely *on what matters.* So when my schedule gets full of meetings and work/writing deadlines, I have to adjust for family time: drinking coffee with my parents; carving out time for my husband and my kids, including reading to Stella, fishing with Harper, piano with Adelaide, running with Grace.

As I follow Jesus around through the Gospels, one thing that interests me most is how He spends His time. His calendar gives us a clear picture of who He was. He's visited by shepherds. A man who eats locusts prepares the way for His ministry, and His best friends are smelly fishermen. Here's the list from Matthew 4:14 of who He's concerned about: "all who were ill with various diseases, those suffering severe pain, the demon-possessed, those having seizures, and the paralyzed" (NIV). Children. Prostitutes. Tax collectors. Samaritans. Gentiles. Slaves. I could go on. If I was there to follow Jesus around, I'd be afraid of the people and places He encountered. And He didn't only see them. Over and over again: He touched them. *I do choose. Jesus stretched out His hand.*

If Jesus is the embodiment of God's will on earth, then it's clear what His will is for us as His church, His people. What does our calendar show the world about who we are? —GWEN FORD FAULKENBERRY

FAITH STEP: *Get out your calendar and take inventory of where you spend your time. Offer it to Jesus and follow where He leads.*

THURSDAY, JANUARY 23

*In the world you will have tribulation; but be of good cheer,
I have overcome the world. John 16:33 (NKJV)*

DO YOU EVER FIND YOURSELF uncertain of how to console someone who is going through a difficult time? Today I spoke with someone who is in a difficult emotional place. She doesn't live near me, but whenever I speak with her about her problems, I want to run to her and wrap my arms around her to erase her pain. At times I get confused as to how to reply. *Do I need to offer words of comfort every time we speak, or does she just need to talk?* Quietly I will ask Jesus for a word of encouragement to give to her. *Do I say some popular Scripture that can almost appear to be trite?* I want to comfort and encourage her but not be so busy giving encouragement that it seems I am not acknowledging her pain. There are times I just simply say, "I love you, and I am praying with you through this tough time." Or I just pray with her on the phone.

Despite those questions swirling through my head when I talk to my friend, I often feel compelled to mention a Scripture or let her know the desire of Jesus to comfort her. Jesus is the healer of broken hearts. When He was surrounded by masses of hurting people, He had compassion for them. Jesus tells us to "be of good cheer" even when we are facing turbulent times. We can do that because He has overcome the world. Whether we are comforting people who share our faith or others who are struggling, we should put them in remembrance of the sweet, tender words of Jesus that are able to sustain. —TRACY ELDRIDGE

FAITH STEP: *The next time you speak to someone in need of compassion, point them to Jesus, who can heal their brokenness.*

FRIDAY, JANUARY 24

He took our sicknesses and removed our diseases. Matthew 8:17 (NLT)

I WOKE UP ONE MORNING with a headache from my stressful work the day before. My initial reaction was to cry out, "Jesus, please take away this pain!" A few minutes later when I rose from bed, my headache was gone just as easily as I'd cried out.

There are times when answers to my prayers do not manifest as soon as I want them to, so it still surprises me when I experience instant relief from Jesus. But the New Testament is filled with stories of how Jesus showed compassion to the sick and suffering, and often they received their healing immediately. When Jesus touched the hand of Peter's mother-in-law who was nursing a high fever, immediately the fever left her (Matthew 8:14–15). Or there was that instance when He told the crippled man to rise and pick up his mat. The man quickly jumped up, grabbed his mat, and walked out of the scene, leaving everyone astonished (Mark 2:1–12). And who could forget the story of Jairus, whose heart sank when he heard his daughter had died? Jesus comforted him with a promise of healing and brought back his daughter to life with the touch of His hand (Mark 5:35–42).

Jesus cares for all of us—men, women, young, old, privileged, and underprivileged. Jesus was crucified on the cross for the forgiveness of our sins and the healing of our sicknesses and diseases. We can cry out to Him and expect His healing touch. The pain may be gone right away as it happened to me or the healing may come much later. But one thing is for sure, Jesus is always concerned with our well-being. —MARLENE LEGASPI-MUNAR

FAITH STEP: *Meditate on the stories of healing mentioned above. Trust Jesus to heal your ailment. Trust Him to heal a friend who may be physically or emotionally suffering. Share these Scriptures on healing to encourage that person.*

SATURDAY, JANUARY 25

*Again I say unto you, That if two of you shall agree on earth as touching
any thing that they shall ask, it shall be done for them of my Father
which is in heaven. Matthew 18:19 (KJV)*

I HEARD HEART-WRENCHING SOBS AS I walked down the hospital hallway. A distraught mother sat alone in the waiting room, crying and
calling out to Jesus. I knew who she was. I was a pharmacy technician
and had just been to her son's room to get his orders. I'd cringed when
I flipped through his chart. *Diagnosis: Alcohol Overdose. Condition:
Critical.* He lay deathly still amid tubes, wires, catheters, and moni-
tors in the ICU. Now as I passed by and heard the mom's cries, I
knew that I should go pray with her, but I was too upset.

I felt guilty. That could be me. My twin sons were the same age as
her boy. I should've offered to pray with her. *Dear Jesus, please heal
him. Give me the words to comfort his mother.*

During lunch, I went to her despite my anxiety. "I have sons the
same age as your son. May I pray with you?" She nodded, her eyes
glassy with tears. We held hands, prayed, and asked for a miracle.

When she was summoned to the consultation room to meet with
the doctor, she asked me to come along. Suddenly everything had
changed. The doctor's words were life-giving. "Jesus performed a
miracle! He has no permanent damage." The power of Jesus was
palpable. The prayers of two mothers were answered.

Jesus says that if two or three of us agree in prayer, His Father will
do what we ask. Prayer is an invitation to see Him work in amazing
ways. When we pray together, our prayers usher in His presence.
—KATIE MINTER JONES

FAITH STEP: *If you need a miracle today, find a prayer partner and pray.*

SUNDAY, JANUARY 26

And it shall be, that thou shalt drink of the brook; and I have commanded the ravens to feed thee there. 1 Kings 17:4 (KJV)

ONE SUNDAY AFTER CHURCH, MY husband's aunt requested his help with a leaking faucet. Since we had plans to visit a new Thai restaurant for dinner, I went home to wait on Mick's return. The time to repair his aunt's plumbing took longer than expected. And as I sat on the couch waiting, my stomach began to growl from hunger. I had two options. I could cook dinner or jump in the car to purchase our meal at a nearby fast-food restaurant. Neither option was desirable.

Right when I opened a carton of milk to prepare a bowl of cereal, the phone rang. It was my neighbor Mrs. Mack. "Alice," she said, "I made rutabagas and corn bread for Mick and you."

I thanked her, slipped on my shoes, and ran across the street to receive her kindness.

I love rutabagas! My mother served them often when I was a child. However, in my adult life, it is a vegetable that I seldom cook. Mrs. Mack remembered a conversation we'd had when I had mentioned my fondness for the vegetable. When she saw them at the market, she purchased enough to share.

How can I ever fret over hunger or lack again? I refuse to do it. You must refuse to do it too. Jesus told the disciples that God knows what we need before we ask for it (Matthew 6:8). And on that Sunday, my Lord's intimate knowledge of my hunger and His immediate ability to command the arrival of sustenance became apparent to me. What do I know for sure? Jesus is forever ready to feed our needs. —ALICE THOMPSON

FAITH STEP: *Visit the market today and ask the Lord to guide you in making purchases that will feed your family and a neighbor's family too.*

MONDAY, JANUARY 27

I hope in the Lord Jesus to send Timothy to you soon, that I also may be cheered when I receive news about you. I have no one else like him, who will show genuine concern for your welfare. Philippians 2:19–20 (NIV)

WHENEVER FRIENDSHIP BLOSSOMS IN MY life, I know Jesus is there. Each time I can point to a moment when I felt Jesus giving me the gift of true friendship. In the case of our next-door neighbors Lon, Jen, and their son, Owen, I even have a scar to remind me!

I was cooking and began to clean the blade of a handheld blender. My mind was miles away—with my dad, who had just been hospitalized. In that moment, I cut my finger badly. My husband, Tony, rushed into action, knocking on our neighbors' door, asking if they could watch our kids while he took me to the emergency room. Our very young children didn't know Lon and Jen that well, but we knew they'd be safe. A minute later Tony returned, saying, "They had a better idea: Lon can take you to the ER, I'll stay with the kids."

That was the day we learned what true friends our neighbors were to become. Lon—a carpenter with lots of experience with blade injuries—was a calming presence as we waited in the ER. He distracted me with stories as I got stitched up. Jen had Tony and the kids around her kitchen table and served a dinner more delicious than the one I was planning to make!

Almost a decade later, my kids remember that as the day they got to play at the kitchen table of their now-best-buddy Owen. I remember it as the day Jesus led me from suffering to friendship and expanded our family by three. —ELIZABETH BERNE DEGEAR

FAITH STEP: *Plan a get-together with friends who've become like family. Give thanks!*

TUESDAY, JANUARY 28

This is the confidence we have in approaching God: that if we ask anything according to his will, he hears us. 1 John 5:14 (NIV)

A FRIEND SENT ME A pretty graphic with the statement "Those who put everything in God's hands eventually see God's hand in everything." I've also heard, "Pray and pay attention."

I've been a Christian for a long while now, yet the tangible proof of these maxims has only recently come fully to life for me. I now see Jesus answering my prayers so plainly and undeniably it often fills me with quiet awe. I'll ask Jesus a very specific question and soon see answers everywhere: A friend unexpectedly shares a relevant experience that answers my prayer. A series of disconnected devotionals or podcasts echoes a theme. A door closes or opens decisively.

Why now? Is Jesus suddenly answering my prayers more than before? Am I praying "better" somehow? Well, yes. And no.

Elsewhere in Scripture, God assures me He will change me to conform me to Christ's likeness. He will. My cooperation hastens this lifelong process. I believe that as I've matured, my prayers more closely align with Jesus's heart, and my eyes are more attuned to how He works. Moreover I've become convinced, through sometimes very painful lessons, that Jesus's way is always best, so I'm more submissive to the stream of His will.

His way is so much easier than ours. Behold, the quietly miraculous answers to prayer—affirming, melodious, and wonderful. I pray and receive, trusting He's listening and answering. —ISABELLA YOSUICO

FAITH STEP: *Get a pretty journal and call it "Jesus in My Life." Note answers to prayer, following God's direction, and those "coincidences," signs, and wonders that Jesus sends your way.*

WEDNESDAY, JANUARY 29

As the heavens are higher than the earth, so are my ways higher than your ways and my thoughts than your thoughts. Isaiah 55:9 (NIV)

I SPENT FOUR DECADES PRAYING a prayer Jesus didn't want to answer. My prayer was framed by what I knew was possible, not by reliance on the limitless creativity of Jesus. The always faithful One knew He should ignore my idea and go with His own plan!

A strip club stood at the edge of town, a disturbing first impression. Its presence was a constant reminder of the depravity of humankind, destructive choices, threats to marriages, and a host of other ungodly activities. My prayer? *Lord, would you burn that place to the ground? One lightning strike is all it would take.*

Storms—and years—came and went. Nothing.

Then Jesus showed His Hand.

First, several women from our church were impressed to show love to the women who worked at the club, many of them convinced they had no other option. The miraculous began to unfold. The heart of the owner softened, changing dramatically. He asked our church if we would buy the property from him. It wasn't the legacy he wanted to leave for his kids.

So our church bought a strip club. The acreage will one day be a hub of ministry lifting up the name of Jesus. He's redeeming even the soil on which the building once stood.

If I'd had my way, a lightning bolt might have gotten the glory, and insurance would have been provided to rebuild depravity. Instead, Jesus had a radical plan of redemption in mind. What a story it's making for His glory! —CYNTHIA RUCHTI

FAITH STEP: *Have you asked Jesus to frame your prayers for a long-held need? Today surrender your brilliant solution to His better idea.*

THURSDAY, JANUARY 30

I can do all things through Christ who strengthens me. Philippians 4:13 (NKJV)

THIS VERSE IS A STRENGTHENING support when we face a difficult task. When a situation is too hard for us to handle. When we feel we can't go on. It's another version of *nothing is too difficult for Him; nothing is impossible with God.* It's a shot in the arm sometimes. A power verse we gulp down like a vitamin smoothie.

But sometimes what a verse doesn't say is just as important as what a verse says. I was recently reminded that while I can do all things through Jesus, He never said I have to do it all. I'm the one who puts that kind of pressure on myself. Sometimes the thing He wants to give me strength for is speaking that powerful little word, "No."

I think women are especially prone to thinking we have to do it all. Maybe it's because we're good at multitasking. You want me to start a load of laundry while I'm cooking dinner while I'm washing dishes while I'm supervising a piano lesson while I'm helping someone else with homework after I've worked eight hours as a teacher? Sure. No problem. I am supermom. I love to be needed. But the honest truth is that it feeds my pride monster to do all this. And I think our culture creates that monster. *I can bring home the bacon and fry it up in a pan.* We prove our value by doing it all.

But Jesus wants us to get our value from Him. Not from doing all things. But from resting in His love for us and letting His strength shine through our weakness. How can He do that if we never admit we have any weaknesses? We can do all things through Him. But that doesn't mean we need to do everything. —GWEN FORD FAULKENBERRY

FAITH STEP: *What's the hardest thing you have to do today? Receive the strength to do it through Jesus. Even if that thing is saying, "No. I don't need to do that."*

FRIDAY, JANUARY 31

Many of his disciples said, "This is very hard to understand. How can anyone accept it?" Jesus was aware that his disciples were complaining, so he said to them, "Does this offend you?" . . . At this point many of his disciples turned away and deserted him. John 6:60–61, 66 (NLT)

OUR SOCIETY IS RAPIDLY ADOPTING attitudes and behaviors contrary to Jesus's teachings. I struggle with knowing how to respond. Politely posting my opinion about controversial issues has prompted strangers to leave scathing comments and call me names.

Fear engulfed me the first time this happened. *Oh no! I didn't mean to offend anyone. What should I do? Maybe I should delete the comment and ban that individual from future contact, but then he'd feel even more offended.*

I asked Jesus for wisdom. He reminded me that He offended others too. Even those who professed to be His disciples disagreed with His teachings. Others flat-out rejected Him and walked away.

Offending others when standing for truth is inevitable. People interpret our words through their upbringing, their personal experiences, their woundedness. Their interpretations may be completely skewed, and they may respond with anger and false accusations.

We can't control how others receive our words, but we can control the manner in which we present them. Jesus never stooped to name-calling or verbally shredding those who disagreed with Him. Neither should we. Our role is to follow His example and trust His Holy Spirit to change the hearts of those who take offense. —GRACE FOX

FAITH STEP: *Magazines and newspapers provide plenty of prayer fodder. Scan headlines for an article that demonstrates society's rejection of Jesus's truth. Read it and ask Jesus to turn people's hearts toward Him.*

SATURDAY, FEBRUARY 1

And the Lord said, If ye had faith as a grain of mustard seed, ye might say unto this sycamine tree, Be thou plucked up by the root, and be thou planted in the sea; and it should obey you. Luke 17:6 (KJV)

MY MOTHER STILL DRIVES AT eighty-one years old. She's steady at the wheel. However, one day she was so caught up loading her car for our road trip that she left her purse and Bible on top of her luggage rack as she started her car. We zipped to my speaking engagement at a rural church, just outside the city. When we arrived, Mother moaned, "I left my purse and Bible on top of the car!"

During my presentation at the church, I couldn't focus on my talking points about faith. I imagined Mother's checkbook, cash, and credit cards in the hands of a city rogue. After the event, a church member approached me. She explained that during my presentation, the fear in my eyes and stress in my voice revealed my lack of faith. She said, "Stand still and see the salvation of the Lord."

Two days later, a stranger returned everything. When he found the items scattered in the street, he said Mother's driver's license photo reminded him of his granny. He researched Mother's name until he found her phone number. The checkbook, cash, and credit cards were untouched.

I learned the meaning of faith. It's trusting Jesus to save the day, even when I see no evidence of His immediate power. According to the Bible, only a tiny speck of faith is required to reap miracles. When anxiety sends my heart racing, I stop what I'm doing and gather myself in stillness. Then I continue my task as I wait on Jesus to move the mountain. —ALICE THOMPSON

FAITH STEP: *Give Jesus all your pressing fears. Stand still and wait for Him to fix what worries you today.*

SUNDAY, FEBRUARY 2

He will yet fill your mouth with laughter and your lips with shouts of joy.
Job 8:21 (NIV)

THE OTHER DAY, I HAD the pleasure of going for a walk with my good friend Lindsey. I had a hard time going up the hills because she was making me laugh so hard. I love her perspective. Neither of us is above sharing a humiliating story about ourselves if we think it will make someone laugh. It is a bond we share. Laughter is powerful. If I can make a few people laugh while I am figuring out this life-thing, if I can usher in some joy, if I make some friends hold their sides when I tell a story, I want to do that. Because joy lets us breathe. And we all need that. This journey of life can be difficult, but in the presence of the One who loves us most of all, what we find is…joy.

Psalm 16:11 says, "You make known to me the path of life; you will fill me with joy in your presence, with eternal pleasures at your right hand" (NIV). I have an inkling that Jesus really liked to laugh. All kinds of people, young and old, rich and poor, men and women, liked to hang around Him. He was a favorite at parties. Children were drawn to Him. The outcasts and downtrodden overcame their fear to get close to Him. They must have been filled with joy, just by being close to Him. Jesus has passed this gift of joy onto you and me. Until He comes again, we are the ones who get to share His joy with others. His love at work in us spills over into joy. Joy unspeakable and full of glory! —SUSANNA FOTH AUGHTMON

FAITH STEP: *Make a coffee date with a friend who makes you laugh. Enjoy every moment of being together and remember that the love of Jesus at work in you ushers in joy.*

MONDAY, FEBRUARY 3

. . . whoever wants to become great among you must be your servant, and whoever wants to be first must be your slave—just as the Son of Man did not come to be served, but to serve, and to give his life as a ransom for many. Matthew 20:26–28 (NIV)

I'M A KID AT HEART. And what child doesn't love a kaleidoscope? I know I do. Nestled on my porch rocker, I peek through the lens of a child's toy, watching colors and shapes dance and play. As I twist the tube, patterns transform and change. Blue chips blend with red to become an irresistible violet. Yellows harmonize with aquamarines, a flower one moment, a sparkling crown the next.

In my mind's eye, I see another picture reminding me how different we are as individuals and especially as Christians. Each of us adds something new to this everchanging creation, displaying the touch of the Master's hand. One might resemble the bright yellow chips as he visits bedridden members of his church; another, the soft green bit as she calms babies in the nursery. Right now I'm that purple diamond, writing my passion for the Lord.

If we follow Jesus, our "colors" will change according to whatever form of service we're called to during that season of life. Our responsibilities may vary, but our purpose—furthering Jesus's kingdom—doesn't. We are created to serve with the humility and love Jesus shared.

When we work together in harmony, the product of our labor is ageless and beautiful. Because our service is blessed by the Lord, we become a greater blessing to Him, part of a vast and timeless host of worshippers. I can't think of any job more vibrant! —HEIDI GAUL

FAITH STEP: *Spend some time today reflecting on the artwork in your home. How is each component significant yet dependent on the others to complete the piece? What part will you play in Jesus's masterpiece today?*

TUESDAY, FEBRUARY 4

---

*Be full of love for others, following the example of Christ who loved
you and gave himself to God as a sacrifice to take away your sins.
And God was pleased, for Christ's love for you was like sweet perfume
to him. Ephesians 5:2 (TLB)*

I MET MARGARET B. AT a mission hospital in Nepal in the eighties.
By that time, she'd already served thirty years as a trained mid-
wife. She was old enough to be my mother, yet she became my
dear friend. Her love for people was one of the characteristics that
intrigued me most.

That love led Margaret from a comfortable life in England to a
sacrificial life in Asia. She lived in a house without electricity or
running water. She trekked more miles than we'll ever know to help
women in isolated villages safely deliver their babies. She invested
countless hours doing prenatal checkups and deliveries. In fact, she
assisted with the births of my first two children.

When my second child was born with hydrocephalus, Margaret
did everything in her power to care for me and my newborn daughter until we left Nepal to return to North America for medical help.

Margaret eventually retired and returned to England, where she
led Bible studies and prayer services. Every year until Jesus called
her to heaven, she blessed my eldest two kids with birthday cards
and assurance of her prayers.

Margaret modeled today's key verse. She lived a life full of loving
others with joy. She reflected Jesus, and her example turned many
hearts toward Him. No doubt her sacrificial love was like sweet
perfume to God. —GRACE FOX

FAITH STEP: *Margaret loved others. How might you love others right where you
are today?*

WEDNESDAY, FEBRUARY 5

Everything on earth has its own time and its own season. Ecclesiastes 3:1 (CEV)

"THANK YOU FOR INSPIRING ME. I was really blessed by your book!" Another reader sent me a message telling me how much *How to Be a Happy Working Mom* helped her. Of course, I'm always thrilled by the positive responses of readers, but occasionally, their messages remind me of how difficult it was for me to get published.

Eighteen years ago, while I was still a young pastor's wife and mom to two schoolchildren, I sent a book proposal to a publisher about my experiences as a mother. The publisher rejected my proposal, citing my "lack of marketability" as the reason. I admit, during that time, except for some magazine articles, I had no other published work to my credit.

I was hurt by that rejection, but that didn't stop me from pursuing writing and exploring other opportunities to write for print, radio, and the internet. I continued to write throughout the years while homemaking, raising two kids, and volunteering at church.

Two decades later, a different editor from the same publishing house I sent my first proposal to contacted me. "Our team has come up with some book ideas that might be right for you." One of the ideas was about being a freelancer and a homemaker. That idea gave birth to *How to Be a Happy Working Mom.*

Now I understand Jesus's insistence on doing things according to His timing—there's a season for everything. He Himself came here in the fullness of time and refused to do any thing prematurely. Seasons are important. He makes everything happen at the right time. —MARLENE LEGASPI-MUNAR

FAITH STEP: *Ask Jesus to help you do what's He's calling you to do now. What you do today is preparation for your next assignment.*

THURSDAY, FEBRUARY 6

*You keep him in perfect peace whose mind is stayed on you,
because he trusts in you. Isaiah 26:3 (ESV)*

MY HUSBAND JOKES THAT MY mind is a scary place. My thoughts dart from subject to subject. I'm prone to spinning out imaginative possibilities. Because of my busy brain, I often think of potential obstacles and solutions before I encounter them. That can be a gift, since it helps me be prepared. However, sometimes my mind lingers on potential problems, and I spin myself into worry. Dwelling on worst-case scenarios can bring unnecessary stress.

Whether our stressors are imaginary (all the what-if worries that never come about) or real and overwhelming (job loss, illness, fractured families, natural disaster, etc.), there is One who is our Rock, One who is not thrown into despair by the hugeness of our needs or fears: Jesus.

Keeping our mind stayed on our Savior can take practice. When I'm faced with a new problem or crisis, I reach for my phone to call my husband or text a friend. I might go online to research solutions. I create a list or chart to set up a step-by-step plan. I evaluate my own resources and strength and tend to put my trust in those. Putting all trust in myself leads to the heavy pressure and weight of responsibilities too large for me to carry.

From now on, when a difficulty arises, I want to stop my hand from reaching for my computer or phone first and instead clasp my hands in prayer. No matter where my thoughts wander, if I bring my focus back to Jesus, my Savior, my mind can find a place of peace. —SHARON HINCK

FAITH STEP: *What are your most troublesome thoughts today? Bring them to Jesus and trust them to His care, then focus your mind on Him.*

FRIDAY, FEBRUARY 7

[The rich man] thought to himself, "What shall I do? I have no place to store my crops. . . . I will tear down my barns and build bigger ones."
Luke 12:17–18 (NIV)

A PINE TREE WE ESTIMATED to be more than one hundred years old is on the ground in our yard. Sixty or seventy feet tall when upright, it was felled by an eight-inch-tall squirrel.

And his or her nesting instincts.

One day we noticed wood chips at the base of the tree. Thirty feet up was a massive squirrel condo—without a permit. Evidence of woodpecker damage suggested the squirrels had help.

But the elbow room the squirrels created in their penthouse destroyed the tree's integrity. Its core. We had to cut it down before it fell and took with it other trees or our house.

Our family once pondered a career decision for me. The job would've provided financially but would've kept me from God's plan. What did we need the money for? Literally, to build a bigger barn. Tripping over that verse from Luke 12 and the parable of the rich man, we knew our answer. I can't imagine what life would have been like if we'd chosen to "hollow out the pine tree" to make space and in the process destroyed the integrity of our building.

Jesus's parable concluded with the rich man's life ending suddenly that same night, and his wealth useless. Jesus said, "This is the way it will be for those who hoard things for themselves and aren't rich toward God" (Luke 12:21, CEB).

Rich toward God. *Jesus, may that remain the core of our desire.*
—CYNTHIA RUCHTI

FAITH STEP: *Is there anything eating away at your spiritual structure? Are you trying to build strong character but unwilling to make integrity a priority? Timber!*

SATURDAY, FEBRUARY 8

Then the servant with the one bag of silver came and said, "Master, I knew you are a hard man, harvesting crops you didn't plant and gathering crops you didn't cultivate. I was afraid I would lose your money, so I hid it in the earth. Look, here is your money back." Matthew 25:24–25 (NLT)

BECOMING INTENTIONAL ABOUT MY PHYSICAL health required a change in my thinking. One of the most important changes was to assume responsibility for my eating behaviors and exercise.

In times past, I made excuses and even blamed others for my habitual overeating. At a buffet-style restaurant, I'd say, "This place has far too many options. I'll just have to try a little bit of everything." At a friend's house, I'd say, "This dessert is amazing. You've outdone yourself. You've forced me into eating a second helping."

I blamed the weather for my sedentary lifestyle: "I'd walk today if it wasn't so cold (or hot, muggy, rainy, snowy, overcast) outside."

I played the blame game instead of assuming responsibility. Jesus taught about a servant who did the same thing. Rather than investing or wisely using the silver his master had given him, the servant buried it and then blamed the master for his behavior. Sadly he paid the consequences.

So did I. I struggled with obesity and chronic pain until Jesus convinced me to take ownership of my habits. Facing the truth that I lacked self-discipline wasn't easy. Neither was admitting that I was lazy about exercise, but He helped me do it. Taking that step helped me understand how easily I deflected responsibility for other areas of my life, and it put me on the path to transformation and freedom. —GRACE FOX

FAITH STEP: *Do you make excuses or blame others to avoid taking responsibility? Fill in the blanks and see if this is true for you: I would _____ if only _____ .*

SUNDAY, FEBRUARY 9

And let us consider one another in order to stir up love and good works, not forsaking the assembling of ourselves together, as is the manner of some, but exhorting one another, and so much the more as you see the Day approaching. Hebrews 10:24–25 (NKJV)

I GO TO CHURCH TWICE on Sunday and again on Tuesday night. Occasionally we have additional services such as revival, our church anniversary, and other celebrations. It doesn't seem excessive to me; however, some of my family members and friends think I go to church too often. They tell me going to numerous weekly services so frequently is not necessary to serve Christ.

They don't understand that I love going to church to assemble with the saints, to hear a Word from the Lord, and to worship Jesus Christ. I am fine with the multiple weekly services. Sometimes I may be tired or not feeling my best, but I go to support the ministry. When I do go to church, I always leave feeling energized, empowered, and encouraged. I prefer those optimistic feelings over the chronic hopelessness I used to experience before I started following Jesus.

When we come together in the church as an assembly, Paul wrote, we are to help each other to "stir up love and good works." We need love and good works to be able to reach the unsaved in this world today. At times, we need to just surround ourselves with the love of one another and encourage each other, knowing that our hope for all things is in our Savior, Jesus. —TRACY ELDRIDGE

FAITH STEP: *If you don't have a church home right now, make a list of nearby churches and visit them. Ask Jesus to show you which one you should join, so you can be with like-minded believers, strengthening and encouraging each other.*

MONDAY, FEBRUARY 10

No discipline seems pleasant at the time, but painful. Later on, however, it produces a harvest of righteousness and peace for those who have been trained by it. Hebrews 12:11 (NIV)

THE MEDICAL REPORT I RECEIVED was discouraging. Since my last annual visit, I'd gained weight and lost bone mass. My doctor examined my blood work. He said, "You need to change your daily routine." Diabetes and heart disease have plagued my family for several generations. According to the doctor, these illnesses would be my fate and devastation if I did not lose twenty pounds.

I worked a full-time job. My hours after work were dedicated to writing books. Hours before work were set aside for my morning devotion and quiet time with Jesus. How would I fit daily exercise in my schedule? Wake up earlier? Yes! It was the only way. And with my alarm set for 3:30 a.m., I rose before the sun to drive to my neighborhood gym. During each visit, I exercised for an hour. Then I returned home to shower and read my morning devotion.

Exercising in the morning did not make me tired. It had the opposite effect. Exercise readied my mind to receive God's Word, and it lifted my energy and enthusiasm all day. The dedication to rise earlier and exercise didn't happen instantly. I didn't lose weight right away. However, over several months, I developed discipline as I prayed to Jesus for help. And with greater discipline, my health improved.

Self-control and discipline dismantle the negative habits that disrupt our joy, peace, and long life. So ask Jesus to bring discipline to the areas in your life where it's missing. Live well. Live long. *Live.*
—ALICE THOMPSON

FAITH STEP: *Make a list of health goals for this year and ask Jesus for the discipline to achieve them.*

TUESDAY, FEBRUARY 11

And so, from the day we heard, we have not ceased to pray for you,
asking that you may be filled with the knowledge of his will in all
spiritual wisdom and understanding. Colossians 1:9 (ESV)

I FELL ON THE ICE earlier this year and injured my shoulder. My church family has frequently asked me for updates, offered help, and lifted me up in prayer. My shoulder has improved. I am thankful that I belong to a church who believes in the power of prayer. We lift up one another in prayer, but we also pray for others outside our church and community. Praying together for each other's needs draws us closer to Jesus and binds us together as a church family. First Thessalonians 5:11 tells us to encourage one another and build one another up. A prayer list with people's names and their concerns is printed in our church bulletin and updated during the week. This enables us to call people by name and make their petitions known to Jesus.

Many of our church members are included in our prayer chain. Whenever there is a prayer concern or a praise report, text messages are sent to those in the group. Technology has allowed us to contact each other quickly and keep everyone updated.

Praying also brings us closer to Jesus; praying for others is good and pleasing in the sight of our Savior. Jesus honors the prayers of those who love Him. He unleashes hope, healing, mercy, and grace for those that we pray for. —KATIE MINTER JONES

FAITH STEP: *Join together to lift up those in need. Call, text, or email prayer requests to your friends or members of your church.*

WEDNESDAY, FEBRUARY 12

Let him have all your worries and cares, for he is always thinking about you and watching everything that concerns you. 1 Peter 5:7 *(TLB)*

As MY MOM STEPPED INTO the grocery store one day, a man coming out paused and said, "You have the most peaceful-looking face. You look like you don't have a care in the world." My mom answered, "That's because I gave them all to Jesus!"

I understand that you can't always tell how a person feels on the inside by looking at her facial expression, but then again, sometimes you can. That man's comment didn't surprise me in light of recent phone conversations I'd had with my mother. But *he* might have been surprised to know that when I was growing up, my mother qualified as a worrier—like I tend to be today.

My dad passed away in 2016, the day before my parents' sixty-ninth anniversary. Naturally widowhood has made some things more difficult for my mom and brought new problems and issues. Mom often will tell me about a difficulty or even scary incident that happened, but she always ends by saying, "I just prayed about it and turned it over to the Lord. He'll take care of it."

Just before His crucifixion, Jesus told His disciples, "Don't let your hearts be troubled" (John 14:1, NLT). How can we obey that in a fallen world where terrible things happen every day? Jesus gave the secret at the end of the verse: "Trust [*Believe* in some translations] in Me." Do we trust Him with a scary medical diagnosis, a wayward spouse or child, a sudden job loss? If we trust Jesus to take care of everything that concerns us, then our faces will reflect that.
—DIANNE NEAL MATTHEWS

FAITH STEP: *Glance at yourself in a mirror. What message does your face reflect? Peace and trust in Jesus, or stress? Recite aloud John 14:1 until you smile.*

THURSDAY, FEBRUARY 13

For the Spirit God gave us does not make us timid, but gives us power, love and self-discipline. 2 Timothy 1:7 (NIV)

EVERY TIME I SEE THIS verse, I read it twice. Usually I'm able to absorb the wisdom and conduct my life accordingly. But sometimes it's like the mirror mentioned in James 1:23–24, and I forget this truth as soon as I step away. *How I wish these precious words stayed with me longer.*

I wasn't always afraid, but during my teens, I learned life can be complex and unfair—and ugly. I'm not alone. Many of us bear wounds that leave us vulnerable and anxious at times. Now, when fear and shame engulf my spirit and I sink beneath the weight of those emotions, I cry out in faith for rescue. Jesus yanks me free from the darkness entangling me.

How can these transgressions—most of which I was a victim to—have such power over me, when I know I'm not only saved, I'm chosen, and I'm not only chosen, I'm...do you see where I'm going? I'm redeemed, called by name (Isaiah 43:1). I'm a child of God (John 1:12), a friend of Jesus (John 15:15), a new creation (2 Corinthians 5:17), and a citizen of heaven (Philippians 3:20).

My favorite identity tag is found in Ephesians 2:10. I prefer the New Living Translation for this verse: "For we are God's masterpiece..."

Beauty is often only achieved and appreciated through pain. Love can be witnessed in suffering. Courage is won in faith. I am loving, beautiful, and brave. I'm His masterpiece. —HEIDI GAUL

FAITH STEP: *Divide a sheet of paper into two columns. On one side, list fears you've overcome. On the other, note your current fears and beneath each one, write ways Jesus has armed you to face it.*

FRIDAY, FEBRUARY 14

Jesus said . . . "'You shall love the LORD your GOD with all your heart, with all your soul, and with all your mind.' This is the first and great commandment. And the second is like it: 'You shall love your neighbor as yourself.'" Matthew 22:37–39 (NKJV)

I MEMORIZED THESE VERSES AS a child and always thought of them as two complete thoughts that sum up the Christian imperative. Love God. Love others. It was not until I became an adult that someone pointed out to me that third essential part: love yourself.

For me this is the hardest. And I believe it's because, had I considered it at all when I was younger, I would have thought loving myself a vain, prideful thing to do. In other words, not a Christian thing. And I think that is a travesty. But that was my impression of Christianity. The emphasis was always putting others before yourself, not being arrogant or prideful or thinking too highly of yourself. Being a servant. The teachers in my faith community taught humility. But humility is not the opposite of loving yourself. Pride is.

I wish that instead of that impression, I'd learned that it grieves God when we treat ourselves poorly. Just as it would if we treated a brother or sister in Christ poorly. I wish that just as I'd learned to love others and treat them well, I'd learned to treat myself well, and love myself too. After all, Jesus said we should. In these verses, it seems like it's so obvious it's an assumption. The way we know how to love others best is to love ourselves first. —GWEN FORD FAULKENBERRY

FAITH STEP: *When you find yourself being too critical, negative, or demanding with yourself today, ask yourself: Is this how I would treat my best friend? Then be kinder to yourself. Remember Jesus loves you and wants you to love yourself too.*

SATURDAY, FEBRUARY 15

I will praise You, for I am fearfully and wonderfully made; Marvelous are Your works, And that my soul knows very well. Psalm 139:14 (NKJV)

THERE IS A LONE BLUE heron that visits the lake on the trail I walk. It comes and goes throughout the year. It's the only one of its kind among the ducks and geese. The fact that it's a loner doesn't stop it from coming to the lake periodically. Sometimes I look at it and feel sorry for it. *Does it feel lonely?* Maybe it just hangs out at the lake every now and then for nourishment. We seem to be alike, the heron and I—socially awkward. In a crowd of familiar or unfamiliar faces, I sometimes feel as if I don't belong or I feel lonely. If you invite me to your party, I will come, but I already have my escape mapped out. Sometimes I just don't know what to say or what to do…you know…it's awkward. Maybe I am socially challenged because of my perceptions of myself.

As I mature in Christ, this Scripture gives me comfort, because Jesus assures me that I was made with tender loving care. Not only that, I am a marvelous creation! Therefore, I can hold my head up high in every social situation.

Jesus was unique in that He was the Messiah with human qualities, but He showed confidence in social settings. Jesus had to be approachable to all types of people in order for Him to be influential. We too should allow our confidence in Christ to help us in social situations to reach the lost. Take heart in the knowledge that Jesus already knows all about us, and we are all created uniquely and marvelously and made acceptable in Christ. —TRACY ELDRIDGE

FAITH STEP: *If you're socially awkward, next time you get invited to an event, be prepared by speaking this Scripture repeatedly until you believe it. We are precious in Jesus's sight, and He wants us to know just how special we are.*

SUNDAY, FEBRUARY 16

*Jesus responded, "Didn't I tell you that you would see God's glory
if you believe?" John 11:40 (NLT)*

I'D WAITED ANXIOUSLY TO FIND out who'd won the writing contest.
I'd prayed and asked God to help me win so that I could use the prize
money to go to a publishing conference in Brazil. With the registration fee, airfare, and hotel, the trip was going to be expensive.

I truly believed that God would provide the contest money, so I
was discouraged after I lost. But I really wanted to go to the conference, so I asked Jesus to increase my faith. I decided to be more
open and submissive to His ways and means.

The following day, I checked with the bank about a friend's love
offering. I was pleasantly surprised to learn that not only had the
money been deposited into my account, but it was a generous gift.
Two hours later at the grocery store, I bumped into a couple that
I've known for a few years. Before we parted, the wife handed me
some money—another contribution to my trip to Brazil. Soon family members and friends sent support, enabling me to participate in
the conference after all. Jesus provided for me in a completely different way than I'd expected, but He provided for me nonetheless!

Sometimes I second-guess how Jesus answers my prayers. But time
has proven that He's got plenty up His sleeve. I've learned that despite
apparent circumstances, it's best for me to simply trust Him. When
I do, I come out a winner in the end. —MARLENE LEGASPI-MUNAR

FAITH STEP: *Recall the times when Jesus answered your prayers in ways you
didn't expect. If you're praying for something right now, don't keep Him in a box.
Expect Him to answer beyond your expectations.*

MONDAY, FEBRUARY 17

You study the Scriptures diligently because you think that in them you have eternal life. These are the very Scriptures that testify about me, yet you refuse to come to me to have life. John 5:39–40 (NIV)

"MAKE A U-TURN AND CONTINUE to the route," my husband's smartphone insisted. The GPS was angry with us because we'd pulled off the freeway to get gas. We appreciate the electronic map, but often our GPS misses the point. To reach our destination, we need to stop for gas, food, and bathroom breaks. We may also pause to take in beautiful scenery and enjoy the journey. Yet the mechanical voice scolds nonstop, trying to steer us to the target.

Like the Jewish leaders Jesus spoke to in John 5, I desire eternal life. It's a great goal. I want a new life after death. I want to reunite with loved ones. I want to spend forever in the presence of my Savior. Jesus acknowledged the Jewish leaders dug into the Scriptures with that goal in mind.

Despite best intentions, they criticized Jesus for healing someone, questioned the good news He was sharing, and followed the laws of Moses instead of listening to the Messiah who'd come. They were missing the Giver of eternal life standing right before them.

Our lives aren't just about the clamoring GPS of the law pushing us to the final destination—not if that makes us miss our true Savior. Jesus leads us on a rich path. Each day, each moment, is an opportunity to commune with Him, to learn to follow Him, to allow Him to change us. Yes, He grants eternal life. But He also grants eternal purpose to our present days. —SHARON HINCK

FAITH STEP: *Thank Jesus for these days on earth to draw closer to Him. Ask Him to reveal His purpose for you today.*

TUESDAY, FEBRUARY 18

Then they [the religious council] became insistent. "But he is causing riots by his teaching wherever he goes—all over Judea, from Galilee to Jerusalem!" Luke 23:5 (NLT)

WORDS MATTER. TO THE AUTHOR—AND to readers. Finding the exact word is a writer's constant quest.

Jesus was brought before Pilate. The council—jealous, angry, and afraid of losing its standing—tried fiercely to persuade Pilate, insisting that Jesus was dangerous, that His ministry should be stopped. At the cost of His life, if necessary.

The Bible tells us they became so desperate they chose a word they knew Pilate would react to. *Riot.* Jesus had—in their words—been "causing riots everywhere."

Is that what He'd been doing? He certainly drew crowds. Most in those crowds returned home healed, amazed, faith-filled, or wanting to hear more. He caused a lot of wonder and soul-searching. He pricked a lot of consciences. But He rarely raised His voice.

It was the doubters, the stubborn, and the rabble-rousers who caused the riots. Those who refused to believe fueled fires of controversy.

Jesus, the Rebel whose resistance was against the enemies of God and soul-condemning sin. Jesus, the Healer, Shepherd-King, the One who welcomed children onto His lap and restored the slashed ear of one of His captors—hours before He was accused of causing riots.

I wonder how many of those desperate council members were transformed by Christ's death and resurrection. How many later longed to reword their complaints against Him, saying, "He caused a riot in my soul, and I'll never be the same again"? —CYNTHIA RUCHTI

FAITH STEP: *What one word describes the riot Jesus caused in your life? Redeemed? Restored? Alive? Hopeful? Live it!*

WEDNESDAY, FEBRUARY 19

Return to your rest, my soul, for the LORD has been good to you. For you, LORD, have delivered me from death, my eyes from tears, my feet from stumbling, that I may walk before the LORD in the land of the living.
Psalm 116:7–9 (NIV)

I WAS WORKING AND WAS suddenly flooded with shame. In the midst of preparing a presentation for my fellow chaplains about the use of the Hebrew Bible in pastoral work, I felt completely unworthy to offer anything; I was convinced that I would end up humiliated in my efforts.

And then a memory floated back to me. In my mind, I heard the voice of a friend who had faced ovarian cancer, telling me how much Psalm 116 meant to her. I let go of my slideshow and my fretting. I went to read Psalm 116 in a translation by Nan C. Merrill called *Psalms for Praying*. Enveloped by the psalm, I was instantly comforted—by the spiritual accompaniment of my dear friend, by the translator of this edition of the Psalms, by the ancient psalmist, and, of course, by Jesus's love.

Accompaniment. That's what Jesus was all about. And that's why His invitation, "Follow Me," is so simple and so powerful. The shame I had been feeling melted away in this sense of connection. Now I could see a simple truth: we are all in this together. The work I was doing wasn't about my success or failure, it was about accompaniment.

When the time for the presentation came, I began with a prayer and read Psalm 116. Jesus was with me and was with us all. There was nothing to fear. —ELIZABETH BERNE DEGEAR

FAITH STEP: *Next time you fear that your reputation is on the line, take some time with Jesus. Ask Him to show you all those walking by your side and ask Him who needs you to accompany them right now.*

THURSDAY, FEBRUARY 20

There's an opportune time to do things, a right time for everything on the earth. Ecclesiastes 3:1 (MSG)

SEVERAL YEARS AGO, WHEN I lost my job, I decided to renew my attempts to start a home business. The extra time gave me an opportunity to learn how to make Christian journals and other gift books. In between interviews and applying for jobs, I immersed myself in the task of learning how to make my dream come true by watching videos and using craft books from the library. Jesus supplied me with ideas and designs, which was reassuring. After many tries, my handcrafted journals were ready to sell. My cousin, who started her own business, was my first customer and a huge encouragement. I rented space at flea markets and craft shows and started selling my wares. I didn't sell much, which was discouraging. I was determined to not give up because I believed that Jesus stirred up the yearning in me to have a business that would glorify Him.

This experience showed me the importance of seizing opportunities. Not only did I find an industrious way to occupy my time as I awaited a job offer, but I also started what I hope is only the beginning of a new financially sustaining self-employment opportunity. Now I know I can do it. When Jesus gives us an opportunity, we must be diligent to pursue it in a timely manner, because when we do, great things will happen. —TRACY ELDRIDGE

FAITH STEP: *Has Jesus placed a yearning inside you for something? Use a planner to schedule appointments for you to work on the vision. There's no better time than now!*

FRIDAY, FEBRUARY 21

The LORD shall open unto thee his good treasure, the heaven to give the rain unto thy land in his season, and to bless all the work of thine hand: and thou shalt lend unto many nations, and thou shalt not borrow.
Deuteronomy 28:12 (KJV)

THERE ARE TIMES IN LIFE when we're not sure how we're going to make it. When I found myself overwhelmed by staggering credit-card debt, I turned to Jesus for help. My prayer was quick and to the point: "Help me, Lord!"

I was forced to confront my lack of discipline, such as shopping weekly for unnecessary clothes. While I only purchased sale items, my credit cards' interest rates required me to pay more than the clothes were worth. Then there were my tithes. Some months I would give. Other months, I used every dime from my paycheck to pay bills...and buy small luxuries like nail polish and pricey lattes.

In daily prayer, Jesus gave me specific instructions to reduce my debt. I started tithing and increased my monthly credit-card payments. I budgeted for charitable donations and eliminated incidentals.

The Bible says in Luke 6:38 that when you give, God gives to you in compound measure. I didn't see this principle unfold until I tried this Word for myself. When I followed a budget and dedicated a portion of my salary to tithes and charity, opportunities to write and earn extra income fell at my feet like manna. I was also awarded a series of merit pay raises on my job. Within eighteen months, I paid off my credit-card debts. I discovered that abundance and debt-free living belong to the faithful, who surrender their money and resources to the Lord. —ALICE THOMPSON

FAITH STEP: *Is there a looming debt causing you to despair? Meditate today on Luke 6:38 as you seek wisdom to pay your debt.*

SATURDAY, FEBRUARY 22

So all of us who have had that veil removed can see and reflect the glory of the Lord. And the Lord—who is the Spirit—makes us more and more like him as we are changed into his glorious image. 2 Corinthians 3:18 (NLT)

MY YOUNGEST GRANDDAUGHTER, RUTH, IS a week away from her third birthday as I write this. This petite blue-eyed blondie loves helping her mommy in the kitchen. When she isn't standing on a stool to stir whatever's in a mixing bowl, she's practicing her organizational skills on her five older siblings or playing mommy with her doll or younger brother.

My daughter-in-law, Cheryl, posts pictures of the kids on Facebook. A woman who's known Cheryl her entire life often comments, "Ruthie acts and looks just like you did at that age."

The fact that Ruth mirrors her mom's looks and personality as a child isn't surprising. After all, they share DNA. A resemblance between mom and daughter is to be expected, but it's fun to see the degree to which it's happened in this family.

A similar expectation holds true for the family of God. His Spirit lives in us and works in us to shape our character. His goal is for us to resemble Jesus more and more in all we say and do. Romans 8:29 says, "For God knew his people in advance, and he chose them to become like his Son, so that his Son would be the firstborn, with many brothers and sisters" (NLT).

Our becoming like Jesus—mirroring Him in all we say and do—is God's desire. The degree to which this happens is our choice. Let's choose well so the family resemblance is obvious to all. —GRACE FOX

FAITH STEP: *Study a family photo for fun. Who resembles who and in what way? On your family's behalf, ask Jesus to work in their lives so they will become more and more like Him in word and deed.*

SUNDAY, FEBRUARY 23

For Zion's sake I will not be silent, for Jerusalem's sake I will not keep still, Until her vindication shines forth like the dawn and her salvation like a burning torch. Isaiah 62:1 (NABRE)

ONE OF THE NEW PROJECTS I took on this past year at my church was coleading a social justice study. We named the course "How Are We Called?" What I didn't realize during the planning was that this seven-week class would work its way into my soul on a deep level. It offered me very personal and surprisingly new, answers to this basic vocational question.

As the class was coming to an end, I helped initiate a new movement at our church. National organizations picked up on it, and soon there was movement in other parts of the country too. The pace and the spread of this new thing were out of my control, and every morning I had to keep coming back to the simple question, "Okay, Jesus, how am I called today?"

This year I have been learning that when we follow Jesus, "new" is a big part of what we sign up for. In the words of a leader in a volunteer corps that I joined in my twenties: "Jesus wasn't crucified because the good news was *good*. He was crucified because it was *new*."

New isn't just different, it can be disorienting and scary. Not just for you when you step into the challenge of the new, but for those around you who don't know what to expect. Looking back at this year of new discoveries and risks, I realize that when you take to heart Jesus's invitation to follow Him, it doesn't always look to the rest of the world like following. Sometimes it looks a lot like leading.

—ELIZABETH BERNE DEGEAR

FAITH STEP: *Ask Jesus if He is calling you to something new. Pray for the courage to follow Him.*

MONDAY, FEBRUARY 24

Instead, be kind to each other, tenderhearted, forgiving one another, just as God through Christ has forgiven you. Ephesians 4:32 (NLT)

MY HUSBAND'S A THIEF. EVERY night as he lays sleeping, he steals the covers. When I try to pull them back over me, his hold tightens to a vise-like grip. I lie there shivering on the outside and steaming on the inside, yanking with all I've got for an extra bit of blanket. I, in turn, snore up a storm, leaving my husband's nerves as frayed as an old pair of jeans. He shushes me and sometimes it works. Every morning we wake, innocent smiles shining past the bags beneath our eyes, clueless to the midnight battles we've waged. We can't stay angry. We love each other.

Our nightly struggle reminds me of how Jesus loves me and forgives my sins, even those I'm unaware of. In His infinite grace, He doesn't fuss and complain. He releases my sins as if they never existed. Every morning I'm washed pure and white as snow.

It's easy for me to forgive my spouse. It's harder to do the same for people I'm not drawn to. The man who cut in front of me in line at the department store. The woman at church who insulted me for no reason. The doctor who lacked compassion when he gave me a negative diagnosis.

But Jesus forgave everyone, from the hypocrites judging Him to the soldier that nailed Him to the cross—to you and me. I want to forgive like Jesus, to love the way He did. Like a comforter covering everyone's sin and blanketing them in understanding. With His help, I can. —HEIDI GAUL

FAITH STEP: *Every day this week as you make your bed, pray for Jesus to soften your heart toward someone who's hurt you. And then forgive that person, just as He has forgiven you.*

TUESDAY, FEBRUARY 25

Jesus replied, "This is the work of God—that you believe in the One He has sent." John 6:29 (HCSB)

A FRIEND'S DAUGHTER MET HER husband while serving as a missionary in India. Now they're serving together. I've known Victoria since she was born but only recently met Ronen. I was excited when I got to spend time with them on their recent trip home.

I asked Ronen to tell me about his life. It was a fascinating story. He was born in Israel to Romanian parents and then immigrated to the US as a child. His mother is Jewish and his father is Catholic, and in college he became a believer in Jesus. He told me this story: "I was in a fraternity. Life was stressful. There was one guy who was peaceful no matter what. I wanted that."

He asked the guy how he could be peaceful when pledging a fraternity was so stressful. The guy introduced him to Jesus. Now Ronen is a missionary because he wants everyone else to know Jesus too.

I've been a believer as long as I can remember. But as I listened to Ronen's story, I thought about what it'd be like to live without Jesus, to not know His presence and that He loved me and cared about my life. And it dawned on me what good news it was to learn about Him—to receive Him as my Savior—to have His peace in my life.

Ronen's story helped me remember something important. Even though I've known Jesus forever (or so it seems), I always want to keep experiencing Him. —GWEN FORD FAULKENBERRY

FAITH STEP: *How long has it been since you've experienced Jesus? Write down your story and share it with a friend.*

ASH WEDNESDAY, FEBRUARY 26

But thank God! He gives us victory over sin and death through our Lord Jesus Christ. 1 Corinthians 15:57 *(NLT)*

CALIFORNIA'S RAGING WILDFIRES INCINERATED WHOLE neighborhoods so completely that there remained little visual evidence they'd existed. The ash was so fine it left only a dusting over the footprint of each lost home.

Sobering as those scenes were, more sobering is the assurance that my sins have been incinerated; a fine layer of ash is all that remains—and that layer is blown away by the breath of Jesus's mercy.

Ash Wednesday ushers in Lent—a time of reflection, self-sacrifice, spiritual discipline, and fasting to prepare the heart for Easter. Ash Wednesday reminds us of our mortality (ashes to ashes, dust to dust) and our sinfulness but also that our mortality and sin have been conquered through the death and resurrection of Jesus Christ.

According to custom, the ashes used to form a small cross on the forehead of the repentant are created from incinerated palm branches from a Palm Sunday service. The hosannas—"Blessed is He who comes in the Name of our Lord"—had turned to cries of "Crucify Him" days later, leading to Jesus's death on the cross, which culminated in His conquering death and rising to new life. The cross made of ashes is a small symbol with layers of meaning as we follow Him on a forty-day path toward the reason for our hope—Resurrection Sunday. —CYNTHIA RUCHTI

FAITH STEP: *Our humanity and our sinfulness have been conquered in Jesus and we are free. Ashes to joy. Dust to life. Live victoriously.*

THURSDAY, FEBRUARY 27

Jesus answered, "It is written: 'Man shall not live on bread alone, but on every word that comes from the mouth of God.'" Matthew 4:4 (NIV)

MY HUSBAND LOVES OUR TWO cats. He buys them cat food and sardines. He carries them close to his chest and pets them. I don't have the same affection for felines as he does, but I do feed them. One morning as I opened a can of sardines, they ran toward me meowing loudly. They milled around me, obviously hungry, and couldn't wait to be fed.

Our hungry cats remind me of how we should be hungry for God's Word. Jesus fed those who came in contact with Him, physically and spiritually. He said, "Man shall not live on bread alone, but on every word that comes from the mouth of God." While He was here on earth, Jesus explained portions of the Old Testament. He revealed new truths about Himself that would be the foundation of the New Covenant that was about to come to pass. His words were transformative and powerful.

Jesus is the Word who became flesh and dwelt among us. He encourages us with His promises. When we need direction, He gives us principles to live by. He fills us with joy and peace as we trust Him, and this makes us overflow with hope (Romans 15:13). Jesus is the Bread of Life, the food for our soul. Each day we can dive into God's Word and read the life-giving words of Jesus. As our hungry cats approach my husband and me with the expectation of being fed, let's come to Jesus in the same way. He's waiting to feed us with fresh manna from heaven. —MARLENE LEGASPI-MUNAR

FAITH STEP: *Have you read the Bible from cover to cover? Get a daily Bible reading guide or a one-year chronological Bible. Use the guide to help you delve deeper into the Words of Jesus and let Him fill you with up with His goodness.*

FRIDAY, FEBRUARY 28

Therefore, since we are surrounded by so great a cloud of witnesses, let us also lay aside every weight, and sin which clings so closely, and let us run with endurance the race that is set before us. Hebrews 12:1 (ESV)

SPORTS OFFER ENDLESS INSTRUCTIVE ANALOGIES. Even the apostle Paul recognized it! Endurance is a major athletic theme, whether for the Olympian or my thirteen-year-old Pierce's basketball league. I'm amazed by the amount of heart these kids muster, win or lose.

Endurance is more than just trudging to the finish line and collapsing in a heap. Endurance is playing your heart out until the very end, whether you're ahead by twenty points or losing.

I watch with awe when there are seconds on the clock and the coach calls a time-out. My son's team huddles for instruction on how to finish strong no matter what. We parents and fans, the witnesses in the bleachers, cheer on our team, regardless of the final score.

Jesus endured the cross (Hebrews 12:2) and the challenges of each "play" that led to it. In those final hours, He endured without devoted fans or coaches. Jesus was alone in the final redemptive act, until He rose again.

With the encouragement I enjoy in my spiritual race, from cheering friends, fellowship, countless uplifting resources and the Holy Spirit Himself, can I too face my race with the heart of an athlete? With the heart of Jesus? By Christ's grace and example, along with that of five sweaty preteens, I can. —ISABELLA YOSUICO

FAITH STEP: *If you're weary from running your race, seek and enjoy the encouragement of our heavenly Coach along with the "great cloud of witnesses." And cheer on someone else today, too.*

SATURDAY, FEBRUARY 29

*Yea, though I walk through the valley of the shadow of death,
I will fear no evil: for thou art with me; thy rod and thy staff
they comfort me. Psalm 23:4 (KJV)*

WE ARE OFTEN UNAWARE OF how Jesus protects us. Have you ever arrived late and realized if you had been on time, you could have been in an accident? Or felt uncomfortable and decided not to go somewhere? Or avoided someone or something you felt just wasn't right? It wasn't fate or luck; Jesus was protecting you. Jesus has wrapped His arms around me and protected me from harm, evil, illness, and death several times. A babysitter left me alone when I was four. A burglar came in and told me to watch television. He ransacked the house but didn't harm me. Once a tornado damaged other houses in my neighborhood but spared ours. A man tried to break into my car one night when I stopped at a traffic light, but I was able to drive away. One day I remembered the stove was left on and rushed back home. The kitchen was filled with smoke, but nothing had caught fire yet. Our small car was crushed in an accident, but Jesus spared us.

I have survived cancer twice. During the time I was recovering from surgery and undergoing treatments, I was extremely weak and tired. However, I was never worried about recovering. I literally felt the arms of Jesus around me. I felt His love, grace, and protection. I remembered the times He had protected me and knew I was safe in His arms.

Jesus is so careful with those He loves. He is constantly guarding us, saving us, and lifting us up. He is our shield and rampart. He is our light in the dark. Under His wings, we find refuge. Know that He is protecting you today. —KATIE MINTER JONES

FAITH STEP: *Ask Jesus to put a hedge of protection around you and your loved ones.*

SUNDAY, MARCH 1

Search me [thoroughly], O God, and know my heart; Test me and know my anxious thoughts; And see if there is any wicked or hurtful way in me, And lead me in the everlasting way. Psalm 139:23–24 (AMP)

FOR THE PAST SEVERAL YEARS, one of my former students has been featured in a TV commercial promoting orthotic and prosthetic services. My first introduction to him was memorable for all the wrong reasons. As an elementary school librarian, I often read aloud to students while they sit on the floor. One day after the story-time reading was finished, all the other students stood up...except for him. He remained on the floor. Naturally I thought he was being defiant. I reprimanded him, telling him again to get up, but he just stared at me. Finally my assistant whispered to me, "He can't get up because he is missing a leg." I hadn't seen him when he walked into the library. He was sitting on his other leg, so I hadn't seen his prosthetic. Ashamed and regretful that I had humiliated him in front of the class, I apologized and allowed him to get up at his own pace.

Sometimes we think we see the whole picture, but in reality we need someone to help us see those things we can't see. Oftentimes in my prayers, I ask Jesus to reveal those things in me that are unpleasing in His sight, those things that I cannot see. It's important to me that my thoughts and actions are pleasing in His sight. Jesus alone can test my thoughts and shape my heart to look like His.
—TRACY ELDRIDGE

FAITH STEP: *Today, when you pray, ask Jesus to reveal your heart to you. Then ask Him for guidance in those areas that He reveals to you which are unpleasing in His sight.*

MONDAY, MARCH 2

This is the day that the LORD has made. Let us rejoice and be glad today! Psalm 118:24 (NCV)

ONE MORNING, MY DAUGHTER TEXTED me a photo of my six-year-old grandson eating breakfast. Roman sat at the table drinking a mug of milk and wearing a gray T-shirt, a clip-on necktie, and a navy blazer. *Does he have a job interview before school?* I texted. Holly responded, *No, he said he just wanted to dress up "for Monday."*

What a contrast to the cartoons and memes that portray Monday as a horrible day. So when I shared the photo on social media, I added, "Wouldn't it be great if we could all feel that enthusiastic about Mondays?"

But wouldn't it be great if we could feel that enthusiastic every day? Arising in anticipation of what Jesus has in store for us to see, do, and learn. Moving through the day, determined to be our very best for Him. Embracing even mundane activities because we know they represent opportunities to serve and honor Him.

You're probably thinking: *It's easy for six-year-olds to have unbridled enthusiasm. They don't have adult responsibilities, and they have parents who meet their needs.* Yes, our responsibilities can be heavy, but don't we have Someone meeting our needs better than any earthly parent can? On a tough day, we can remember that Jesus offers guidance, wisdom, and strength. When we're sick we can reflect on the promise of a new, perfect body someday. On an empty and lonely day, we can meditate on the many reasons our loving Savior gives us to rejoice. —DIANNE NEAL MATTHEWS

FAITH STEP: *Start your morning by quoting Psalm 118:24. Thank Jesus for whatever He has in store for you today.*

TUESDAY, MARCH 3

He must become greater and greater, and I must become less and less.
John 3:30 (NLT)

MORE THAN TWENTY YEARS HAVE passed since I received my first invitation to speak at a women's event. Word of mouth spread, and invitations increased. It seemed obvious that Jesus was opening these ministry doors, so I walked through them despite feeling woefully inadequate. My stomach knotted and my knees knocked every time I got up to teach.

One weekend while in my hotel room between meetings, I experienced an *aha* moment. It was like Jesus removed a veil from my eyes, so I could see the reason behind my fear: pride.

The revelation shocked me, but I knew it was true. I was more concerned about making a good impression on my audiences than about making Jesus famous. I wanted women to like me, and I wanted them to think I was a skillful Bible teacher. In my selfish pursuit, I'd sought to make myself—not Jesus—greater and greater.

The *aha* moment humbled and grieved me, and I confessed my pride as sin. From that day forward, I purposed, as a speaker, to make Jesus great.

Before I go onstage, I form two fists and then slowly open them, palms down. I silently pray, *Jesus, I release all personal ambition and selfish motives.* Then I turn my hands over, palms up, and pray, *Fill every cell and fiber of my being with Your Holy Spirit. You must increase, and I must decrease.*

More of Him; less of me. That's the way I want it to be. That's the way it must be. —GRACE FOX

FAITH STEP: *If you think pride is an issue for you, pray the prayer I mentioned above, doing the hand motions. Do this often and sincerely, and it will make a difference.*

WEDNESDAY, MARCH 4

*Ask, and it shall be given you; seek, and ye shall find; knock,
and it shall be opened unto you. Matthew 7:7 (KJV)*

I AM PRIVILEGED TO WORK with Christian believers. On a trying day
when I need a Scripture to settle me, I can depend on colleagues to
give me a timely word. I can also depend on them for inspiring conversations. One day, the school secretary started a dialogue about
miracles and wanted to know if I had witnessed one. I explained
that no one I knew had "walked on water." However, while I was
teaching at my previous school, a miraculous thing did happen.

The secretary raised her brow with heightened interest as I recalled
an unforgettable time. Jean, a first-grade teacher in my building, had
adopted three children and needed a van to replace her aged and sput-
tering compact car. As an unmarried woman with only one income,
Jean had opened her heart and home to the children. But she needed
help to purchase the proper vehicle to transport the family.

One day during my lunch break, I sat at my computer and wrote
a letter to Oprah Winfrey on Jean's behalf. I wrote the letter anony-
mously and never spoke of it to anyone. Two months passed. On
the third month, a miracle happened. Oprah Winfrey contacted
Jean and purchased a new van for her and the children.

I believe that miracles happen every day. And while Jesus knows
what I need before I make my requests, I am still required to pray
and open myself up to a personal relationship with the Savior. As I
make bold requests from the Lord, I boldly receive His abundance
and provisions for family, friends, and myself. —ALICE THOMPSON

FAITH STEP: *Come boldly to the throne of grace this morning. Ask Jesus to supply the needs of a friend. He will do it.*

THURSDAY, MARCH 5

You make known to me the path of life; you will fill me with joy in your presence, with eternal pleasures at your right hand. Psalm 16:11 (NIV)

WHEN I HUGGED MY FRIEND Tanya goodbye after our spiritual catch-up at a local café, I made my way home feeling lighter, smiling in the early June sunshine. What is it about connecting with a friend who is also listening to Jesus say, "Follow Me," that makes the day brighter?

When I rounded the corner where I live, my apartment building looked dramatically different than when I'd left it a couple of hours before. Workers were in the midst of putting up scaffolding for impending work on our brick facade. Rows and rows of metal beams framed the sidewalk, extending from where I stood all the way to my front door. They had yet to cover the crossbeams at the top with wooden planks. So in this not-yet-finished moment, the beams, glinting silver in the sunlight, looked like a trellis for the lush green trees and bushes that grew alongside and above this new structure. Scaffolding is notorious for ruining the architectural aesthetics of New York City streets, but this scaffolding was beautiful.

This, I thought, is what it is like to follow Jesus. He offers a structure, open to the heavens, framing my pathway home in a way that adds clarity, beauty and a hint of majesty. But He still allows room for the natural growth already in progress. It's all about the on-the-way-there moments. Around every corner, even in the aspects of our lives that are most ordinary and familiar, we may come upon surprise and delight—as if Jesus is smiling and saying, "Thanks for following Me!" —ELIZABETH BERNE DEGEAR

FAITH STEP: *When Jesus asks you to follow, how does He help guide you on your path? Spend some time journaling about what the road looks like and how you know Jesus is with you on it.*

FRIDAY, MARCH 6

Be dressed for service . . . . Be like people waiting for their master to come home. Luke 12:35–36 (CEB)

I WAS A LATECOMER TO the *Downton Abbey* craze a few years ago, but soon became fascinated with the vast differences between high society and servant status and the similarities between their hearts' longings, strengths, and weaknesses. Staff members took their responsibilities seriously. I was humbled by their quick response times, how they anticipated the needs of their masters and mistresses and made accommodations for the smallest or most inconvenient requests.

Then I reread this passage from Luke 12. Speaking to His close followers, Jesus told them to be "dressed for service . . . . like people waiting for their master to come home." What does that mean to a twenty-first-century servant of Jesus Christ? Am I ready for whatever He asks of me? Could that mean that I need to devote myself to match the Scriptures I know with the references where they're found in the Bible, so I'm ready to share them with others without a Google search? Could it mean taking an online Bible study? Or filling my pantry with extra food so I'm ready to be hospitable, inviting someone into our home, preparing a meal for a family in need, providing for people without food?

From the context of that passage, it's obvious "dressed" didn't mean wearing an apron at all times or dressing in what used to be called "Sunday best" in case Jesus returns before our next breath. And it seems clear He meant it to include anytime He calls on us, not just when He calls us home. I'm going to spend time today considering how I can be royal-ready for whatever He requires. —CYNTHIA RUCHTI

FAITH STEP: *Do you own a small bell? Keep it on your desk, worktable, or counter to remind you to be ready whenever your Master Jesus has a request of you.*

SATURDAY, MARCH 7

Two men went up to the temple to pray, one a Pharisee and the other a tax collector. The Pharisee stood by himself and prayed: "God, I thank you that I am not like other people—robbers, evildoers, adulterers—or even like this tax collector." Luke 18:10–11 (NIV)

I WAS AHEAD OF SCHEDULE for a writing deadline and had been working faithfully every weekday. Friday, I returned home from a doctor appointment exhausted. My body felt that feverish-flu sensation as if dozens of little elves were hitting me with tiny bats. The sensible choice would be to take a sick day and rest. Yet even as I considered that option, I told myself I needed to be diligent. Write every day. Push myself harder.

When I stopped to pray about my choices, Jesus challenged me to look at my motivations. He reminded me of the Pharisee praying in the temple. Prayer is a good thing. Yet Jesus used the story as an example of wrong motivations.

Writing faithfully was a good thing, but in my case, I hesitated to take a day off out of fear. Fear that if I missed a day I'd forget how to write. Fear that everyone else in the world was getting ahead of me. And the root of that fear was a lack of trust in Jesus. Could I trust Him to help me resume my work if I dared take time off?

Like the Pharisee, we can be influenced by mixed motives in our daily lives: pride, fear, winning the praise of people, or a desire to control.

We can often do the right thing for the wrong reasons. Jesus challenges us to go deeper. To make choices motivated by trust and love. At times, He will encourage us to step forward boldly. Other times, He'll call us to step back and rest. Both actions require trust. —SHARON HINCK

FAITH STEP: *Look at your calendar. Are there any activities that you are doing for wrong reasons? Ask Jesus to help you make wise choices for the right reasons.*

SUNDAY, MARCH 8

Jesus asked Simon Peter, ". . . do you love me more than these?"
John 21:15 (CEB)

"YOU CAN COUNT ON ME, babe," my husband said. "Unless I'm not paying attention."

It's one of the reasons I call him Wonderhubby. He's a wonder.

Once again, humor defused what could have been an incendiary situation. Laughter is good marriage medicine.

I've discovered an additional reason why the Bible urges us not to be "unequally yoked together with unbelievers" (2 Corinthians 6:14, KJV). The reason is that only a devoted follower of Jesus understands that the other person's relationship with Him is a higher priority than the marriage, that the only One who will never fail, disappoint, neglect, and never "not pay attention" is Jesus.

His faithful, unchanging nature is a rock-solid truth we can count on. When Jesus invited us by saying, "Follow Me," He was also saying, "You can count on Me. The road may be treacherous, but I'll keep you safe. I'll light the way for you, and you can rely on My strength. I don't mind carrying you. And I don't get distracted, consumed by other issues, or relax my grip on you."

Jesus resisted every self-serving thought. Humans often fail each other, even when we're well-intentioned, even when love is involved. But Jesus—ah, Jesus. The flawless Spouse. —CYNTHIA RUCHTI

FAITH STEP: *Jesus has vowed to never leave you or forsake you, and to love you forever. What are your vows to Him?*

MONDAY, MARCH 9

Jesus replied, "Foxes have dens, and birds have nests. But the Son of Man doesn't have a place to call his own." Matthew 8:20 (CEV)

A WOMAN I WORK WITH couldn't give me her home address. I imagined the possibilities. Homeless? Evicted? Memory loss? Living out of her car? Sleeping on a friend's couch? Witness protection program?

The answer was much simpler—and more complicated—than that. She and her husband were in the process of moving. Their current address wouldn't be viable for long and her new address wasn't "hers" until they signed the final papers.

Jesus had a home with His earthly parents while growing up. But as an adult, after His ministry began, He had no home, according to Scripture. Not even a "tiny house" in a friend's backyard. Have you wondered why?

In biblical times, a home was a cultural sign of manhood. Owning property indicated that one was established, successful, part of the community.

I believe Jesus didn't have an earthly address because He didn't fit in with this world. He was—as we are—a temporary sojourner. He couldn't afford the upkeep—the time or attention—of a home on earth. It would've distracted from His primary purpose—to serve, speak God's truths, and show God's heart. He belonged to all people, not one community or one neighborhood. And He belonged on the throne.

Jesus didn't need a temporary earthly address during His ministry years. He stayed on the move. And He had a permanent address. We'll share His zip code for eternity. —CYNTHIA RUCHTI

FAITH STEP: *Are you fussing over upkeep when He's calling you to open your home for outreach?*

TUESDAY, MARCH 10

They asked . . . "Why does He eat with tax collectors and sinners?"
When Jesus heard this, He told them, "Those who are well don't need a
doctor, but the sick do need one." Mark 2:16–17 (HCSB)

I LEAD THE PRAISE TEAM at my church. We have a group text for sending practice schedules and stuff like that.

Last Sunday, one of our members wrote, "I won't make it to the service today. I just don't feel like singing. I may not come back to church until I get a grip on my problems."

People responded: "Let me know if I can do anything to help." "Praying for you." "You will be missed." All kind attempts at support in an awkward situation. I thought about it for a while and prayed. Being a private person, I feel weird in these situations. It's like I'm embarrassed for the person because I would never share something like that in a group.

As soon as I had that thought, I felt convicted. It was as if Jesus Himself spoke to my heart. *Why would this be awkward? It's exactly what I want you to do. It's exactly what the church is for.* Suddenly it seemed like this actually was the church. It actually was a praise team. The church is more than a service. Music is more than praise.

I wrote back: "We love you. You don't have to be in a good mood or have a grip on your stuff. We are for you, and Jesus is too."

From now on, I'm going to try to be more "awkward" at church instead of acting like I have it all together. Maybe if we do that, more people will feel safe enough to be vulnerable like this girl was, and church can be a more healing place for all of us.
—GWEN FORD FAULKENBERRY

FAITH STEP: *Do you try to "get a grip" instead of resting in the grip of Jesus? Call or text a buddy to ask for prayer about whatever ails you.*

WEDNESDAY, MARCH 11

Sing and make music from your heart to the Lord, always giving thanks to God the Father for everything, in the name of our Lord Jesus Christ.
Ephesians 5:19–20 (NIV)

I STEPPED OUTSIDE EARLY ONE morning after a rough night of severe storms. Lightning, rolling thunder, pounding rain, and high winds had kept me up most of the night. The morning news showed the destruction from the storms. As I surveyed our property, I could see that we'd been spared any real damage, but our lawn was littered with pine cones, small limbs, and other debris. I grumbled out loud as I started cleaning up the mess. "This is no way to start a Saturday morning! I have so much to do today!"

But while picking up the debris, I saw a bird's nest on the ground. Instantly I was aware of the sound of birds singing from the tree limbs above. I stopped and looked up to watch and listen to the birds. They sounded as if they were praising Jesus for protecting them from the storm! Two blue jays, busily rebuilding their nest, stopped to sit on a branch to sing praises. Job 12:7 (NIV) says, "But ask the animals, and they will teach you, or the birds in the sky, and they will tell you."

Those wonderful birds reminded me that I hadn't stopped to thank Jesus or praise Him for protecting us and our property from last night's storm. Despite the damage the storm had caused the birds' nests, they were still singing and praising Him! I felt convicted, so I stood still and thanked Jesus for His protection through last night's storm, and His enduring protection through all the storms of life. And I thanked Him for the birds, who taught me a valuable lesson about faith and praise. —KATIE MINTER JONES

FAITH STEP: *Remember to thank Jesus for your blessings every day. If the birds praise Him, shouldn't we?*

THURSDAY, MARCH 12

*My sheep listen to my voice; I know them, and they follow me.
I give them eternal life, and they shall never perish; no one will
snatch them out of my hand. John 10:27–28 (NIV)*

MY HUSBAND AND I LOVE cats. Our home is full of them. We live close to a river where people often leave their unwanted pets. One day, some kittens made their way to our porch. These little lions —Timmy and Johnny—were soon joined by another abandoned marmalade, Tommy. He's mild as a lamb.

Next, we adopted a local farmer's female kitten. At only six weeks old, our feisty Ivy quickly ruled the household. Later, we added Milo to our brood. This little tuxedo couldn't resist tormenting his farmer-owner's chickens. Now he spends time in good-natured wrestling with the other cats. A variety of circumstances brought these felines into our home. We don't know much about their pasts or how they survived. We only know they belong with us and we'll always care for them. They're part of the family. They trust us and come running whenever they hear our voices calling them.

Before I found my way to Jesus, I felt lost and my life seemed empty. I was starving for a love that was true and Someone I could depend on. When He called me by name (Isaiah 43:1), I started walking in His direction, but soon my slow steps gave way to a full run.

Jesus has given me an eternal home, a place where I can live within His glory forever. No one can harm me. Nothing can steal me from the safety of His hand. I've been adopted into a kingdom beyond anything I'd ever dreamed possible, where hope and power and love reign. And I need never go hungry or fear again. —HEIDI GAUL

FAITH STEP: *Visit your local animal shelter. Donate pet food or your time. Meditate on the mercy you were shown at your adoption in Jesus's family and give thanks.*

FRIDAY, MARCH 13

*Again he sent other servants, saying, "Tell those who are invited, 'See,
I have prepared my dinner, my oxen and my fat calves have been
slaughtered, and everything is ready. Come to the wedding feast.'"
But they paid no attention and went off, one to his farm, another to
his business. Matthew 22:4–5 (ESV)*

I WOKE UP EXCITED FOR a writers' retreat I was hosting. Then I
checked my emails. "Sorry, something came up." "Can't make it."
Several people canceled for valid reasons, but I still felt deflated. I
prayed for Jesus to fix my attitude.

The story of the wedding banquet came to mind. Jesus understood feeling disappointed when guests couldn't or wouldn't arrive.
As I read His parable again, something even more remarkable stood
out. He put Himself in the position of being rejected, ignored, or
stood up. That's how much He loves us. He was willing to suffer the
pain of preparing salvation, even though some would turn away—
all because He cares so much about having a relationship with us.

I continued to pray for Jesus to fix my attitude, but I also asked
Him to give me the courage to keep risking, reaching out, and planning activities where people might not show up. Because that's what
love does. And I asked Jesus to forgive me for the times He waited
for me and, like the guests in the parable, I didn't pay attention.

We've accepted Jesus's invitation to the eternal wedding feast that
awaits us in heaven, but let's also accept His daily invitation to commune with Him. Let's follow His example and reach out to others.
—SHARON HINCK

FAITH STEP: *Take a risk and invite someone to spend time with you. If they are
too busy, ask Jesus for the love to reach out to the next person.*

SATURDAY, MARCH 14

I know your deeds, that you are neither cold nor hot. I wish you were either one or the other! So, because you are lukewarm—neither hot nor cold— I am about to spit you out of my mouth. Revelation 3:15–16 (NIV)

I STOOD IN THE MOTEL shower, dripping wet and shivering. At first, the water ran steamy hot. But as I applied shampoo to my hair, a sense of foreboding came over me. Seconds later the stream cooled to lukewarm and the pressure reduced to a trickle. I raced to rinse off the suds. The next moment, an alternating medley of cold-to-tepid blasts of water splashed my body. I shrieked.

Hurrying from the stall, I toweled dry. I was furious. Which felt worse? The freezing temperature because it shocked me? No. At least it invigorated me. The half-warm spurts annoyed me more, neither soothing my muscles nor jarring me into alertness.

After dressing, I remembered Jesus's response to the wealthy, complacent church at Laodicea. His anger raged against a lukewarm faith that neither blazed nor burned out, its embers barely red, smoldering. And I understood. He was talking to me. And it wasn't a whisper.

I've endured dry seasons when I allowed my faith to slip into the background, when I forgot that my life is from, to, and through Him. This was one of them. I hadn't noticed how far I'd strayed from His side as I scurried to claim control of my life.

Seeking forgiveness, I begged to once again experience the closeness with Jesus that I'd come to take for granted. How could I have forgotten His worth? Jesus knows my motives and sees into my heart. He welcomed me back with open arms—He always does!
—HEIDI GAUL

FAITH STEP: *Take a lukewarm shower for as long as you can stand. Use that temporary discomfort as a reminder of how not to believe.*

SUNDAY, MARCH 15

---

*He calls his own sheep by name and leads them out. After he has gathered
his own flock, he walks ahead of them, and they follow him because
they know his voice. John 10:3–4 (NLT)*

ON A LEDGE ABOVE THE desk where I write sit two stuffed toy sheep
approximately eight inches tall. One is dressed like a shepherd from
biblical times, cloaked in a brown striped robe and head covering. He
hugs a staff in the crook of one elbow, and he wears lace-up sandals
on his hind feet. The other wears four lime-green socks with purple
toes. Two wee daisies—yellow and pink—are tucked behind one ear.

These comical lambs survived my household purge because they
convey a vital message: I constantly need Jesus, the Good Shepherd.

Sheep aren't exactly the smartest animals on the farm. They're
easy prey. They wander off safe paths to places where they become
lost or hurt. They're prone to becoming "cast"—rolling onto their
backs when their center of gravity is displaced—and dying in that
position if not rescued. They're unable to care for themselves. Apart
from their shepherd's vigilance, they're in constant jeopardy.

Every day my little woolly lambs silently remind me that I'm not
much different from them. Apart from Jesus, I'm in jeopardy too. I
dupe myself into believing I'm smarter or stronger than I am, and I
venture down paths that seem right but lead to danger.

Everything changes when I regard Jesus as my Shepherd. He protects,
guides, and provides for me. Knowing I don't have to fend for myself
floods me with a sense of security, and I find peace. —GRACE FOX

FAITH STEP: *Read Psalm 23 as a prayer to Jesus. Verses one and two might
sound like this: "Jesus, You're my Shepherd and provide everything I need. Thanks
for letting me rest in green meadows and leading me beside peaceful streams."*

MONDAY, MARCH 16

Ship your grain across the sea; after many days you may receive a return.
Ecclesiastes 11:1 (NIV)

I WAS EXCITED WHEN THE newspaper reported that a famous author would visit our city to give a lecture. I bought seven copies of her book and gifted them to a variety of friends and family members. My loved ones were delighted to receive the books, and they were more thrilled when I gifted each of them with a ticket to attend the writer's lecture. I was so focused on purchasing books and tickets for others that I failed to buy a book for myself.

Two days before the lecture, I was invited to speak with a local youth group. At the conclusion of the program, the leader of the group called me to the podium and presented me with a gold bag filled with gifts. I did not open the bag until I arrived home. The gifts were dressed in delicate white tissue paper. Inside I discovered an embroidered scarf from Guatemala, two bracelets made with turquoise stones, and the brand-new book that I had failed to purchase for myself.

The abundance of gifts that I received that day called to mind a song written by Doris Akers. No matter how we try, we cannot "beat God's giving." The more we share with others, the more love and blessings we receive from heaven's shore. Therefore, let us make it our daily goal to live with caring hearts. We can never be at a deficit in this way. As we pour into the lives of others, Jesus pours blessings into our lives. —ALICE THOMPSON

FAITH STEP: *Go through your home today and collect a variety of brand-new items that you purchased some time ago and still have not used. Gather the items and donate them to a person or organization in need.*

TUESDAY, MARCH 17

Be still, and know that I am God. Psalm 46:10 (ESV)
Be holy because I am holy. Leviticus 11:44 (GW)

ONE MORNING IN MY LADIES' small-group Bible study, we began talking about our obsession with making to-do lists. Two of my friends admitted that on more than one occasion they had written down a chore they had already done, just to get the satisfaction of crossing an item off the list. I laughed at that idea—until I remembered on the drive home that I had actually done it once or twice myself.

Lists do come in handy, but if we concentrate too much on a to-do list, we can forget the importance of simply *being*. God calls us to be many things: joyful, thankful, kind, forgiving, and patient, just to name a few. But the most important "be" command is sprinkled throughout the Bible: be holy; in other words, be like Jesus. Sounds impossible, but the secret is revealed in another "be" verse: be still. If we want to become Christ-like, we need to schedule quiet moments each day to settle our spirit, meditate on His qualities, and ask Him to give us strength to honor Him in everything we say and do.

The most important use of our day is to practice being like Jesus. Even when our day doesn't turn out like we'd hoped or planned. Even when we have to deal with a difficult person or when we receive bad news. Every day we can expect to encounter plenty of opportunities to choose between behaving like Christ would and acting on the basis of our natural instincts. In those moments, what we *do* will reflect who we are *becoming*. And that's much more important than crossing off every item on the longest to-do list.
—DIANNE NEAL MATTHEWS

FAITH STEP: *Take a few moments to review your written or mental to-do list for the day ahead. At the top add these words: "Be like Jesus."*

WEDNESDAY, MARCH 18

In all my prayers for all of you, I always pray with joy because of your partnership in the gospel from the first day until now, being confident of this, that he who began a good work in you will carry it on to completion until the day of Christ Jesus. Philippians 1:4–6 (NIV)

THIS PAST YEAR I LAUNCHED myself back into the workforce—as a middle school teacher. I know. It was a wild idea. In preparation for this new career, I met with my fifth-grade teacher, Mrs. Cox. (*Best. Teacher. Ever.*) I asked her, seriously, "How in the world am I going to do this?" In her calm way, she set my feet on the path of teacher wisdom: "Be firm. Explain EVERYTHING. Set boundaries. Have routines. Share procedures. Be prepared. Be ready to improvise because teaching is fluid." As she spoke, I thought, *I want to be just like you.* I said, "I have a lot to learn." She said, "Keeping thinking that. The teacher who thinks she knows it all is finished."

I am far from finished. This truth is mirrored in my walk with Jesus. I am still learning to follow His ways and His voice. Still learning how to trust Him and lean into the hope of who He is. The lessons keep coming. Every day is a new opportunity to become more like Him. When I read the life-altering words Jesus shared, I think, *I want to be just like you.* And the crazy thing is? That's His promise to us. We still have a lot to learn, but He is transforming us moment by moment. As we follow Him, we become like Him. We can be confident that He is completing the work He began in us. —SUSANNA FOTH AUGHTMON

FAITH STEP: *Journal about how Jesus has changed you in the past year. Thank Him for the good work that He has started and is going to complete in you!*

THURSDAY, MARCH 19

The LORD has made everything for his own purposes. Proverbs 16:4 (TLB)

I LOVE SPRING, BUT THERE are a few things that bother me. Pollen, for one, and another thing would be those pesky, buzzing, stinging insects called bees. On this pretty day, while attempting to complete this writing, I can see and hear those dreaded insects through my window. I wonder what I always wonder... *why did God create bees?* They always chase me back inside. I run and slam the door on them. Once I'm safe in the house, I remind myself again that bees have a purpose just like everything does on this earth. Bees pollinate fruits and vegetables, which provide nutrition for us. They also provide honey. Bees are an intricate part of the natural world and are needed... even though I could do without them.

Jesus's purpose on earth was to preach the gospel, heal the sick and brokenhearted, and set captives free. He had an appointed time to work on earth before He fulfilled His other purpose, which was dying to save us. When He left, Jesus purposed us with continuing the work He started on earth with each of us working uniquely to bring hope, beauty, and His truth to the world. Like the bees that spread pollen, we're meant to spread the love of Jesus. When we seek Jesus, He helps us to fulfill our purpose in our jobs, churches, families, and communities. —TRACY ELDRIDGE

FAITH STEP: *Look at the beauty of the ecosystem right outside your window where everything is working together to fulfill its purpose. Now imagine us working together and creating beauty as we fulfill our purpose on earth.*

FRIDAY, MARCH 20

The LORD is my shepherd; I shall not want. He makes me lie down in green pastures. He leads me beside still waters. Psalm 23:1–2 (ESV)

WHILE WAITING TO BOARD MY plane, I tapped the screen of my smartphone and Psalm 23 appeared. I've probably read this popular psalm a hundred times, but its pastoral imagery has never come so vividly to me as it did when I reached the Vayang Rolling Hills. These beautiful hills are located on the west side of Basco, Batanes, the northernmost island-province of the Philippines.

The Vayang Rolling Hills are a vast series of low hills covered with green grass and hedgerows, as far as one's eyes can see. And from where I stood, I saw cows dotting the landscape—a few were standing still on the slope, some were grazing, others were just lying down as the sun was setting. This was one of the reasons I came to this place—to see this breathtaking view that travelers rave about.

My eyes feasted on the green hills as winds from the sea swept my hair. A different kind of calmness filled my heart. I wanted to take more photos, but after snapping a few, I stopped and gazed at the pastureland. *If I were a cow or a sheep, I wouldn't lack grass to eat. The grazing area is so huge I couldn't possibly consume it all.*

That thought struck me. Seeing these animals in this vast meadow reminded me of Psalm 23:1. If I believe that Jesus's resources are boundless and if I consider Him my Good Shepherd, then I need not worry about lacking anything. I can be content knowing Jesus cares for and provides for me. —MARLENE LEGASPI-MUNAR

FAITH STEP: *Refuse to be worried by thoughts of lack. Instead, thank Jesus for taking care of all your needs and experience the peace that comes from that belief.*

SATURDAY, MARCH 21

Your prayers and your compassionate acts are like a memorial offering to God. Acts 10:4 (CEB)

MY HEART SWELLS WHEN I hear about exceptional acts of compassion. The little girl who designed a bracelet to raise funds to help pay for a friend's lung transplant. The eleven-year-old who returned his Christmas presents so he could purchase gifts for children of the incarcerated. The four-year-old hero who asked his parents to take all the money he earned as an allowance and what they would normally spend on toys for him, so he could buy chicken sandwiches for the homeless, whom he served personally while wearing a superhero cape, telling each recipient, "Don't forget to show love."

The grieving mom who—days after her daughter died following a long battle with cancer—sat in a hospital waiting room crocheting hats for premature babies, praying for each one with each stitch.

The readers who write to say, "I pray for each of you who write a *Mornings with Jesus* devotion."

Such compassion! Such beautiful gifts! Jesus would be so proud.

Jesus *is* proud. Today's verse from the book of Acts refers to Cornelius, a Roman centurion who was singled out for special assignment because his "prayers and compassionate acts" were noticed and applauded by heaven. His generosity and caring heart—which no doubt to him seemed simple things—effectively rose as the fragrance of a memorial offering to the Holy One.

Jesus's life was consumed with prayer and compassionate acts. Can the same be said of mine? —CYNTHIA RUCHTI

FAITH STEP: *Show compassion today. In the words of a four-year-old—and the Jesus he imitates—"Don't forget to show love."*

SUNDAY, MARCH 22

For I want you to understand what really matters, so that you may live pure and blameless lives until the day of Christ's return. Philippians 1:10 (NLT)

I HAVE THIRTEEN-YEAR-OLD AND TEN-YEAR-OLD boys. Pierce, my bright, witty, and athletic older one, is starting middle school and is showing signs of "tween-itude." My nine-year-old Isaac, a joy and fun-filled fellow with Down syndrome, presents some unique challenges that are somewhat less predictable.

I read parenting books, swap strategies with pals, and pray a lot. I mostly just do my best. Some days I feel like a pretty good mom—just the right balance of loving discipline, attention, and fun. Other days, I feel like a failure. I know this is normal.

My particular challenge when it comes to parenting is control. I've struggled with this, but it can look pretty awful with my kids. I catch myself adopting a harsh, graceless tone. I hate it and apologize. I've found solace from someone who knows what it's like. I once heard a lady preacher, who was a single mom to four boys, express similar frustration and self-loathing. Jesus granted her a sweet insight that she used whenever she remembered. She'd pause and ask, "God, is this bothering You or just me?"

In other words, does this behavior, choice, activity, bother You or *just me*, Lord? Now I ask myself, *Does it matter if my older boy wears flip-flops to church? Does Jesus care if his clothes don't match? Is Jesus concerned that Isaac plays with a toy in an unconventional way?* How much correcting and relentless nagging could I avoid if I asked this simple question and humbly listened for the answer? Jesus's grace-filled, unconditional love is my inspiration and aspiration. —ISABELLA YOSUICO

FAITH STEP: *When inspired to correct your spouse, kids, or friends, ask, "God, does this bother You or just me?"*

MONDAY, MARCH 23

Peter turned and saw that the disciple whom Jesus loved was following them. (This was the one who had leaned back against Jesus at the supper and had said, "Lord, who is going to betray you?") When Peter saw him, he asked, "Lord, what about him?" Jesus answered, "If I want him to remain alive until I return, what is that to you? You must follow me."
John 21:20–22 (NIV)

YESTERDAY I DISCOVERED A COLLEAGUE of mine had been given a position I felt I deserved. I heard it from a friend. Struggling to maintain composure, I regulated my voice to hide my emotions.

After the shock wore off, I spent time alone, stoking fires of indignation and jealousy. *Does Jesus love her more than me?* Dark thoughts clouded my mind as I muffled the Holy Spirit's urgings to pray. I was determined to stay angry. I dredged up other situations in which the Lord had seemed to reward others, leaving me in the background. *Poor me!*

In the next moment I felt as if I'd been shaken from the inside out. I hung my head, suddenly aware of a fresh sin I thought I'd conquered long ago. Praying, I asked Jesus to forgive my covetous spirit. I thanked Him for all He'd already given me and acknowledged it was more than enough, much more than I deserved.

Like an invisible hug, a song came to mind, and I smiled. *Jesus loves me. The Bible tells me so.* True. His limitless love more than quells my desires. What more could I want? —HEIDI GAUL

FAITH STEP: *Think about how Jesus has blessed you. Write down how these gifts are perfect for you. Give thanks!*

TUESDAY, MARCH 24

For God so loved the world, that he gave his only begotten Son, that whosoever believeth in him should not perish, but have everlasting life.
John 3:16 (KJV)

ONE MORNING I OVERSLEPT. THEN, while rushing around the kitchen, I spilled a glass of orange juice all over the counter. After that, I got stuck behind a slow driver and was late for work.

When I got to work, it was hectic. The phone was ringing. The computer kept crashing. Customers were waiting. And there was a stack of orders to be filled. I was anxious.

So I took a deep breath and said a quick prayer. *Dear Jesus, please calm me, and help me adjust my attitude.*

I started ringing up customers in the pharmacy. "That will be three dollars and sixteen cents," I said. Hmm…$3.16. John 3:16 popped into my mind. Later, I picked up a bottle of medicine. The number 316 was in the stock number. It couldn't be a coincidence. That afternoon, I looked at the clock. It was 3:16. Again, I repeated the promise of John 3:16 and thanked Jesus for His grace.

That crazy morning at the pharmacy changed me. When I asked Jesus to change my attitude, He reminded me that He loved me enough to die for me so that I could have eternal life. I don't ever want to forget that. Now I set my phone alarm for 3:16 p.m. every afternoon. When I see the number 316, I thank Jesus for His love.

Jesus constantly reminds us to focus on Him. He wants our thoughts anchored in His mercy and grace. He etches His words upon our hearts because He wants us to remember just how much He loves us. —KATIE MINTER JONES

FAITH STEP: *Set your clock or phone alarm for 3:16 p.m., then focus on Jesus's sacrifice and His promise of eternal life.*

WEDNESDAY, MARCH 25

Lift up your eyes and look about you: All assemble and come to you;
your sons come from afar, and your daughters are carried on the hip.
Then you will look and be radiant, your heart will throb and swell
with joy; the wealth on the seas will be brought to you, to you the
riches of the nations will come. Isaiah 60:4–5 (NIV)

As a CITY GIRL, I never learned about birdsong. But then, I spent a year volunteering in Alaska and got an education I'll always treasure. On long walks in marshes surrounded by lush woodlands, one of the school teachers I worked with taught me how to recognize the calls of different birds. I slowly began to distinguish the different notes and rhythms that alerted me to the presence of pintails and plovers, ptarmigans and Pacific loons. The sounds of nature became a rich symphony to my ears.

When I returned to New York City, I thought I wouldn't use my new birding skill. But I was wrong. Now when I ride the crowded subway, I tune in with my listening skills, and I hear sounds reminiscent of birdsong! In what before used to be noise, I can now discern a variety of languages and dialects. I hear families interacting, tourists from around the world speaking, and teenagers laughing together.

My commute has become special as I savor the sounds around me and realize that the sound of humanity is a gift from God, just like birdsong or a babbling brook. I hear Jesus speaking to me in this diverse human chorus, and I marvel at His beauty and wisdom.
—ELIZABETH BERNE DEGEAR

FAITH STEP: *Spend time with a sense you take for granted—sight, hearing, touch, taste, or smell. Can you use it today to become more aware of Jesus communicating directly with you?*

THURSDAY, MARCH 26

The thief comes only to steal and kill and destroy; I came that they might have life, and have it abundantly. John 10:10 (NASB)

SOMETIMES MY KIDS CRACK ME up around the dinner table. Especially the little one. She'll get way more food on her plate than she needs or could ever eat. (Unless it's bacon; she can eat all the bacon!) I'm trying to teach her how to get the right amount and that she can get more if she needs it. She doesn't have to worry that there won't be enough for her. But I remember my kids all going through this stage. It seems natural, especially when you're small, to worry you won't get your portion.

Some of us never grow out of it. I think many of our problems, between people as well as nations, come from this mind-set of scarcity. We think we have to grab everything we can for ourselves lest we'll run out or someone will take it from us. But it doesn't only apply to things. Maybe it's attention. We think that if someone else gets attention from the boss about good work or another parent's kid wins an award or another church gains members, these things take away from us.

But our God is a God of abundance. Jesus came for that very reason—to give us life to the full (John 10:10). In Him, there is no such thing as scarcity. He has no limits to His resources, including the love and attention He lavishes on us. There's plenty to go around.

What would it look like if we really believed that? What kind of people would we be? What kind of nation could we build?
—GWEN FORD FAULKENBERRY

FAITH STEP: *Pray, Lord Jesus, You are the source of everything good. In You, I find everything I need. I commit myself to trust You, not to fear scarcity. Make me a vessel that Your abundance flows through into the lives of others.*

FRIDAY, MARCH 27

Pray without ceasing. 1 Thessalonians 5:17 (KJV)

I DROVE TO MY COUSIN'S home to deliver her birthday gift. I noticed that the green oak tree that loomed over her roof was now gray and stripped of leaves in the middle of spring. The hundred-foot tree was *dead*. My cousin reported that she and her husband did not have money to pay a tree trimmer.

I drove away consumed with fear because my cousin and her husband have two small children. One ferocious wind or rainstorm had the potential to topple the brittle tree. My mind ran wild with tragic scenarios. I wanted to help my cousin and her husband pay to have the tree cut. My mother stopped me. "Leave them alone!" she said. "Let those young people handle their own problems."

Over time the tree began to shed and dismantle itself onto my cousin's roof. In rainstorms, I worried that her family would not survive the night. Due to my mother's ultimatum, prayer was my only recourse. I prayed for the young family's safety every day. As I entered a second year of fervent prayer, my cousin and her husband, with the Lord's help, finally found the means to hire a company to raze the tree before it destroyed their roof.

My mother called to say, "That big tree was cut down today." I thanked Jesus for answered prayer and offered up a shout of praise.

There are times that we are able to physically and financially help others. But sometimes Jesus permits us to only offer them prayers of faith. Why? He wants us to witness the power of fervent prayer. He wants our loved ones to know Him as their personal Savior. —ALICE THOMPSON

FAITH STEP: *Write down a problem that seems to have no end and mark it with today's date. Tuck this note away, and no matter how long it takes, pray over the problem until Jesus sends a solution.*

SATURDAY, MARCH 28

Suppose one of you has a hundred sheep and loses one of them. Doesn't he leave the ninety-nine in the open country and go after the lost sheep until he finds it? And when he finds it, he joyfully puts it on his shoulders and goes home. Then he calls his friends and neighbors together and says, "Rejoice with me; I have found my lost sheep." Luke 15:4–6 (NIV)

I GET LOST. A LOT. Even when I use my GPS, I often manage to take a wrong turn. My most recent adventure landed me on a dirt logging road blocked by a fallen tree, not quite sure where I went wrong. And as I listened to Madam GPS, her voice sounded the tiniest bit frustrated, as she said, "Recalculating."

There are times I get lost in my personal life as well. Last month, I failed to follow Jesus's directions on loving others, and as a result, I almost allowed a friendship to die from lack of attention. Without meaning to, I'd hurt someone and disappointed the Lord. Like my driving blunders, it wasn't something I'd set out to do. I'd just taken a wrong turn and wound up where I shouldn't have.

The regret I felt was tremendous. But as He carries me back to the fold, I'm certain that whatever sin I've committed, whether accidental or intentional, is forgiven. The moment I repent, He erases it. As I sigh, grateful for the Good Shepherd's patience and love, I imagine His relief in finding me. He's as happy to welcome me back as I am to return to the flock.

The longer I live in faith, the deeper this understanding is driven into my heart. When I walk close beside my Shepherd, I'm less likely to stray and become lost. But those times when I do stray, I'm so glad I can depend on Jesus. —HEIDI GAUL

FAITH STEP: *Purchase a Bible and leave it somewhere you think a lost soul might find it. Help the Good Shepherd add another sheep to His flock.*

SUNDAY, MARCH 29

One of them, an expert in the law, tested him with this question:
"Teacher, which is the greatest commandment in the Law?" Jesus replied:
"'Love the Lord your God with all your heart and with all your soul
and with all your mind.' This is the first and greatest commandment."
Matthew 22:35–38 (NIV)

MY HUSBAND FILLS OUT OUR tax forms each year with organized files of receipts and computer spreadsheets. I try to stay involved, but my head throbs on the first page: subparagraphs; special exclusions; rules, and more rules. According to some sources, the US tax code includes seventy thousand pages. And still people find loopholes. Rules have a way of multiplying and growing more burdensome. Their original purpose gets buried. The notion of everyone chipping in to help each other has been lost along the way.

The Pharisees had over six hundred regulations and argued endlessly about them. The ceremonial laws became more burdensome and controlling. The notion of living every moment of the day in relationship with God was often lost along the way.

The expert who questioned Jesus probably assumed his question would stump anyone. After all, who could sort out the mess now? Who would have the authority to decide the most important of all the laws? Jesus, of course, the only One to fulfill the law perfectly. He reminded the Pharisees, and He reminds us, that when we feel overwhelmed by commands and rules, we can come back to the core truth. Our God wants to be in relationship with us. Because of Jesus, that relationship is restored. We never go wrong when we pour our heart, soul, and mind into love for our Lord. —SHARON HINCK

FAITH STEP: *Write Jesus's greatest commandment on a three-by-five card and carry it with you. Think about how to apply it to every part of life.*

MONDAY, MARCH 30

I'm reminded of how sincere your faith is. That faith first lived in your grandmother Lois and your mother Eunice. I am convinced that it also lives in you. 2 Timothy 1:5 (GW)

TODAY I RETURNED TO SCHOOL after spring break, and learned that my coteacher's grandmother had passed away. Sometimes when I speak with someone who's lost a loved one, I hesitate to ask questions. I don't want to be intrusive. But today I remembered the tremendous hurt I felt when my beloved maternal grandmother died, so I asked my colleague about her grandmother. She told me about the treasure of journals, Bibles, photo albums, and keepsake books that had been discovered in her grandmother's house. For years, her grandmother had written prayers of blessings and protection for her children, grandchildren, and great-grandchildren, speaking life, healing, hope, and prosperity into the lives of her family. Her grandmother left a legacy of faith for her family, just as Lois did for Timothy in the New Testament.

In Paul's second letter to Timothy, he let Timothy know that the same faith his mother and grandmother had in Jesus Christ lived inside Timothy, and he needn't be fearful starting his ministry. I'm sure that Timothy's grandmother and mother prayed for Timothy as he was growing up, trusting that he'd live a life for Jesus. Seeing the faith of our loved ones in action shapes our lives. It's shaped mine. I'm experiencing the faith in Christ that first lived in my grandmother on a higher level. I desire to leave the same faith legacy to my daughter and future grandchildren, so they, too, will trust Him as they work for Him. —TRACY ELDRIDGE

FAITH STEP: *Speak life! Leave your loved ones a legacy of faith—a treasure of written prayers.*

TUESDAY, MARCH 31

*Happy are those servants whom the master finds waiting up when
he arrives. . . . he will dress himself to serve, seat them at the table
as honored guests, and wait on them. Luke 12:37 (CEB)*

WHEN MY HUSBAND SAYS, "LET'S eat out," he usually means a place
with plastic lids and straws for our beverages, ketchup in little plastic saucers, and brown paper napkins—made from recycled paper,
a counterpoint to all the plastic.

The first time I ate at a four-star restaurant, a waiter took my linen
napkin—*What? Napkins come in linen?*—then laid it across my lap.
When the first course was over, he removed all my silverware, all of it,
and replaced it with a whole new set. If I dropped my napkin on the
floor, the waiter was there with a fresh one before I could reach to pick
it up. A finger bowl to clean my fingers. Sorbet to cleanse my palate.

It was over-the-top service. But I felt...cared for. Someone was
watching to make sure my every need was met. It made a great
memory to feel like an honored guest for those few hours.

Jesus asked us to be dressed and ready, like a well-trained and
beloved servant anticipating our Master's arrival. But He added
more to that story from Luke 12. He said that the servants who are
"waiting up" when He arrives home, no matter the hour, are happy
and blessed. Not tired. Not exhausted. Not impatient. Happy.

Then the tables turn. The Master dresses Himself to serve, seats
us in a place of honor, and waits on us. I can't imagine a more humbling experience than having Jesus serve me that way. Won't that be
something to write home about? —CYNTHIA RUCHTI

FAITH STEP: *Allow yourself a few moments today to create a visual image of
what it will look like to have Jesus pulling out a chair for you at His table. Thank
Him for that promised gift of grace.*

WEDNESDAY, APRIL 1

He called out to them, "Friends, haven't you any fish?" "No," they answered. He said, "Throw your net on the right side of the boat and you will find some." When they did, they were unable to haul the net in because of the large number of fish. John 21:5–6 (NIV)

I COUNTED THE NUMBER OF children on the list again, and then re-counted the number of Bibles, gifts, and stuffed animals. Easter was fast approaching, and we didn't have enough items for the baskets.

My husband and I direct a ministry, Baskets of Joy, that provides Easter baskets to children living in children's homes, foster homes, and shelters. Each basket contains a Bible, a stuffed animal, candy, and several gifts, and is a tangible representation of Jesus's love, so each child feels special and knows someone cares—most of all Jesus.

Each year after Easter, we start preparing for the next year. We purchase Easter sale items and other clearance merchandise and donations start to flow in. But as I stood over the baskets one Easter season, I started to worry. Despite our best efforts, we were missing lots of items. We needed a miracle.

But then my friend Belinda reminded me that if we trusted Jesus He would provide. So we prayed. The next day we prayed some more. Nothing happened, but we kept on praying. Then one day people started dropping off donations, some by the carload! It reminded me of the disciples and the big haul of fish they caught after trusting Jesus's command to let down their nets.

That year we received so many unexpected donations that we had extra supplies for the following Easter. That was also the year I learned not to worry and to trust Jesus for miraculous provision.
—KATIE MINTER JONES

FAITH STEP: *Ask Jesus to teach you to trust Him to provide for you.*

THURSDAY, APRIL 2

Jesus traveled through all the towns and villages of that area, teaching in the synagogues and announcing the Good News about the Kingdom. And he healed every kind of disease and illness. When he saw the crowds, he had compassion on them because they were confused and helpless, like sheep without a shepherd. He said to his disciples, "The harvest is great, but the workers are few." Matthew 9:35–37 (NLT)

A FEW WEEKS BEFORE EASTER, our church gave each member ten door hangers to hand out in our neighborhoods. We were supposed to invite people to our Easter service, but to my shame, I didn't give any to my neighbors. I gave one to a coworker and the rest sat on my table. Initially I told myself I'd deliver the door hangers in the evening when most folks would be home. But I never went. I used my injured knee as an excuse, but the real reason was that I didn't want to talk to anyone when I dropped off the door hangers.

Lives could have been changed and souls saved by that one simple act.

Jesus was and is moved by the condition of people's lives. Jesus willingly gave His life for me to experience salvation and life everlasting. Before He ascended into heaven, He told us in the Great Commission that we were to go out into the world and preach the gospel, telling the world of His saving power. The truth is, the harvest is great—so many people need to know our risen Savior. Jesus's boundless love and His faithfulness toward me should compel me to *want* to share His good news with everyone I meet—whether I feel like it or not. —TRACY ELDRIDGE

FAITH STEP: *How can we witness to people about Jesus the Savior when we don't want to talk to them? Make a decision to fulfill the Great Commission. Be a willing worker because the harvest is great.*

FRIDAY, APRIL 3

And I pray that you, being rooted and established in love, may have power, together with all the Lord's holy people, to grasp how wide and long and high and deep is the love of Christ, and to know this love that surpasses knowledge—that you may be filled to the measure of all the fullness of God.
Ephesians 3:17–19 (NIV)

THIS PAST YEAR WE MOVED to Daly City, California. Bordering San Francisco, it sits thirty miles north of Redwood City, our home for the past thirteen years. Redwood City's motto is "Climate Best by Government Test." But Daly City does not pass the "climate best" test because of all the fog that settles in over the surrounding bay. The fog is dense, cold, and gray. I miss Redwood City's warm, clear days. But the gray days of Daly City speak to my spiritual journey. So much of life...is fog. Mysterious. Uncertain. Nebulous. It can be difficult for us Christ followers to navigate. We never know what is coming next. The brightness of Jesus's love has to cut through the gray. When we are lost in life's storms, He warms our wind-swept hearts with the light of His hope. Confused and anxious? He bursts in with clarity and guidance. Bone-weary? He makes us lie down in green pastures, giving us rest. We forget that the penetrating gray fog of life is sitting over the unending ocean of Jesus's love. It is so vast we can't wrap our minds around it. The truth is we are surrounded by His love. Jesus loves us completely...even in the fog, even when life feels gray. He is with us, holding us, keeping us, preserving us, lifting us up, in this moment in time.
—SUSANNA FOTH AUGHTMON

FAITH STEP: *Find a picture of the Pacific Ocean online. Ponder its endlessness. Meditate on the truth that Jesus's love for you is wider and deeper and stronger than any ocean.*

SATURDAY, APRIL 4

Let us not become weary in doing good, for at the proper time we will reap a harvest if we do not give up. Galatians 6:9 (NIV)

WRITING IS MY CALLING. EVEN without compensation, I would write. My latest book explores the life of Dr. Martin Luther King Jr. I wrote the first draft in 2005. Countless editors rejected it. Over ten years, I rewrote the manuscript no fewer than eight times. Each new revision was denied for publication.

As an orator and Bible scholar, Dr. King said, "Faith is taking the first step even when you don't see the whole staircase." I was tempted to quit on many days as my manuscript received mountain-high rejection notices. Isaiah's words comforted me, "But they that wait upon the LORD shall renew their strength; they shall mount up with wings as eagles; they shall run, and not be weary; and they shall walk, and not faint" (Isaiah 40:31, KJV).

Ultimately I did not quit or cave to self-defeat, and my book was finally published in 2018. The decade that I spent revising the text proved to be a priceless exercise in learning patience and sharpening my writing skills. My dream was deferred, but it was not denied. And here is a spiritual nugget that was gleaned from my ten-year writing journey: The soul will grow weary when it toils toward an unseen promise. Yet, as I labor to attain the vision that I hold for myself, the Spirit of the Lord strengthens my heart and emotions as I press ahead.

What are you laboring to achieve? If you refuse to quit, Jesus will touch you with His unwavering perseverance. Despite what happens in the process, never give up on yourself. Press onward. Jesus will bring you to a successful finish. —ALICE THOMPSON

FAITH STEP: *Today when you are tempted to quit or give up, go to Jesus and pray for the determination to keep moving forward until the task is accomplished.*

SUNDAY, APRIL 5

As the time drew near for him to ascend to heaven, Jesus resolutely set out for Jerusalem.... But the people of the village did not welcome Jesus because he was on his way to Jerusalem. Luke 9:51, 53 (NLT)

PALM SUNDAY MARKS THE FIRST day of Holy Week, the day we celebrate Jesus's entry into Jerusalem amid the crowd's fanfare. We focus on waving palm branches and cheers that quickly turned to derision. But there's another angle to this story—one that deserves a closer look.

Scripture tells us that Jesus resolutely set out for Jerusalem. Some Bible versions say He "was determined to go." Without doubt, Jesus had made up His mind to travel there, and no one could convince Him otherwise. Here's the nugget: He did so knowing that His triumphal entry marked the beginning of the end of His time on earth. He knew He'd die there, yet He went.

If I knew that visiting a particular city meant death for me, I'd change my plans. Wouldn't you? But Jesus would never have considered such a cop-out. He delivered Himself to His executioners, and He did so by choice. "No one can take my life from me," He said. "I sacrifice it voluntarily." (John 10:18, NLT).

Why would Jesus do such a thing? Because love compelled Him. He said, "The greatest love is shown when people lay down their lives for their friends" (John 15:13, NLT).

Christ's love for us led Him to Jerusalem and then Golgotha. God ordained the events that took place for His glory and our good, and Jesus willingly played the leading role despite the cost. —GRACE FOX

FAITH STEP: *Think of a loving act you can do for someone. Don't do something super easy. Stretch yourself and do something that requires a sacrifice.*

MONDAY, APRIL 6

And so, dear brothers and sisters, we can boldly enter heaven's Most Holy Place because of the blood of Jesus. By his death, Jesus opened a new and life-giving way through the curtain into the Most Holy Place. And since we have a great High Priest who rules over God's house, let us go right into the presence of God with sincere hearts fully trusting him. Hebrews 10:19–22 (NLT)

I LOVE RECEIVING PHONE OR FaceTime calls from my kids. They catch me in the middle of writing articles, preparing messages for speaking events, and fixing meals, but that's okay. The moment I hear their voice, I turn my focus from work to them because I cherish them and care about what's happening in their lives.

I receive calls from other people too, but they're usually scheduled. My coaching clients, for instance, set up appointments in advance. The nature of our relationship doesn't allow the freedom to call at their convenience just to chat.

Holy Week lends itself to reflecting on Jesus's death and resurrection and the difference both make in our lives. It's now possible for us to become members of His family. When we accept that invitation, we become children of the living God and we can connect with Him anytime. What a privilege!

God finds great pleasure in our desire to talk with Him. He's never too busy, and He'll never turn us away. We can enter His presence anytime, confident that He welcomes us, thanks to what Jesus did on the cross. —GRACE FOX

FAITH STEP: *Set a timer to beep every hour you're awake today. When the timer sounds, thank Jesus for welcoming you into His family and giving you unlimited access to His Father.*

TUESDAY, APRIL 7

"Come now, let's settle this," says the LORD. *"Though your sins are like scarlet, I will make them as white as snow. Though they are red like crimson, I will make them as white as wool. Isaiah 1:18 (NLT)*

AS A MOM TO EIGHT active kids, my daughter-in-law does laundry several times a week. She recently discovered a cleaning solution that treats stains more effectively than any other product she'd previously used. Grass, blackberry juice, spaghetti sauce, ink—you name it—no longer ruin her children's clothes. She rubs a teeny bit of this gel-like cleanser into the fabric and presto! The stain's gone.

I marvel at the parallelism between physical stains and spiritual stains. Whereas soap removes stains from our clothing, so Jesus's shed blood removes stains from our hearts and minds.

What types of stains cover us? A common one is shame for either wrong things we've done or hurtful things that others have done to us. It leaves us feeling like we belong in the discard pile. The list includes but isn't limited to jealousy, pride, unforgiveness, impure thoughts, gluttony, prayerlessness, and discrimination.

We might try to wash away our sin stains using man-made remedies. We immerse ourselves in church activities, donate to charities, or attempt to be an outstanding citizen. But the only effective cleanser is Jesus's blood.

A well-known older hymn says, "What can wash away my sin? Nothing but the blood of Jesus. What can make me whole again? Nothing but the blood of Jesus." Indeed, Jesus's blood is the only cleanser that removes our sin stains. Nothing else will do. —GRACE FOX

FAITH STEP: *Read Colossians 1:21–23. Verse 23 says we must continue to believe the truth that Jesus's blood cleanses us and we must not drift from it. Think of a creative but simple way to celebrate this truth during Holy Week.*

WEDNESDAY, APRIL 8

He saved us, not because of the righteous things we had done, but because of his mercy. He washed away our sins, giving us a new birth and new life through the Holy Spirit. He generously poured out the Spirit upon us through Jesus Christ our Savior. Titus 3:5–6 (NLT)

ON THIS DAY OF HOLY Week, let's rejoice in the gift of the Holy Spirit who lives in us thanks to what Jesus did on Calvary.

Jesus was called "the lamb without blemish." His death on the cross satisfied the blood sacrifice needed to atone for our sins. When we place our faith in Him for salvation, we nail our sinful nature to His cross and crucify it there (Galatians 5:24). Our old self dies with Him, and just as He rose from the dead, He raises us to new life.

There's only one problem: our old nature and habits don't give up without a fight. They want to rule as they've done in the past. We need help to resist their negative influence.

God knows our weaknesses, so He sends the Holy Spirit to dwell in us and help us live that new life. Slowly but surely, the Spirit transforms us. He makes us more and more like Jesus as we give Him control over our thoughts and desires. He develops in us godly characteristics such as love, joy, peace, patience, kindness, goodness, faithfulness, gentleness, and self-control (Galatians 5:22–23). He teaches, equips, and empowers us to say *no* to temptation and *yes* to following Jesus.

Jesus gives us a new life and then He sees to it that we have the Holy Spirit to help us walk it out. "And I will ask the Father, and he will give you another Advocate, who will never leave you," Jesus said to His followers. "He is the Holy Spirit, who leads into all truth" (John 14:16–17, NLT). —GRACE FOX

FAITH STEP: *Thank Jesus for asking the Father to send the Holy Spirit to help you live a godly life.*

MAUNDY THURSDAY, APRIL 9

There is more than enough room in my Father's home. If this were not so, would I have told you that I am going to prepare a place for you? When everything is ready, I will come and get you, so that you will always be with me where I am. John 14:2–3 (NLT)

I WAS EIGHT WHEN MY sister told me about heaven. "No one gets sick," she said. "Everyone has food. No one fights or cries!"

Images of happy, healthy people filled my mind. *Nice place to go when I die,* I thought. Decades later, heaven means infinitely more.

As I reflect on Christ's death and resurrection, I realize that I'd have no place in heaven apart from Him. I thank Him for giving me citizenship there (Philippians 3:20).

Apart from what He's done, I'd languish without hope. But because heaven is real, I know my heartaches will pass. Someday Jesus will wipe away my tears (Revelation 21:4). I'll see clearly His purposes for my pain.

Apart from what Jesus has done, the thought of aging and dying would be much more daunting. But heaven is real, and so is His promise to transform my body: "He will take our weak mortal bodies and change them into glorious bodies like his own, using the same power with which he will bring everything under his control" (Philippians 3:21, NLT).

Heaven is real, and if you believe in Jesus, we'll experience it someday and meet Him, the One whose work on Calvary makes the hope of heaven real even as we tarry here on earth. —GRACE FOX

FAITH STEP: *Listen closely to the song "I Can Only Imagine." Worship Jesus for making heaven a possibility for you.*

GOOD FRIDAY, APRIL 10

At about three o'clock, Jesus called out with a loud voice, "Eli, Eli, lema sabachthani?" which means, "My God, my God, why have you forsaken me?" Matthew 27:46 (NLT)

I CANNOT FATHOM THE PHYSICAL, mental, and emotional pain Jesus felt. His body crucified like the criminals hanging beside Him, His spirit crushed by the weight of the world's sin, He cried to His Father, "Why have You forsaken me?" In His deepest, darkest hour of need, He felt abandoned by His Father. What agony could compare?

Only once have I felt like God had removed Himself from me. A dear friend perceived something I'd said through the lens of her broken past and took offense. She cut me out of her life despite my repeated efforts to address the situation. I prayed, wept, and pleaded with God to restore our relationship, but nothing happened. "Where are You?" I cried one day. I heard only silence.

Because Jesus suffered as He did, we have a Savior who feels our pain. He knows how quickly doubts and despair descend on us when we're facing a dark hour. He knows our need for hope and reassurance, and He brings it to us through the Word. On this day of Holy Week, meditate on this truth from Romans 8:35–38:

"Can anything ever separate us from Christ's love? Does it mean he no longer loves us if we have trouble or calamity, or are persecuted, or hungry, or destitute, or in danger, or threatened with death? (As the Scriptures say, 'For your sake we are killed every day; we are being slaughtered like sheep.') No, despite all these things, overwhelming victory is ours through Christ, who loved us. And I am convinced that nothing can ever separate us from God's love" (NLT). —GRACE FOX

FAITH STEP: *Draw two stick figures—one for you and the other for Jesus. Draw a heart around them. Thank Jesus that He'll never abandon you.*

SATURDAY, APRIL 11

Our old sinful selves were crucified with Christ so that sin might lose its power in our lives. We are no longer slaves to sin. For when we died with Christ we were set free from the power of sin. Romans 6:6–7 (NLT)

BEING INVOLVED IN WOMEN'S MINISTRY and global missions means I hear people's life stories. Some are victorious; some aren't.

My heart breaks for Jesus followers who live trapped in destructive attitudes and behaviors such as fear, jealousy, unforgiveness, pride, lust, greed, and gluttony. Some recognize their plight and seek biblical counseling to break free. Others seem content to live as captives of the enemy.

I can relate. For several years my physical appetite held me hostage. I overate three times a day and gorged on junk food in secret, all while struggling with obesity. I knew gluttony was sin, but I felt helpless to stop.

I identified with Paul, who wrote, "I love God's law with all my heart. But there is another law at work within me that is at war with my mind. This power makes me a slave to the sin that is still within me. Oh, what a miserable person I am! Who will free me from this life that is dominated by sin and death?" (Romans 7:22–24, NLT).

Paul answered his own question: "Thank God! The answer is in Jesus Christ our Lord" (Romans 7:25, NLT). I found freedom from gluttony when I finally acknowledged that Christ's work on Calvary ended sin's control over me. Allowing it to defeat me was akin to saying His death was not enough.

Jesus's suffering and resurrection have empowered me to say no to temptation and to make wise choices. I am free. Are you? —GRACE FOX

FAITH STEP: *Dare to live freely, empowered by Jesus!*

EASTER SUNDAY, APRIL 12

So they went in, but they couldn't find the body of the Lord Jesus. . . .
Then the men asked, "Why are you looking in a tomb for someone who is
alive? He isn't here! He has risen from the dead!" Luke 24:3, 5–6 (NLT)

HOLY WEEK CLIMAXES WITH THE angels' proclamation at Jesus's empty tomb. His unexplainable absence affirmed His credibility and proved that He was who He said He was—the Son of God. He'd battled evil and won. Heaven threw a victory party that Sunday morning; Satan and his henchmen sulked in defeat.

The resurrection validated a promise Jesus made: "I am the resurrection and the life. Anyone who believes in me will live, even after dying. Everyone who lives in me and believes in me will never ever die" (John 11:25–26, NLT).

Jesus emerged the victor; and we're victors too. Not just over physical death someday, but over the enemy's attempts to defeat us now.

The enemy wants nothing more than to destroy us and seal us in an emotional, mental, or spiritual tomb. Alone. Afraid. Helpless. Dead to joy, peace, purpose, and passion. Dead to God's purposes for us and to all things related to His kingdom. But Jesus made a promise and staked His life on it, and that changes everything.

Jesus said, "The thief's purpose is to steal and kill and destroy. My purpose is to give them a rich and satisfying life" (John 10:10, NLT). His resurrection confirmed this truth. He burst from the grave fully alive and victorious. Let's follow in His steps.

"Jesus, we worship You. Thank You for everything You've done to give us life. Amen." —GRACE FOX

FAITH STEP: *Do something for Jesus that brings you and others joy!*

MONDAY, APRIL 13

Why do you seek the living among the dead? Luke 24:5 (NKJV)

THE RESURRECTION IS EVERYTHING, ISN'T IT? It's a metaphor for the whole Christian life. Without it, what's dead is just dead. Over. Finished. Buried forever. No hope of new life springing forth.

But in Jesus, we have the promise that death is not the final word in our stories, not only in an eternal sense but every day. In the accidents, the bad choices, the disappointments, the thousand other deaths that make up a lifetime.

The worst death of this kind that I've ever suffered is the death of a relationship. It's too painful now to even write the details. But someone I loved and trusted with all my heart broke that trust. And in turn, broke me. It's as if I were crushed into particles of dust. It has taken years to put the pieces back together. And what I've found is that sometimes when you've been broken and put back together, you don't fit back into your old life. At least not in the same way you once did. It's like pouring new wine into old wineskins. It just doesn't work.

The problem for me is that I loved my old life. It suited me perfectly. And so, the temptation even now at times is to look back and long for what was. To try to find what I once had. Because the way forward is unfamiliar. Like starting over, it feels harder.

That's when I hear the voice of the angel: *Why are you looking for the living among the dead? You won't find it. That thing is over. Finished. Gone. But see over here? Where you are? New life is happening. Watch the flowers appear. Listen. It's the season of singing. Don't look back. That's not where you're going. With Jesus, you rise.* —GWEN FORD FAULKENBERRY

FAITH STEP: *You know that one death, loss, or failure that you just can't get over? It's time to scatter the ashes to the wind. Don't keep them any longer. It's time to begin rising with your living Savior.*

TUESDAY, APRIL 14

Jesus said . . . "Mary!" She turned and said to Him in Hebrew, "Rabboni!" (which means, Teacher). Jesus said to her, "Stop clinging to Me, for I have not yet ascended to the Father." John 20:16–17 (NASB)

CAN YOU IMAGINE WHAT IT would have been like to be Mary on that day? Faithfully and quietly going to the tomb to be near Jesus's body, to tend to unglamorous, needful things. It was an act of worship, in her own way. Some say she was lacking faith because she looked for Him at the tomb—she should have known He was risen, after all. But I don't judge her. She was limited, human, fallible.

Her world ended with His death. He was her teacher, but much more. Jesus loved her not only for what she was, but who she wanted to be. The world looks at the outside—God sees the heart.

His love had changed her utterly, freed her from her past. But now He was gone. And with Him, her joy and light.

Mary!

She turned and saw her Jesus. And all she can do is hold on.

Stop clinging to Me.

This seems like such an odd thing to say. I believe Jesus saw her desperation, how lost she was without Him. And though (because?) He felt compassion, He wanted her to move on from that place. Not to cling to His physical presence, to what their relationship had been, but to grow stronger. To walk in communion with His Spirit from that point onward. —GWEN FORD FAULKENBERRY

FAITH STEP: *Are there aspects of your faith you need to release in order to move onward and upward with Jesus? Don't cling to the past, even if it's been good. There's more.*

WEDNESDAY, APRIL 15

And when all the crowd that came to see the crucifixion saw what had happened, they went home in deep sorrow. Luke 23:48 (NLT)

As I SIT HERE WRITING, my son, Isaac, is singing the soundtrack from *Frozen* at the top of his lungs. He brings truly immeasurable and uniquely delivered love and joy to me, my family, and many others. Yet, when he was born with Down syndrome just after Easter ten years ago, I confess it was one of the darkest times of my life—an agonizing and humbling admission for a mom to make. Now I can say with complete honesty that Isaac is one of the greatest joys of my life, a precious and continuous gift. His guileless and generous affection, unprejudiced enjoyment of the littlest things, keen emotional intuition, and innocent yet profound faith are priceless blessings. Plus, he's just plain fun.

As I remember those early, dark moments of my pregnancy and those first months after Isaac's arrival, I think about the last few days of Jesus's life. How unspeakably dark that time must have been for His followers. The hope Jesus offered was seemingly extinguished on that hill. I found myself unexpectedly but joyously pregnant at forty-three with the heart-welling anticipation of new life; then that joy was suddenly, confusingly, agonizingly gone.

Did the apostles feel the same way? Were they lost in despair? But we're wrong to underestimate God's omnipotence and His love for us! The empty tomb and then Jesus's appearance in the upper room heralded joy, just as Isaac does for me today. If you are at what seems like a terminal low point, look to the cross. Recall how hopeless it all seemed. Then remember Easter. Thank you, Jesus, for Easter! —ISABELLA YOSUICO

FAITH STEP: *Read Luke 22–24, imagine being in each scene, the fears, and ultimately the joy. Think of a time when Jesus resurrected you.*

THURSDAY, APRIL 16

But the fruit of the Spirit is love, joy, peace, patience, kindness, goodness, faithfulness, gentleness, self-control; against such things there is no law.
Galatians 5:22–23 (ESV)

MY FRIEND MARIE WAS IN a rehabilitation center while recuperating from a major surgery. "I can't wait for you to meet my favorite nurse, Crystal," she said. "You'll love her. She's such a good Christian lady." When Crystal came into the room, I was immediately impressed by how friendly and caring she was. "Crystal came to check on me on her day off," Marie said. Crystal smiled at me and said, "I was concerned about Marie, so I brought my daughters to visit." Later I realized Crystal had driven over eighty miles to visit Marie. When I asked why she'd traveled so far, she answered, "Jesus put me here for a purpose. I want to spread His love to the people who need me. I could work closer to home, but I am following His will."

Marie and I sat in the lobby visiting. Many of the people who lived at the facility looked forgotten. I watched Crystal as she walked down the hall, an aura of kindness surrounding her as she smiled and talked to the patients. She stopped and readjusted someone in a chair or gave someone water. As we sat there, she kneeled beside one lady and prayed. She rubbed the woman's back and hugged her. Crystal was being Jesus to these people. It was a beautiful thing to witness.

The fruit of the Spirit is love, joy, peace, patience, kindness, goodness, faithfulness, gentleness, and self-control. When Jesus is at work in us, the fruit of His Spirit is evident, as it was in Crystal.
—KATIE MINTER JONES

FAITH STEP: *Let the fruit of Jesus's Spirit be evident in your life today. If you know someone is sad or lonely, reach out with a phone call or stop by for a visit. Let her know she is loved.*

FRIDAY, APRIL 17

At this, many of his disciples turned away and no longer accompanied him. Jesus asked the Twelve, "Do you also want to leave?" John 6:66–67 (CEB)

NOT KNOWN FOR MY ATHLETIC skills, I was surprised when my answer to a trivia question about my life included having hiked in Colorado, Arizona, Alaska, Wisconsin, as well as the Utah desert.

The desert hike with my youngest sister took a lot out of me. Like hydration. All of it. And endurance I didn't think I had.

The heat beating down on us from above, the distance that had seemed manageable before we embarked, the constant watch for snakes and scorpions, and being a few years shy of well-trained for the hike contributed to the agony.

I brushed off the question every time my sister asked, "Do you want to turn back?"

No. I wanted to find the air-conditioned car. I wanted a tall glass of iced tea and a cold, bracing shower. But most of all, I wanted to finish, to show that I could do it, to press through the difficulties, knowing they were temporary.

Some of the teaching Jesus offered seemed harsh to His followers. Hard truth. And following Him meant attracting unwanted attention, as well as requiring unwavering devotion.

Among the saddest words in Scripture are these: "Many of his disciples turned back and no longer followed him" (John 6:66, NIV). I wonder how they felt on Good Friday, on Resurrection Sunday, when they stood before Him, at the end of their lives.

I hear a beloved song in my head: "I have decided to follow Jesus. No turning back. No turning back." —CYNTHIA RUCHTI

FAITH STEP: *Search for the story behind the song "I Have Decided to Follow Jesus." Whether true or legend, it confirms what a privilege and honor it is to follow Jesus.*

SATURDAY, APRIL 18

When he was at the table with them, he took bread, gave thanks, broke it and began to give it to them. Then their eyes were opened and they recognized him, and he disappeared from their sight. Luke 24:30–31 (NIV)

JUST AFTER JESUS'S TRIUMPH OVER death, Cleopas and another disciple traveled the road to Emmaus, discussing our Lord and His empty tomb. As they walked, Christ joined them, but they didn't recognize Him. After reaching town, they invited Him to join their table, and He accepted. As Jesus gave thanks and broke the bread with them, their eyes were opened, and they saw Him for who He truly was.

Jesus often chose mealtimes for sharing His wisdom, encouraging others to deepen their relationship with Him. I feel that way about having friends over. The table is a great place to take part in mindful conversation. We all need food and drink to survive, but our daily bread involves so much more than what we put in our stomach. The thoughts and feelings filling our hearts and minds are every bit as important. *As Jesus gave thanks, what did He say that revealed His true identity to the apostles?*

I wonder. Because after they recognized Him, He disappeared. *Had He told them all they needed to hear and cut the meeting short, so His prayer would remain embedded in their minds?*

When company comes over, I strive to show my guests that Christ lives inside me. I want to radiate Jesus's love as we break bread. I trust Him to supply the right things to say so friends will welcome Him into our visit. This time He won't disappear because now He sits at the right hand of God, and says, "Surely I am with you always, to the very end of the age" (Matthew 28:20, NIV). —HEIDI GAUL

FAITH STEP: *Invite some friends over for a meal. As you give thanks, consider the words of Jesus. He's at the table with you. How can you share that fact?*

SUNDAY, APRIL 19

But Jesus often withdrew to lonely places and prayed. Luke 5:16 (NIV)

ONE DAY I SUGGESTED THAT my husband and I visit New York City to attend a Broadway play, but work prevented him from going. The idea of navigating the busy city without him was frightening. What was I to do? The play was getting rave reviews, with one month left on Broadway. Like King David, I encouraged myself. I put fear under my feet and purchased my plane ticket.

When I arrived in New York, the hotel desk clerk upgraded my room from the seventh to the thirty-first floor. The play was excellent. But that night in the hush of my hotel room, thirty-one floors above the Hudson River, the twinkling skyline reflected in the glassy waters rendered me speechless. High above the city street, I imagined myself alone on a mountain. For most of the night I didn't sleep but sat at the window to watch and pray.

While Jesus traveled in groups, the Savior also highly regarded His alone time with the Father. Without family or friends, Jesus would steal away to pray on a mountain. Self-isolation spent in prayer fortified His spirit and equipped Jesus with power to heal the sick, feed the hungry, and surrender to His death on the cross.

Take a solo getaway to pray and revive your soul. My trip gave me an opportunity, like Jesus, to commune with the Father, and I returned home refreshed, ready to fulfill my daily obligations.
—ALICE THOMPSON

FAITH STEP: *Jesus often left the clamoring crowd to be alone in prayer. Today, steal away to spend a few minutes alone with Him.*

MONDAY, APRIL 20

Thereafter, Hagar used another name to refer to the LORD, who had spoken to her. She said, "You are the God who sees me." She also said, "Have I truly seen the One who sees me?" Genesis 16:13 (NLT)

I GREW UP IN THE country outside a small town in Tennessee. I never dreamed it was possible to pass someone face-to-face without making eye contact and offering at least a perfunctory greeting, which often led to a full-blown conversation. When I grew up and moved away, I learned that's not the common practice everywhere. At first it shocked me to see someone turn their head away at the moment we passed each other, just when I had my friendliest smile and comment ready. It made the loneliness of moving to a new place cut even deeper.

Maybe that's why I love that Hagar called God "the One who sees me." Many Bible scholars identify the angel of the Lord in this passage as Jesus. Even before He was born on earth, Jesus came down from heaven to tell a servant girl, "I see you and I care about you." During His years of earthly ministry, He communicated that same message over and over: "I see you. I know what's going on with you, and I can help."

Nobody likes to feel invisible. But we've become a more transient society due to the job market. Also, studies reveal that many people substitute social media for real-life personal interaction. Moving around the country several times as an empty nester has made me aware of the power of a smile and friendly greeting to ease loneliness. It's also taught me to find comfort in knowing that even when people ignore me, Jesus loves me so much that His eyes never leave me. —DIANNE NEAL MATTHEWS

FAITH STEP: *If you haven't done so already, develop the habit of acknowledging strangers you encounter with eye contact, a smile, and a silent prayer that they will come to know the One who sees and loves them.*

TUESDAY, APRIL 21

The King will reply, "Truly I tell you, whatever you did for the least of these brothers and sisters of mine, you did for me." Matthew 25:40 (NIV)

I NOTICED A THIN, YOUNG man sitting alone at a small table near the door of the fast-food restaurant. He appeared homeless and hungry. A backpack was on the floor beside him. Although the weather was freezing, he wore a thin jacket and sandals. His socks were dirty and had holes in them. "If he doesn't buy something soon or bothers anyone, he'll have to leave," I overheard the manager say. I ordered my food and sat down.

I can't sit here and eat when I see someone who looks hungry. If not for your grace, God, that could be me. Please touch the manager's heart so he lets the young man stay inside, I prayed. I went to the counter and bought a restaurant gift card. I discreetly laid the card on the table where the man sat. "Jesus told me to bless you," I whispered, and went back to my seat. He bought a meal and quickly devoured it. Remembering I had some donations for the homeless shelter in my car, I went outside. I put a thick jacket, a New Testament Bible, and some socks in a bag. I went back into the restaurant and placed the bag by his bag. He thanked me as I walked away, but I was just grateful that I was given the opportunity to bless someone, as so many people have blessed me in the past.

Acts 20:35 says it is more blessed to give than receive. Every day we have the opportunity to reach out in love to those around us. When we do this, we mirror Jesus's love for humanity. We fulfill His purpose for us. And in the blessing of others, we are blessed.
—KATIE MINTER JONES

FAITH STEP: *Pray that Jesus will give you opportunities to bless those around you.*

WEDNESDAY, APRIL 22

. . . and, lo, I am with you always. Matthew 28:20 (KJV)

MY NEPHEW HUNTER IS THREE years old. His mom plays a Kari Jobe worship album a lot, and he's picked up on some of the songs. His favorite is called "I Am Not Alone." It says a lot of other nice things, but the chorus repeats the truth of the above verse. Hunter likes to tell me to watch his show, which means he's going to stand in the middle of the room, use his sister's hot-pink Trolls microphone, and sing at the top of his lungs: "I am not awone! I am not awone! You will go for me! You will never weave me!" And then I clap. And then he does it again. And I clap again. We've been engaged in this scenario on a daily basis for the past week.

Last night, he was playing in my yard when it came time for the show. I sat on my porch steps, and he stood out on a stage of grass. It was twilight, and the first stars shone in the sky like lights in the dome of a great cathedral. Hunter seemed tinier than ever as he began, "I am not awone!" His big brown eyes melted my heart.

Hunter was born premature—he weighed four pounds and spent a month in the NICU. We couldn't stay with him there, but he was not alone. Jesus went before him. Jesus never left him. He'll go to school in a few years, and then he'll become a teenager. He'll go to college, get married, and have a family. One day, he'll be forty-six like me. And then he'll be an old man. And he will never, ever be alone. —GWEN FORD FAULKENBERRY

FAITH STEP: *Draw a timeline of the significant moments of your life. Thank Jesus for never leaving you. And as you imagine what the future might hold, thank Jesus that He is already there.*

THURSDAY, APRIL 23

*For out of His fullness [the superabundance of His grace and truth]
we have all received grace upon grace [spiritual blessing upon spiritual
blessing, favor upon favor, and gift heaped upon gift]. John 1:16 (AMP)*

I OPENED THE GROCERY STORE's freezer and saw the choicest array of
sausages and franks. There were a variety of European sausages, but
I particularly noticed those big, bulging orange-brown tubes labeled
Hungarian Sausage. It'd been a while since our family had enjoyed
Hungarian sausages for breakfast, but after looking at the price I
realized they weren't in our budget. *Maybe next time,* I sighed.

Two days later, I saw my cousin, who excitedly told me about his
new business. He'd shifted from fish processing and diversified into
processing high-end meat products. I was delighted to learn that
after months of struggling financially, business was picking up.

As I turned to leave, he said, "Wait, I'll give you some of our
products." He opened his freezer and took out a chunk of raw salmon
and several smoked chicken breasts. Then he brought out sausages,
franks, kielbasa, chipolata, and chorizo *Mexicano*. All mine for free!
I didn't have to buy them from the grocery store. Now our family
could have Hungarian sausage for breakfast and so much more!

I love savoring incidents like this that demonstrate the favor of
God in daily living. We are able to receive such grace—unearned
and undeserved favor—only because of Jesus Christ. Yes, we are
saved by Him for eternity, but we are also sustained by Him daily.
And believe me, Jesus also will surprise us with His lavish gifts.

—MARLENE LEGASPI-MUNAR

FAITH STEP: *Do you have a lingering suspicion that Jesus is stingy? Be assured
that Jesus is gracious toward you and that you can ask Him for favor.*

FRIDAY, APRIL 24

Why, my soul, are you downcast? Why so disturbed within me?
Put your hope in God, for I will yet praise him, my Savior and my God.
Psalm 42:5 *(NIV)*

I'D NEVER BEEN SO GLAD to receive test results! At last, the four-month-old mystery of unexplained severe itching was solved. Sometimes I woke up at night and found myself raking my nails across my body. The skin in some places became so inflamed that the shower water stung. In February, my family doctor ordered blood tests to rule out scary possibilities. He chalked it up to general allergies and recommended anti-itch ointments. They didn't help.

In April, a dermatologist did a biopsy, diagnosed contact dermatitis, and recommended a patch test. For days I wore large patches taped to my back, exposing the skin to thirty-six different substances. When the nurse peeled them off, a bright red square indicated the winner: #17, a synthetic preservative used widely in all types of products today. Two products I used daily contained the offending ingredient.

Skin reactions can be bad, but emotional reactions have potential to cause pain and serious damage if not traced back to the root cause and treated. Sometimes I feel troubled or sad, other times I sense discontent or resentment simmering and I'm not sure why.

Jesus looked at people and knew exactly what they needed. He confronted the Pharisees' hypocrisy (Matthew 23). He knew the woman who touched His robe needed a personal encounter besides physical healing (Luke 8:43–48). Jesus wants to pinpoint the cause of our painful symptoms and show us the cure. He's waiting for us to consult Him. —DIANNE NEAL MATTHEWS

FAITH STEP: *Are you struggling with a negative emotion, but can't pinpoint the source? Meditate on Psalm 139:23-24. Ask Jesus to show you His cure.*

SATURDAY, APRIL 25

You will show me the path of life; In Your presence is fullness of joy; At Your right hand are pleasures forevermore. Psalm 16:11 (NKJV)

TWO WEEKS AGO, MY FRIEND from church Brenda and I started walking. She graciously agreed to meet me at my favorite walking trail, which is lined with trees that provide shade. On the other side of the trail, there is a man-made lake that is lined with small trees and filled with families of duck and geese. When we get to the side of the trail where the lake is, Brenda always comments on the ducks. She coos at the ducklings and counts the ducks and their families. It is interesting to see her reaction when she sees the white ducks and the geese. Since I have been passing by these birds for several years, I don't look at them in awe anymore. I'm too busy completing my miles so I can move on to the next activity of the day.

Several years ago, I noticed that my mind is always churning and I am never fully present in any activity. I can miss out on the pleasures of life because I don't totally focus on the present. At times, not being focused in the moment and not sitting in the presence of Jesus can prevent us from seeing the path that He has for us.

Lately, I have been asking Jesus to help me remain present in His love. Just like my friend Brenda was aware of the beauty of the ducks and geese, I want to be aware of all that Jesus brings to my life each day. When we are aware of His presence, we can experience abundant joy and enjoy all the beauty of life, no matter how big or small. My desire is to be fully present, basking in the pleasures of Jesus as He guides me in life. —TRACY ELDRIDGE

FAITH STEP: *Today, take some time to appreciate all your surroundings. Thank Jesus for making you aware of His presence. Let His joy permeate your soul.*

SUNDAY, APRIL 26

*So Christ himself gave the apostles, the prophets, the evangelists,
the pastors and teachers, to equip his people for works of service, so that
the body of Christ may be built up until we all reach unity in the faith
and in the knowledge of the Son of God and become mature, attaining
to the whole measure of the fullness of Christ. Ephesians 4:11–13 (NIV)*

I WAS RAISED IN A denomination that discouraged visiting other churches, so finding a faith community when I became a Christian eighteen years ago was a quandary. But once I overcame my inhibitions, exploring different denominations became interesting. I even created a spreadsheet to keep track of the churches I'd attended.

Some preachers were a little "fire and brimstone." Others were scholarly. Others were pragmatic and almost therapeutic Bible teachers. Some focused on manifestations of the Holy Spirit, while others sternly warned against them. Some focused on Jesus's love and our service to others. Some shared themes of prosperity, others sacrifice. My survey of churches was initially confusing, and I felt like I had to choose sides.

Today, I listen to an array of Bible teachers, praying for discernment, and looking for core beliefs that unify our faith. I now know that no single preacher (or denomination) can capture the fullness of Jesus and that everyone is likely to get something wrong some of the time. While I guard my mind against wayward teaching, I prayerfully enjoy and benefit from diverse Christian messengers, knowing each is anointed with a particular gift but unified in Christ. My spiritual life is richer as a result. —ISABELLA YOSUICO

FAITH STEP: *This week, listen to a podcast or read a book by a respected preacher who is outside your normal circle. Listen for Jesus and reflect on what you learn.*

MONDAY, APRIL 27

I have told you these things, so that in me you may have peace. In this world you will have trouble. But take heart! I have overcome the world.
John 16:33 (NIV)

I LOVE TO READ—FICTION, NONFICTION, magazines—anything with words. My husband has caught me reading the shampoo bottle when that's all I have handy. But there are occasions I can't bear the level of suspense in a story, the stress of not knowing how things will turn out. My stomach muscles tighten. I can't concentrate, and I find myself reading the same passage over and over. Then, I sneak a peek at the book's ending. It eases my anxiety.

Likewise, when experiencing real-life tense situations, I long to see the future, that things will be fine. Not only is my wish impossible, but it reveals a lack of faith. Challenges to my health and finances, like the conflicts found in the plotline of a good novel, are a necessary part of life. Just as a book's characters develop through their struggles, Jesus uses suffering to build character and produce hope (Romans 5:3–4). Without opportunities to deepen my belief in Jesus, it would remain shallow.

Now, as I face battles common to everyone, I've found peace in the knowledge that He has everything under control. Every day of my life was written in His book even before I was born (Psalm 139:16). He knew me at my beginning, and He's walking beside me as I face the middle. I trust He'll carry me through to a happy ending.

And that will be the start of an even better story—eternity.
—HEIDI GAUL

FAITH STEP: *Next time you open a book, use the time to consider how your life would read as a novel. Is your character deepening as you face hurdles? Is Jesus the central figure in your story?*

TUESDAY, APRIL 28

I and the Father are one. John 10:30 (NIV)

I'M NOT THE SAME PERSON I was in junior high. Good thing. I cared too much about the wrong things, not enough about what really mattered. I treated friendships too casually at times and held too tightly to them at others. I resented too much and was stingy with compassion. And…I would have been considered one of the "good girls."

Who of us would want to be our junior high self all our lives? Many of the changes I've experienced are directly linked to a still-growing devotion to follow Jesus. Not rules, man-made traditions, preconceived notions, or my mood at the moment. Jesus.

I'm a follower of Jesus Christ. I've had to rethink what that means. *Adhere to principles He laid out? Listen when He speaks in His Word? Respond quickly when I know He's asking something of me?* Yes. Working on it.

This one question, though, stopped me in my tracks: Am I love? Not, am I loving? Beyond merely *acting* in loving ways to those around me, am I an embodiment of love the way Jesus is?

The Bible says that God *is* love (1 John 4:8). It also tells us that Jesus and His Father are one, which means Jesus *is* love. We're told to abide in, dwell in Him, which means immersing myself in that vast pool of love until it can be said of me, "She is love."

I'm not the same person I was in junior high. But I still have a long way to go. The good news is that the goal won't come in striving, but in diving in and becoming. —CYNTHIA RUCHTI

FAITH STEP: *Take a look at the thirteenth chapter of 1 Corinthians. Superimpose "I" for the word love: "I am patient. I am kind…" Repeat the practice—and practice love—until you find the statements truer about yourself every day.*

WEDNESDAY, APRIL 29

Therefore do not worry, saying, "What will we eat?" or "What will we drink?" or "What will we wear?" . . . . But strive first for the kingdom of God and his righteousness, and all these things will be given to you as well.
Matt 6:31, 33 (NRSV)

IF WE ARE LOOKING FOR reasons to be stressed in our home right now, we don't have to look far. My husband lost his job and has been looking for work for several months. A close relative on my side of the family is using this crisis to exacerbate tensions with his side of the family. And our children are old enough to pick up on what is going on.

We have been in this situation before, and this time around I can see clearly that all is not lost. Last time Tony was unemployed it seemed like it went on forever, but Jesus kept whispering to us, *Keep following Me.* In retrospect, I can now see that time of "unemployment" was in fact a crucial time in our very young children's lives when the daily love and care their father so attentively offered them allowed them to blossom. And when he did (finally!) find a job, it was a wonderful fit: running residential shelters for formerly homeless families.

So this time around I'm whispering to Jesus, "Yes, we'll keep following *You.*" Our children are now on the cusp of adolescence, and we realize that every day that Tony can be a full-time parent with them is a gift. We see that they are thriving; we both know that this is due in part to the extra time and attention from their dad.

There's a sense of peace in our home right now that I would never associate with an employment crisis, but that I do associate with having Jesus around the house. Time and tenderness with each other bring us closer to Jesus in a way a paycheck never can.
—ELIZABETH BERNE DEGEAR

FAITH STEP: *Ask Jesus to help you find the blessing in your current crisis.*

THURSDAY, APRIL 30

The Lord will rescue me from every evil attack and will bring me safely to his heavenly kingdom. To him be glory for ever and ever. Amen. 2 Timothy 4:18 (NIV)

THE PARKLAND, FLORIDA, SCHOOL SHOOTING—AND SO many other tragedies in recent years—reminded me again that this world is unpredictably and unspeakably unsafe. The ripple effect is powerful and close to home. My own children's Florida schools now have much more stringent security measures in place, including extensive staff training and armed-security details on campus.

Fear of random violence has never topped my list, but this recent spate of terror has ramped it up. I'm more aware now when a real or imagined threat appears. With Jesus's help, I've pushed through fear before. I marinate in Scripture. I dance and sing praise. I share my fear with trusted others. More often, "I feel the fear and do it anyway." But sometimes I cower for a spell. Jesus is still with me.

In the story of the terrified apostles caught on a very windy Sea of Galilee (Mark 6:45–51), Jesus had actually "sent" them on the boat. By themselves. He *put* them in a scary place all alone, and then He walked on the water to silence the wind and their fears. "Take courage! It is I. Don't be afraid," He said (v. 50). It's just that simple.

We can allow our days to be overshadowed by fears large and small, real and perceived... exactly what the true enemy wants—to steal our peace, grace, love, and joy. Or we can hand our fears and ourselves over to the only Safe Place, Jesus. —ISABELLA YOSUICO

FAITH STEP: *Fast from a week of news—TV, print, or the internet—and spend that time with Jesus instead. Journal about your experience.*

FRIDAY, MAY 1

He defends the cause of the fatherless and the widow, and loves the
foreigner residing among you, giving them food and clothing.
Deuteronomy 10:18 (NIV)

ONE DAY BEFORE LEAVING WORK, I was moved to call a member of
my church, Mrs. McGee. Since I was also eager to get home in time
to watch my favorite game show, *Jeopardy*, I told myself, "I will call
Mrs. McGee another day." However, my soul would not rest until
I dialed her number.

When the elderly widow answered the phone, I chimed, "Hello!
How's it going?"

Mrs. McGee explained that she needed someone to purchase and
deliver dinner to her home because her daughter had to work late
that evening. Mrs. McGee went on to say that she was not on any
restrictive diet and whatever I purchased would satisfy her appetite.

I stopped at a local diner to purchase a blue-plate special complete
with iced tea and apple pie for dessert. Mrs. McGee was standing
in her front door waiting on my arrival. After receiving the dinner,
she thanked me and hugged my neck. As I departed she said, "Jesus
sent you here today." I nodded, with tears in my eyes.

Like Jesus used the little boy's lunch to feed five thousand, Jesus
used me to feed a widow. Each and every day, I understand that I
am the Lord's ambassador. My life is not my own, and the Lord is
not coming down from heaven's shore to personally feed and help
the needy. No, He sends me, the believer, to do His bidding. And
so it was. I missed watching *Jeopardy* that evening because Jesus
needed me for a more urgent task. —ALICE THOMPSON

FAITH STEP: *Is there a widow in your church or neighborhood? Today, call and*
offer to assist her with your free time, resources, or creative talents.

SATURDAY, MAY 2

After this, when Jesus knew that everything was now accomplished that the Scripture might be fulfilled, He said, "I'm thirsty!" A jar full of sour wine was sitting there; so they fixed a sponge full of sour wine on hyssop and held it up to His mouth. When Jesus had received the sour wine, He said, "It is finished!" Then bowing His head, He gave up His spirit.
John 19:28–30 (HCSB)

SEVERAL YEARS AGO, I READ studies that revealed the huge amount of chemicals we're exposed to by the different toiletries and personal care products we use daily. Since then I've jumped on the DIY (do-it-yourself) bandwagon. I've been making many of these products at home, using recipes from blogs that focus on healthier living. Some attempts prove successful, like the two-ingredient eye-makeup remover. Others not so much, including the overly greasy moisturizer.

Some people seem to want a DIY faith, creating their own "recipe" by choosing the ingredients that appeal to them. Those attempts will never be successful. That's why Jesus offered Himself as the perfect sacrifice to pay the penalty for our sin.

One of the final words Jesus spoke before He died was *tetelestai*, usually translated as "It is finished." In New Testament times, this word had many uses in everyday life. Ancient documents show that merchants and tax collectors wrote *tetelestai* on receipts for debts that had been paid in full. This single word spoken from the cross assures us that Jesus paid our debt freely, fully, completely. We no longer need to be separated from God or fear death. Our Savior did for us what we could never do for ourselves. —DIANNE NEAL MATTHEWS

FAITH STEP: *Prayerfully examine your attitudes and behavior. Are you still unconsciously trying to earn God's favor? Thank Jesus for paying your debt in full, then write the word tetelestai in large letters on a note card to keep in your Bible.*

SUNDAY, MAY 3

For the message of the cross is foolishness to those who are perishing, but to us who are being saved it is the power of God. 1 Corinthians 1:18 (NIV)

IN MY FIELD—CHRISTIAN WRITING—I CROSS paths with all sorts of people. In many cases, the main thing we have in common is our faith in Jesus. This isn't true of my personal life. Some of my closest friends and family look at Jesus and the cross in a different light than I do. They consider the gospel a fairy tale. Others question the validity of any sort of higher power.

I've prayed and shared my views with them and will continue doing so. Aside from that, I plan to step back and let Christ do His work. That's good news. He often does better without my "help."

Years ago, my father lost a battle against cancer. This highly intelligent man bore a stubborn streak deeper than anyone I've ever met. Cynical retorts blocked any path I'd lay toward our Savior. As Dad lay on his deathbed, I'd all but abandoned hope, considering his salvation an impossibility. It was time to let Jesus take over. Jesus stretched His hand to touch my father's heart. At last, Dad accepted Him and was saved. Jesus's timing was perfect, as always.

No one is beyond His reach. Right now I'm interceding for a specific person's salvation. When we're together, I pull the Lord's name into our conversations. I hope to draw my loved one's interest. Will the Lord grant this friend eternal life? There's no way to know. Jesus alone decides who, what, why, and when of each soul's destiny.

As for me, I'm willing to step aside as He leads—to wait, watch, and hope in faith. —HEIDI GAUL

FAITH STEP: *Make a list of seven people you know who need salvation. Choosing a different name each day, ask Jesus for ways you can play a part in guiding them to Him. Wait, watch, and hope.*

MONDAY, MAY 4

Long ago . . . God spoke to our fathers by the prophets, but in these last days he has spoken to us by his Son . . . through whom also he created the world.
Hebrews 1:1–2 (ESV)

A FRIEND IS A WATERCOLOR artist. She paints peaceful scenes from her surroundings in the beautiful Blue Ridge Mountains of Appalachia.

She posted some of her recent watercolors on social media, a handful of which I owned in a set of note cards she'd given me. Social media went wild over the simple but strikingly beautiful artwork. My artist friend was overwhelmed by the response. Creativity was so much a part of her, but having it recognized by others lifted her heart in a way few other things did.

When Jesus stood on the shore of the Sea of Galilee or surveyed the vast valley from the top of a mountain retreat or walked in the cool of the evening in Bethany and the garden of Gethsemane, He must have been stirred by the beauty of the creative handiwork in which He'd participated.

But when others recognize His artistry . . .

When we appreciate the color variations in a hummingbird's wings, the glitterlike glisten of a daylily's petals, the cobalt blue of the sky, or the delicate ballet of a milkweed seed lifted on a breeze, it must propel His enjoyment to new levels.

And when we pass by, not noticing . . . ?

Jesus, we don't want to only notice what you're doing in the lives of your followers but appreciate the stunning creation you helped set in motion eons ago. —CYNTHIA RUCHTI

FAITH STEP: *What creative pursuits interest you? If it's not your habit, consider making it a routine to begin and end your creative sessions thanking Jesus for setting a standard of beauty for us to reflect.*

TUESDAY, MAY 5

My brothers and sisters, whenever you face trials of any kind, consider it nothing but joy, because you know that the testing of your faith produces endurance; and let endurance have its full effect, so that you may be mature and complete, lacking in nothing. James 1:2–4 (NRSV)

IN JOHN 16:33 JESUS MADE a promise to His followers: "Here on this earth, you will have many trials and sorrows"(NLT). I can understand that, since this world is opposed to Jesus and all He stands for. But I've always had a hard time understanding how I'm supposed to count those trials and sorrows as joy. I do want my faith to become "mature and complete," but still—joy? Then I heard a story from a friend that changed my perspective on trials.

One spring Mike's neighbor gave him some duck eggs and explained how to incubate them. Mike watched the eggs carefully; he couldn't contain his excitement when he saw the baby ducks trying to break their way out. When he noticed that some were struggling, he helped them by breaking off parts of the eggshell. Sadly, those baby ducks died. His neighbor later told him the babies needed that initial struggle to help them gain strength. So despite trying to help, Mike had actually killed some of the baby ducks.

Just as those baby ducks needed the struggle to grow physically stronger, we need trials in our lives to help our faith grow stronger. There is no shortcut to spiritual maturity. To get there, we have to travel a road of trials, difficulties, and sorrows. But we can persevere because of the second half of John 16:33. The One who travels with us declares, "But take heart, because I have overcome the world" (NLT).
—DIANNE NEAL MATTHEWS

FAITH STEP: *Think about your hardest struggle. Thank Jesus that He will use it to strengthen your faith.*

WEDNESDAY, MAY 6

He must increase, but I must decrease. John 3:30 (ESV)

AS A NOVELIST, I HAVE several trusted critique partners who pore over my manuscripts. They suggest places I need more description, flag areas where the pace lags, or let me know when a character's motivation isn't fully developed. They also turn their eagle eyes to typos.

Today I eagerly opened an edited manuscript that arrived in my email. I skimmed through the chapters, and my writing buddy's note caught my eye. She had marked a section where I'd accidentally used capital letters for pronouns where the character referred to herself and lowercase letters for pronouns referring to God—the opposite from what I'd intended.

I made the corrections, grateful she'd caught my error. Then I chuckled. How like human nature it is to get everything backward! In my real life, esteeming Jesus isn't just a matter of capitalizing His pronouns. Just like in my manuscript, I sometimes put my own interests before Jesus.

John the Baptist had the right idea when he said, "He must increase, but I must decrease." This is a big struggle for me. I subtly steer conversations toward topics that allow me to insert an anecdote that makes me look good. Or I spout off my opinion as if a friend's problem would evaporate if she took my advice. I've begun to ask Jesus to change my heart and help me grow in this area. I want to elevate His role in my thoughts, my decisions, and my conversations. Instead of talking about my interests, my experiences, my suggestions, I want to point others to Christ and His answers.
—SHARON HINCK

FAITH STEP: *Are there any parts of your life where you can invite Jesus to increase? Ask Him to help you esteem Him as more important than all else.*

THURSDAY, MAY 7

Then God said, "Let us make mankind in our image, in our likeness, so that they may rule over the fish in the sea and the birds in the sky, over the livestock and all the wild animals, and over all the creatures that move along the ground." Genesis 1:26 (NIV)

I STOOD IN FRONT OF the mirror one morning to comb my hair. As I raised the comb to my temple, for a split second, I saw my mother's face in my reflection. People tell me often I look like her. On that morning it was clear to me too. My small eyes, round nose, and cheekbones were inherited from my mother. I was so moved by our uncanny resemblance that I sat down before work to write the following poem:

The matter is out of my hands.
I am my mother—all over again.

To see my mother in my very own features called to mind Scriptures in Genesis. They tell us we are made in the divine likeness of God and His Son. Because we are created so, the Lord should see Himself in the way we work our jobs, love the people in our communities, and care for our families. Jesus told the disciples to be like Him and emulate Him. He said, "I have set you an example that you should do as I have done for you" (John 13:15, NIV).

Each day, as we live to meet our personal needs and the needs of our families, there is also the body of Christ that deserves our attention and care. Responding like Jesus, where can we offer service or kindness to someone else? For us as believers created in the Lord's image, loving others is our family crest, and Jesus is trusting that our neighbors will encounter His love in our eyes. —ALICE THOMPSON

FAITH STEP: *In the likeness of Jesus, visit an ailing loved one and serve her by cleaning her home or cooking a meal.*

FRIDAY, MAY 8

Cast all your anxiety on him because he cares for you. 1 Peter 5:7 *(NIV)*

FLORIDA, MY NEW HOME, IS one of the nation's leading states for fishing. It's really obvious. Drive by any body of water from dawn to dark, and you'll see many, many people fishing. Men and women, young and old, from piers, off the coast, in waders, up to their necks, from boats and bridges... fishing is everywhere. People who fish (not me) know that casting is not passive. People cast in an athletic stance, forcefully launching their line into the deep. My husband is a longtime fisherman, and I sometimes tag along when he takes our boys. I can testify that casting isn't as easy as it looks.

Today's Scripture tell us to cast our anxiety—our "cares" in some translations—fling it upon the Lord. Talk about hard to do! I need constant reminders that "casting" is a deliberate action I must choose to take. Over time, I've acquired and use a lot of different tools to practice casting. I pause and pray. Sometimes a simple "Help me, Jesus." I journal. I allow myself a fixed amount of time to ponder my cares. I read Scripture aloud, sing worship songs, write down my fear to place in my "God box," surrendering it to the Lord. I call a friend and share my concern or, even better, I help someone else. Sometimes I do several things. Repeatedly.

Waiting for the anxiety to simply vanish on its own has not worked for me. I have to muster my spiritual might to claim this verse and actively entrust my cares to Him who cares for me. Casting, believing, trusting... all actions. —ISABELLA YOSUICO

FAITH STEP: *Pray: "Lord, give me the grace and faith and spiritual strength to cast my cares on Your boundless, loving shoulders." Use one of my "casting" tools this week.*

SATURDAY, MAY 9

There is no fear in love, but perfect love casts out fear. For fear has to do with punishment, and whoever fears has not been perfected in love.
1 John 4:18 (ESV)

HERE'S THAT WORD AGAIN, *CASTS*. Here, love casts out fear. Perfect love. This whole passage appears in a powerful message about loving one another, love empowered and demonstrated by God's love for, and through, us in Christ Jesus.

When I first learned my unborn son, Isaac, would have a genetic condition that we later learned was Down syndrome, I felt terrified. I felt betrayed, and yes, I confess, even punished by God. *How could a loving God let this happen to me and my family after all we'd been through?* Yet now I share as often as I can, Isaac has proven to be an utter blessing; to know him is to love him! My fear, it turns out, was unwarranted. Far from a punishment, Isaac is a gift.

I've returned to this truth over and over. Even difficult challenges can reveal Jesus's love, when filtered through the fearless eyes of love. A fearlessness, this verse reminds us, that can only come when we know we are loved unconditionally. This is the very Good News of Jesus. Jesus bore the punishment I truly deserve—an act of perfect love—so I need never fear.

When I'm in fear or lacking love, it reveals that I have not been perfected in love. I, the fragile, imperfect, and imperfectly loved child, have not fully received the only Perfect Love...yet. It's only when I receive and rest in Jesus that I can surrender my fears and truly love; the two are proportionate and inextricably linked.
—ISABELLA YOSUICO

FAITH STEP: *Pray this prayer to Jesus: "Please, please help me to receive and rest in Your perfect love. Help me experience it with all my senses."*

MOTHER'S DAY, SUNDAY, MAY 10

*But that doesn't mean you should all look and speak and act the same.
Out of the generosity of Christ, each of us is given his own gift.*
Ephesians 4:7 (MSG)

I LOVED THE MOTHER'S DAY floral arrangement that Kevin, my younger son, sent me last year—at first, that is. An assortment of small blooms in several colors spilled over a cobalt blue (my favorite color) vase. I texted my thanks to Kevin along with a picture. He called me immediately, shocked that the flowers looked absolutely nothing like what he'd ordered. Kevin had browsed through pages of arrangements on a website, finally choosing one in colors he thought I'd like, arranged in a vintage-looking pitcher. My local florist delivered something completely different.

The next day some of the flowers had already wilted. I contacted the company. They claimed to have left a voice mail letting my son know the arrangement he ordered was out of stock, but his phone showed no record of the call. Eventually the business refunded half his money and sent me a second, larger bouquet. It was gorgeous, but I still wished I could have received what Kevin had picked out specifically for me.

Jesus has given each of us gifts, talents, and resources we can use to bless and build up others. Some gifts are more visible than others, but they're all equally important. Once in a while, I wish I could serve Jesus like somebody else does. But Jesus designed each of us to fill a special place in His body of believers. Shouldn't we be satisfied with the gifts He's picked out especially for us? —DIANNE NEAL MATTHEWS

FAITH STEP: *Make a list of the gifts and abilities you've been given to serve Christ. Are you using them to the fullest? If you don't know what yours are, ask a staff member at church or an experienced Bible teacher to help you discover them.*

MONDAY, MAY 11

Salvation is found in no one else, for there is no other name under heaven given to mankind by which we must be saved. Acts 4:12 (NIV)

I ONCE ENROLLED IN A short online course about happiness. From time to time, I would receive follow-up emails from the course coach. In one of his emails, he mentioned that the inability to remember passwords is a major source of everyday frustration for millions around the world. "The main purpose of a password is to offer protection," he said. To lessen his students' frustration and increase our sense of security, he gave us a mnemonic device to help us remember our passwords. Then he recommended an app to store our passwords.

As soon as I read the word *password* in my teacher's email message, I instantly recalled the password given to all of us to access the most glorious realm. It's a single word that's so easy to remember. It's the only word that will guarantee our eternal safety and security. *Jesus.* Referring to Jesus, the apostle Peter proclaimed, "There is salvation in no one else! God has given no other name under heaven by which we must be saved" (Acts 4:12, NLT).

Jesus Himself said, "I am the way, the truth, and the life. No one can come to the Father except through me" (John 14:6, NIV). Jesus offers the *only* safe and secure entry into His kingdom, where there is righteousness, peace, and true happiness. The password has been revealed. Jesus is the password to the kingdom. And that's the only password we need. —MARLENE LEGASPI-MUNAR

FAITH STEP: *Express your faith in Jesus by verbally saying that you trust Him as your Savior today. Thank Him daily for saving you and experience a satisfying relationship with Him.*

TUESDAY, MAY 12

If you are angry, don't sin by nursing your grudge. Don't let the sun go down with you still angry—get over it quickly. Ephesians 4:26 (TLB)

LAST THURSDAY IN OUR CHURCH-LEADERSHIP meeting, we completed a lesson on character by Carey Nieuwhof. Nieuwhof suggested that as leaders, we should evaluate our true character by thinking about our responses to stressful scenarios, such as getting cut off in traffic or having to redo a work report. The results from our group were amusing and revealing. Sometimes I don't respond well to stress. A few times, I've left a bad impression. I always apologize when I get upset, but after one such incident, a person said, "And she's supposed to be a Christian." That hurt. I immediately repented because I knew that my behavior was not characteristic of Jesus. Since then, I've been asking Jesus to help me change. He alone can shape me into someone who responds like Him, acts like Him, and speaks like Him. I don't want to get defensive when a stressful situation arises, I want to respond like Jesus.

Sometimes anger can lead us to do things we can't take back, and our apologies are rejected. People are always watching us even when we're unaware, so we have to be conscious of how our actions affect others. Jesus got angry sometimes, but He never sinned. When He faced the ultimate betrayal by Judas, Jesus didn't respond with anger, He showed Judas love. Even more, Jesus forgave *our* betrayal of Him at the cross. Jesus's willingness to quickly forgive, not remain angry, and love are character traits that I want in my life. I want my character to be like His, full of love and grace. —TRACY ELDRIDGE

FAITH STEP: *When you've lost your temper or acted out of character, think about your actions and write them down. Ask Jesus to help you see your true character and help you respond well so He gets the glory.*

WEDNESDAY, MAY 13

*The LORD says, "I will guide you along the best pathway for your life.
I will advise you and watch over you." Psalm 32:8 (NLT)*

MAKING A LIVING FROM WRITING is hard. I haven't earned anything in a month. My situation made me think about the story of Jesus and Simon Peter.

Jesus said to Simon, "Now go out where it is deeper, and let down your nets to catch some fish" (Luke 5:4, NLT).

For a while, I'd considered closing my business, but I cried out to Jesus one more time. *Is it really time to give up? Lord, what's Your will?* Then I came across a Bible verse, and I felt a tug in my heart. "Let the favor of the Lord our God be upon us, and establish the work of our hands upon us; yes, establish the work of our hands!" (Psalm 90:17, ESV). *Establish. Establish. Establish.* The word kept echoing in my mind. *Do You want me to continue?*

"'Master,' Simon replied, 'we worked hard all last night and didn't catch a thing.'" (In spite of an empty catch, Simon yielded to Jesus.) "'But if you say so, I'll let the nets down again.' And this time their nets were so full of fish they began to tear!" (Luke 5:5–6, NLT).

Like Simon Peter, I didn't know what the outcome would be but I followed Jesus's instruction and did what He asked me to do regarding my business. The next day, I received a contract—the biggest one yet. Jesus overwhelmed me with a huge blessing!

When we yield our lives to Jesus, we never know what the outcome will be, but He always comes through for us. When we believe and obey Jesus, in spite of unfavorable circumstances, we receive the tremendous blessings He's already prepared for us.
—MARLENE LEGASPI-MUNAR

FAITH STEP: *What is Jesus instructing you to do? Are you ready to obey?*

THURSDAY, MAY 14

Refresh my heart in Christ. Philemon 1:20 (CEB)

MY FIRST EXPERIENCE WITH A private bed-and-breakfast—the kind where a homeowner advertises a room, suite, or home online—was a raving success. I knew it might be the place for me when I discovered that not only was it in a good location for a good price, but it was called Grace Cottage.

What sold me was the online image of the living room of the sweet little cottage—a small fireplace flanked by two comfy couches. On the mantel perched a blackboard-like sign with one word—Hope.

I did due diligence in researching the rest—other rooms, extra features, quiet neighborhood, positive reviews and recommendations. But the Hope sign had already made the decision for me.

A friend met me at the cottage for three days of work and planning. But the atmosphere in the home was saturated with peace and serenity. We knew it was a place where Jesus was a frequent and honored "guest."

Despite the hours we spent working, we left feeling refreshed in a way that only the presence of Jesus can accomplish.

When the apostle Paul wrote to Philemon, asking a favor—that Philemon would "refresh [his] heart in Christ"—I wonder if he was in need of a spot like Grace Cottage. Verse 22 of that chapter convinced me. "Also, one more thing—prepare a guest room for me."

We can search for a room with luxury amenities. We can scroll the internet looking for a room with a view. But the sweetest luxury of all is to have our soul refreshed in Christ. —CYNTHIA RUCHTI

FAITH STEP: *Take a moment to find an online or magazine image of a room that reflects the idea of serenity. Peace. Soul refreshment. Envision that kind of internal atmosphere as your soul is refreshed in Christ today.*

FRIDAY, MAY 15

*You will keep in perfect peace those whose minds are steadfast,
because they trust in you. Isaiah 26:3 (NIV)*

THE OTHER NIGHT, I HAD a dream. *I was teaching, wearing a long
sweater... but no pants.* In case you didn't know, it's super important
to wear pants when you are teaching! I told my dream to my sister,
Jenny. She said, "I'm no psychologist, but I would say you are feeling vulnerable." That is the understatement of the year. My unfet-
tered dreams are showing the real picture. I am operating out of a
vulnerable and fearful place. This encouraging verse keeps coming
to mind: "You will keep in perfect peace those whose minds are
steadfast, because they trust in you."

My mind is not even close to being stayed on Jesus. It is stayed
on worry and a fear of lost pants. I struggle with trust. I struggle
with believing that Jesus can work in and through me when I doubt
myself. But Jesus promises if I trust Him that He will fill me with
perfect peace. He promises the same for you. Our hearts are designed
to reside in a place of love, knowing that we are cared and provided
for. Our minds are created for peace. Not heart-thumping, mind-
numbing fear. We need to rip our eyes off our proverbial pants (our
lack, our people pleasing, our fear of the unknown) and focus on
Jesus, the One who loves us most of all. The One who casts out fear
with His mere presence. We want our minds to be stayed on His
goodness and strength and purpose. Stayed on His great love and
hope and joy. We desperately need the perfect peace Jesus is offering.

Now that *really* is the understatement of the year.

—SUSANNA FOTH AUGHTMON

FAITH STEP: *Are you in an anxious, vulnerable place right now? Entrust your
fears to Jesus today, knowing that He promises to fill you with His perfect peace.*

SATURDAY, MAY 16

Praise be to the God and Father of our Lord Jesus Christ, the Father of compassion and the God of all comfort, who comforts us in all our troubles, so that we can comfort those in any trouble with the comfort we ourselves receive from God. 2 Corinthians 1:3–4 (NIV)

THIS MORNING I STUMBLED TO the kitchen to pour myself a cup of tea. My body ached, and light-headedness had me gripping the walls for support. It was going to be a "stuck in bed" sort of day. My grandson was sitting in his booster seat at the table and lit up.

"Book?" he asked hopefully. He loves when I read to him, even though we have to squeeze it in around his family's busy routine.

"Not today, buddy. Gramma's not feeling well."

He gave me his most sympathetic look. "Hug?" he asked.

I picked him up, and he nestled into my shoulder, patting my back gently. Bliss and comfort in a little two-year-old package.

The experience left me thinking about the many ways Jesus sends us comfort. When we open our Bible, words may spring off the page that are exactly what we need to hear. A song may open our heart and stir us to worship. A friend may call or text or email with an encouraging note. Or a two-year-old may wrap chubby arms around our neck. In whatever form it takes, we can acknowledge that Jesus is pouring out His love to us. His compassion acknowledges our hurt and never belittles us. His tenderness helps us receive His grace, and His strength empowers us to endure and offer His comfort to others. —SHARON HINCK

FAITH STEP: *List a few unexpected ways Jesus has comforted you. Thank Him, and ask Him to show you someone to comfort today.*

SUNDAY, MAY 17

When Jesus saw Nathanael approaching, he said . . . , "Here truly is an Israelite in whom there is no deceit." John 1:47 (NIV)

THE CALLING OF THE FIRST disciples in John 1 crackles with excitement. You can sense the beginning of something big, something that's going to change the world, as these fishermen see Jesus for the first time and decide to follow Him.

Of course, when it was happening they didn't know how special it was. In fact, one of the men wasn't sure he even wanted to follow Jesus. "Nazareth! Can anything good come from there?" Nathanael asked.

Jesus's response is telling. Rather than being offended, He looked at Nathanael and declared, "Here truly is an Israelite in whom there is no deceit." Nathanael said, "How do you know me?"

He's astonished. Amazed. And, I believe, touched. Jesus answered, "I saw you while you were still under the fig tree before Philip called you."

I saw you. To this Nathanael could only exclaim, "Rabbi, you are the Son of God; you are the king of Israel."

Why did Nathanael change so abruptly from a skeptic to a believer? Jesus saw him as no one has ever seen or known him before, and Jesus welcomed him. Instead of judging him for his doubts, even his rather rude question, Jesus appreciated his honesty. *You're a truth teller,* Jesus said. *I could use a guy like that.*

Jesus was never afraid of a person's honest questions or doubts. They didn't make Him defensive. His response to Nathanael was like it later would be to Thomas. *I see you. Now come and see me.* Jesus knew the antidote to doubt was to invite the doubter in.

—GWEN FORD FAULKENBERRY

FAITH STEP: *The next time doubt visits you in the form of a person or your own fear, remember Jesus's reaction.*

MONDAY, MAY 18

From the end of the earth will I cry unto thee, when my heart is overwhelmed: lead me to the rock that is higher than I. Psalm 61:2 (KJV)

I ENTERED PUBLIC EDUCATION AS a teacher. That first year almost killed me. The principal put me in charge of a fourth-grade class with forty students. Each child was a chatterbox. Every last one was like a wiggly worm and required classroom-management skills that I did not have. I was given a veteran teacher to serve as my mentor. The principal sent me to workshops to help me organize my classroom. Even with additional help, I left work each day in tears.

I was a young woman in my early twenties. My relationship with the Lord was a fickle one at the time. However, I had the good sense to cry out to Jesus in my distress, and He revealed His love for me in Romans 8:1. Despite my immaturity and wavering relationship with Him, I read in the Word that there was no condemnation for me as a believer. There in the book of Romans, the apostle Paul also went on to say that despite my challenges and trouble, nothing could separate me from the Lord's love. And what did I do? I grabbed on to that love and survived a school year that was plagued with flying spitballs, hacky sacks, and paper airplanes.

Jesus held my hand, and He protected my mind and emotions during that first year of teaching. My feeble efforts should have ended in complete failure. But like a strong tower, the Lord sheltered and shielded me. You have this same assurance. Today the Lord will rise up and be a rock for you in the face of what appears to be a crumbling situation. Praise Him. —ALICE THOMPSON

FAITH STEP: *Do you hold feelings of guilt about some personal or professional failure? Be released today from self-condemnation and meditate on Romans 8:1.*

TUESDAY, MAY 19

I saw the Holy City, the new Jerusalem, coming down out of heaven from God, prepared as a bride beautifully dressed for her husband. Revelation 21:2 *(NIV)*

A WELL-KNOWN FASHION MAGAZINE RECENTLY ran an online feature about royal wedding gowns, no doubt prompted by Prince Harry's nuptials. There were dozens of pictures of royals from every continent, dating back to the 1940s. The caption offered just enough information about the bride, groom, and gown to spark the imagination. There were Cinderella and Cinderfella stories. There were elaborate, custom couture outfits that could drain treasuries. There were even simple frocks the royal brides dared to buy off the rack or design themselves.

Having eloped in a simple ivory day dress, I never wore a fancy wedding gown or had a wedding full of fanfare. I tell myself it was my practicality and thrift, but in retrospect I know I felt unworthy of the pomp.

My eternal Bridegroom, the God of all things, says otherwise—and always has. I am, you are, we are *all* His beloved, His bride for whom He gave everything and even now bestows untold treasures.

One of the brides pictured in that fashion feature went on to be married five times. Maybe that first royal bridegroom wasn't quite the prince he seemed to be. Or maybe the bride expected more of her mortal groom than he was ever designed to provide.

Not so with Jesus. In Christ, we have the perfect royal Bridegroom. In Christ, I am the perfect royal bride. Thank you, Jesus, for loving me so much and clothing me in the snow-white gown of glory.
—ISABELLA YOSUICO

FAITH STEP: *Take a few moments to Google wedding gowns, imagining yourself beautifully dressed for Jesus, the Ultimate Bridegroom.*

WEDNESDAY, MAY 20

I will come to you soon, if the Lord wills, and I will find out not the talk of these arrogant people but their power. For the kingdom of God depends not on talk but on power. 1 Corinthians 4:19–20 (NRSV)

I AM INSPIRED BY MY friend Akhita in the way she listens to Jesus as He says, "Follow Me." She is a successful professor and sociologist who intertwines her faith and her work life, even as she respects the boundaries of her secular profession. We went for a hike together the other day, and I loved listening to her muse aloud about how Jesus is working in her life. It was so apparent to me: she lets her relationship with the Lord infuse her work at every turn.

For a woman of faith working in an environment where "God talk" is strongly discouraged, this can be a challenge for Akhita. She feels the worldly expectations of her academic profession as voices within her (*Publish or perish! Join that committee, you need more recognition in the academy!*). But through it all, Akhita is letting Jesus talk *to her*. The other day she put down her research for a few moments to take some time in prayer. When she returned to the task, she suddenly saw how to arrange the material in a way that brought her project alive in a whole new way. Jesus's name might not appear anywhere in her project's bibliography, but she knows the impact their relationship is having on her work.

What I'm learning from Akhita about "God talk" is that it doesn't always have to do with the words we use when we speak with others. It has everything to do with the spiritual ears we use in our relationship with Jesus. That is where the power is.
—ELIZABETH BERNE DEGEAR

FAITH STEP: *Today when you find yourself in a situation where "God talk" isn't appropriate, can you find time to listen with ears of faith and see how Jesus guides you?*

THURSDAY, MAY 21

When Jesus came to the region of Caesarea Philippi, he asked his disciples, "Who do people say the Son of Man is?" They replied, "Some say John the Baptist; others say Elijah; and still others, Jeremiah or one of the prophets." "But what about you?" he asked. "Who do you say I am?" Simon Peter answered, "You are the Messiah, the Son of the living God."
Matthew 16:13–16 (NIV)

ON ONE OF OUR TRIPS up North, my hubby and I found a smooth rock that formed a gently curved bowl. We also discovered a round white stone that fit inside. We brought them home, and marveled at how much they looked like modern sculptures we'd seen.

I called it *Mother and Child*; my hubby called it *Baseball and Mitt*. It's amazing how many different things we see in those two stones. As with abstract sculpture, viewers bring their own perspective.

It's interesting how many different perspectives people bring to their understanding of Jesus. When He walked on the earth, confusion reigned. To some, He was the son of a poor local carpenter. Others saw Him as a potential political leader. Some believed He was a new incarnation of John the Baptist, Elijah, or Jeremiah. Simon Peter proclaimed, "You are the Messiah, the Son of the living God."

Who do we say Jesus is? The way we answer that question is vital. Do we see Him only as a good man or role model? A wise teacher? Or do we fully embrace the identity He reveals? He tells us He is *the* Way, *the* Truth, and *the* Life. When we acknowledge this truth, our view of Him changes. We don't simply honor His teachings, we invite Him to live within us in resurrection power.
—SHARON HINCK

FAITH STEP: *Who do you say Jesus is? Answer for yourself, then thank Him.*

FRIDAY, MAY 22

He cuts off every branch in me that bears no fruit, while every branch that does bear fruit he prunes so that it will be even more fruitful.
John 15:2 (NIV)

TODAY I SPENT TIME OUTSIDE pruning grapes, wisteria, and hydrangea—and remembering my parents. They were landscapers, and as they worked, I'd watch. The care and wisdom they displayed when tending plants fascinated me. *How could they know when and how much to trim off? Wouldn't it hurt the plant? Why were some bushes pruned so hard?*

They taught me by their actions. I learned the proper techniques slowly, until they seeped into my soul. Prune back to the joint to keep visual integrity. Cut on a slant to speed healing. Trim at the right time for that particular bush or vine so it doesn't go into shock, and will blossom or bear fruit next season.

Years later, as an adult, I keep these tips tucked inside my mind like a treasure, ready for referencing in my yard. When pruning, I visualize my parents' hands guiding my own and feel their love.

Thanks to my mother and father, when Jesus disciplines me, I see what He's doing and I understand. Has He removed a hidden temptation from me, trimming way back to its source? Did He cut me free from an unforgiven hurt, allowing me to heal and blossom again for Him? Have I reached a season where He wants me to address a tough issue I've ignored or avoided? All His pruning is necessary, even if it first pains me. I'm learning to accept it with gratitude.

I'm His blessed creation, one of His flowers. With His love, wisdom, and care, I can thrive and bloom to His glory. —HEIDI GAUL

FAITH STEP: *Next time you trim a plant, consider the why and how behind your actions, and apply that knowledge to your relationship with Jesus. Are you currently being pruned? How can you speed the process and bloom for Him?*

SATURDAY, MAY 23

Stay alert; be in prayer so you don't wander into temptation without even knowing you're in danger. There is a part of you that is eager, ready for anything in God. But there's another part that's as lazy as an old dog sleeping by the fire. Matthew 26:41 (MSG)

SOMETIMES I CAN BE LAZY when it comes to prayer. I know it is my time to commune with Jesus, to seek His face for direction and guidance, and to pray for loved ones, lost souls, and world matters. However, there are times I let the busyness of life take precedence over prayer. I don't take the time to spend *quiet* time in prayer. Each time I renew my mission to be more consistent in prayer, I tell the Lord the same thing, "I'm going to make quiet prayer time with You a daily habit." So this week I am starting over again. I am so thankful that Jesus knows my weaknesses and always gives me more chances.

Jesus would often steal away from the crowds to spend quiet time in prayer with His Father. He wrestled in prayer all night before He was crucified. He knew the road ahead would be excruciating, but in the end, Jesus's words to His Father were "Not my will, but thy will be done." Through prayer, Jesus found the strength to endure the pain of the cross. He challenged the disciples to stay alert and be in prayer. He knew they would need that same strength in their own lives.

Paul said we should pray continuously, because there are always forces around us trying to pull us into temptation, away from our walk with Christ. We cannot afford to consider prayer as an option. Rather, it is a daily necessity. Just as Jesus gained strength and clarity in prayer, we can too. —TRACY ELDRIDGE

FAITH STEP: *Are you spending quiet prayer time with Jesus daily? If not, start today. If you don't know what to say, just begin thanking Jesus. He will meet you right where you are.*

SUNDAY, MAY 24

By this we know that we love the children of God, when we love God and obey his commandments. For this is the love of God, that we keep his commandments. And his commandments are not burdensome. 1 John 5:2–3 (ESV)

OUR CHURCH HAS A COMFORT dog, Gideon, who visits shut-ins and others who need a lift. This morning Gideon helped teach the children's message and demonstrated how well he obeys. His example showed me three truths that I can apply to following Jesus.

First, Gideon has a handler. She provides for him, protects him, and takes him to the people who need a visit. Similarly, Jesus cares for me and supplies my needs. He also places me in a community where I can serve. If we listen to our Shepherd, He'll guide us to the right place.

Second, Gideon obeys his handler. He doesn't make a move without a command. I felt humbled as I thought of how often I ignore Jesus's direction to "stay" or "come." Gideon's obedience was cheerful and enthusiastic, qualities I'd like to emulate. I long to bring comfort to the hurting and as I become better at hearing and obeying Jesus's guidance, I'll become a more effective source of comfort to others.

Finally I drew encouragement from another aspect of Gideon's ministry. When he visits with those in pain, he doesn't provide wise counsel. He doesn't worry about whether he has enough talent or skill to serve. He just wags his tail and offers the gift of his presence. As Jesus invites us to care for the hurting, we don't need to worry about our limitations. He simply asks us to share His presence in the lives of others. —SHARON HINCK

FAITH STEP: *What can you learn about obedience and service from Gideon's example?*

MONDAY, MAY 25

Don't be concerned only about your own interests, but also be concerned about the interests of others. Philippians 2:4 (GW)

PARENTS LIKE TO BRAG ABOUT their children, and I'm no exception. So let me tell you how proud I was of my daughter, Holly, when my husband and I visited over a long Memorial Day weekend. My son-in-law's mom was also visiting, so Holly had planned special meals. On Monday, I helped her make side dishes to accompany the brisket smoking on the grill. Then, before dinner, she prepared lasagna from scratch, salad, and homemade rolls for neighbors who had a newborn baby. She started to make a dessert for them, but I talked her into sharing the one she'd already made for us.

The next time we visited, Holly was on crutches from a broken foot, our grandson was facing serious surgery, and our son-in-law had deployed. A few days after we arrived, I learned that Holly had planned to double a recipe for dinner that night so we could share with another neighbor who'd just had a baby. Yes, it was an inconvenient time, but Holly and a neighbor had organized a Care Train for the subdivision, and no one had signed up for the Fourth of July.

Like earthly parents, God feels pleasure when He sees His children doing things worth bragging about. And what better way to please Him than by imitating Jesus? That means serving others with a self-sacrificial love—even when it's inconvenient or costly. Putting others' needs above our own desires. Grabbing every opportunity to be the hands and feet of Jesus. Every day we have the chance to give God more reasons to feel proud of us. —DIANNE NEAL MATTHEWS

FAITH STEP: *Each day, think of ways you can imitate Jesus by setting aside your agenda in order to meet someone else's needs. Imagine the pleasure that gives Him.*

TUESDAY, MAY 26

As for that in the good soil, these are the ones who, when they hear the word, hold it fast in an honest and good heart, and bear fruit with patient endurance. Luke 8:15 (NRSV)

I BET I'VE READ JESUS'S Parable of the Sower a hundred times. Maybe a thousand. I'm Southern Baptist after all. I cut my teeth on a black King James Version Bible, and I thought I had these verses zipped up in my mind. But the other day, some completely different things stood out to me. Specifically those bits about holding fast to the Word and bearing fruit *"with patient endurance."*

I've always seen myself like the seeds in good soil. None of the other options fit my experience. This is more of a credit to my parents than myself. With them around, no birds had a chance to eat the seeds, and thorns were not allowed to choke them out. Rather than rocky dirt, the home where I spent my formative years was a bed of potting soil with "Miracle-Gro," and my parents watered me daily.

But now I'm an adult. I've lived long enough to be broken by the world. To get discouraged. To be tired. To wrestle with doubts and ask questions that don't have answers. And there seems to be something here for this stage of life that I never noticed until I needed it.

The seeds hold fast. They hold on. They spread out and dig deeper into the good soil, so the Word takes root and grows to bear fruit. It's like they're stubborn about it. And apparently the fruit doesn't always come fast and easy. It takes patient endurance. This means we fall down, but we get back up. We doubt, but we refuse to give up our faith. We are tired, but we keep fighting the good fight.

—GWEN FORD FAULKENBERRY

FAITH STEP: *Draw a picture of what speaks to you about this parable. Then hang it on your fridge to remind you to tend your heart's garden and water it with faith.*

WEDNESDAY, MAY 27

The death of one that belongs to the LORD is precious in his sight.
Psalm 116:15 (NCV)

WHEN A NEIGHBOR RENELLA INTRODUCED me to one of her long-time friends and quilting-group buddies, I fell in love with her on the spot. At ninety years young, Laverne's sparkling personality spilled over with joy, wit, and a sense of fun. But soon after, Renella called to say that Laverne had suffered a stroke. Four days later, Laverne passed away.

Renella later sent this email: *When I went to Laverne's wake, all of her family, including the nine "great-grands" were there. Her daughter-in-law, Linda, told us about a conversation she overheard between two of the little boys, ages five and six. "Where IS Gran?" the younger boy asked his cousin. The older one pointed to the casket and said, "She's asleep over there in that treasure chest." I could almost hear Laverne giggling. I thought, "What a fitting tribute. She truly WAS our treasure."*

Little did I know that a month later I would help my mom choose a "treasure chest" for my beloved dad. It helped to remember that my dad had gone to be with the One who loved him far more than we ever could.

Death is ugly. When we lose a loved one, we have to deal with unpleasant realities. But from Christ's perspective, the death of someone who belongs to Him is a beautiful and precious thing. It means being united with our Savior who considers us His treasure.
—DIANNE NEAL MATTHEWS

FAITH STEP: *Do you struggle with a fear of death? Whenever that fear surfaces, think about how much Jesus longs to bring you home to Himself.*

THURSDAY, MAY 28

Jesus said, "I am the living bread that came down from heaven. Whoever eats this bread will live forever. This bread is my flesh, which I will give for the life of the world." John 6:51 (NIV)

"ARE YOU GETTING ENOUGH SUNSHINE?" my doctor asked. He may have noticed my I-work-at-my-desk-all-day pallor.

"I work at my desk all day," I told him. "But I take vitamin D supplements."

He looked at my lab results. "Your calcium is on the low side of normal. Are you eating enough dark greens?"

"Not to worry, Doctor. I'll take a calcium supplement, or two."

This is how the appointment progressed in my mind as I prepared for my annual physical. I was compiling the list of medications and supplements, conscious that I was supplementing much of what the human body can normally get from a healthy diet and ten minutes of fresh air a day.

How often do we try to do the same with our spiritual health? We depend on supplements—someone else's insights, Sunday's sermon, a brief nugget heard on the radio—as our entire spiritual intake for the week. We lean on supplements rather than a rich diet of daily Bible reading, prayer time, and reflection with Jesus.

Jesus no doubt carried on a perpetual internal conversation with His Father, but He still stole away by Himself for extended times of prayer. He said we should "abide" in Him (John 15:7, NKJV), which seems more like a meal than a quick snack, doesn't it? —CYNTHIA RUCHTI

FAITH STEP: *Establish a regular extended time of savoring the Bread of Life, taking time to ensure your spiritual nutritional balance.*

FRIDAY, MAY 29

As water reflects a face, so one's life reflects the heart. Proverbs 27:19 (NIV)

"THIS GLASS IS LIKE A person," our pastor explained, holding up a glass to illustrate his point. "Whatever is inside the glass splashes out when you shake it. If a glass is filled with water, then water will spill out. Tea will spill from a glass filled with tea. A person whose heart is filled with anger will respond with anger. A person who holds fear in their heart will be fearful. A joyful heart will produce a reaction of love and joy."

After hearing this illustration, I began using it as a tool to examine my heart and reflect on how I responded to various trials during different times in my life. When I was in my early twenties and going through a difficult phase, I often responded with anger and frustration. My anger and frustration spilled into my relationship with Jesus as well. But over the years, I have come to know Him more. Jesus's love has healed my heart. I have grown closer to Him and it shows.

When I was diagnosed with cancer a few years ago, my response wasn't anger or bitterness. During this time, my husband, Clay, and I drew comfort from Jesus. Even though we didn't know what the outcome would be, our faith grew. We believed that Jesus was in control and holding us close, and He was. As I look back at that "spiritual checkup" I realize that we responded with love, faith, strength, and hope because of Jesus.

When we face adversity, Jesus wants His love and hope to spill out of us. The only way this can happen is if we draw close to Him. His love fills us to overflowing and changes the way we respond to life and those around us. —KATIE MINTER JONES

FAITH STEP: *Look at the way you respond to circumstances and perform a self-evaluation of your heart. Ask Jesus to fill you to overflowing with His love and hope.*

SATURDAY, MAY 30

Those who weep or who rejoice or who buy things should not be absorbed by their weeping or their joy or their possessions. Those who use the things of the world should not become attached to them. For this world as we know it will soon pass away. 1 Corinthians 7:30–31 (NLT)

MY HUSBAND AND I ARE decluttering our house. He pulled out a wooden box. "This really doesn't hold much, but you gave it to me."

"That's all right," I reassured him. "Put it in the giveaway bag. My turn. I wore this sweater when I was pregnant, so I'm sort of attached to it. Should I keep it?"

"Hon, that was twenty-four years ago. I think it's time to let it go."

It's amazing how difficult it can be to let go of possessions—even those that are broken or useless. Removing clutter involves difficult choices and mental effort to discern what's really important to us. Yet these things we've invested in are so very temporary.

My house often feels cluttered by objects. But my days can also become encumbered by activities and interests that demand my time. I remember hearing a poem when I was young, "Only one life, 'twill soon be passed. Only what's done for Christ will last." Just as my husband and I set aside time to declutter around the house, I can take regular inventory of my interests and passions. Which parts of my life are enabling me to serve Jesus's kingdom more fully? Are they distracting me from Him and causing me to become too enmeshed with the world? How can I use my hobbies or other passions to worship Jesus and share Him with others? Let's surrender our attachments and allow Jesus to transform our interests and possessions into something that brings eternal value. —SHARON HINCK

FAITH STEP: *Declutter a closet or room. Ask Jesus to show you if there are possessions or activities that distract you.*

SUNDAY, MAY 31

Therefore, if anyone is in Christ, the new creation has come:
The old has gone, the new is here! 2 Corinthians 5:17 (NIV)

I'M A BIG FAN OF historic architecture and love the stories behind the buildings. On a recent road trip, I became fascinated with a magnificent old structure located in a city's downtown. Incredible detail graced the windows and balconies, and multiple spires rose like a crown from its rooftop high overhead. Wow!

I investigated, learning the grand hotel had been built in the early 1920s and became the town's social hub. But after only a few years the building suffered financial struggles. It fell into disrepair and was condemned in the 1960s, standing vacant until the 1980s, when it was updated and repurposed to be subsidized housing. Reading about that building's heyday, I remembered myself as a young woman, the embodiment of a "free spirit." Pride and thrill-seeking made up a large part of my personality. But inside, I was derelict. How many years did I present a proud face while remaining hollow inside? Too long.

I needed a second chance —someone willing to rebuild me, bit by bit. When I found Jesus, I discovered new hope, and another way to live. Today I'm able to reach out in kindness, to see worth inside people's hearts just as He did with mine. Sharing His love is part of the way He's repurposed me.

I'm not rich, nor am I young. But still I shine with an inner light and wear a crown. Only now, it's because I belong to the King.
—HEIDI GAUL

FAITH STEP: *Take a walk through a historic district in your town. As you contemplate the changes these buildings have undergone, recognize the ways Jesus has given you greater purpose and made you new.*

MONDAY, JUNE 1

And we all, who with unveiled faces contemplate the Lord's glory, are being transformed into his image with ever-increasing glory, which comes from the Lord, who is the Spirit. 2 Corinthians 3:18 (NIV)

AS A MIDDLE-SCHOOL TEACHER, I find that the end of the grading period is fraught with anxiety. I am rushing to grade end-of-quarter projects while my students keep asking me, "Is there any extra credit?" They are trying to improve their grades. Yesterday, one student asked, "You mean I have done all the extra credit that I can do?" I told him, "You've done everything, buddy." He was crestfallen. He was longing for the glory of all A's.

There are moments in life when we give it all we've got...and we still come up short. The righteousness of Jesus makes this painstakingly clear. Our very best works, attitudes, and accomplishments still aren't good enough to bridge the gap between us and a holy God. There is no extra credit to be found. All have sinned and come short of the glory of God. We can't change our hearts. We can't heal our minds. We can't usher forgiveness and hope into our own lives. That is why Jesus came: to lend us His glory. He knows we have no glory of our own—so He fits us with His. Jesus transforms us from glory to glory. We believe in Him—and He credits us with His righteousness. We trust Him...and He cracks the darkness of our lives with His brightness. We hold on to Him with arms wrapped tight...and He delivers us. All the glory belongs to Jesus. With lives healed and transformed, the only thing left for us to do is shout His praises! —SUSANNA FOTH AUGHTMON

FAITH STEP: *Take time today to share with a friend how the glory of Jesus has changed your life. Shout His praises by telling of His marvelous work in your life.*

TUESDAY, JUNE 2

They have lost connection with the head, from whom the whole body, supported and held together by its ligaments and sinews, grows as God causes it to grow. Colossians 2:19 (NIV)

ON DAYS WHEN I'M ABLE, I use online Pilates classes to stretch and strengthen my muscles. One of the important themes in Pilates is the way each part of the body is connected to the rest. If my hip is torqued, my back can't work properly. If my back hyperextends, my legs aren't as free to move in their sockets. The alignment of each part of the body is important, and even if I'm working on a movement that only uses my feet and ankles, I try to be aware of the placement of my head, neck, shoulders, ribs, etc.

We're all familiar with the image of the Christian community as the "body of Christ." Yet it's easy for me to forget that my actions affect the rest of the body. When I grumble or complain, the person hearing it is affected—just as my neck is affected if I strain my shoulders. When I gossip, I send misalignment through the entire body, harming loving connections. If I give in to worry, it's as if I'm moving without remembering to breathe and others in the body may suffer from that lack of oxygen.

This morning as I exercised, I was sobered by the realization of how the choices I make have impact beyond myself. At the same time, I took comfort in knowing Jesus is the head. When my head turns to the left, my body naturally moves that way. When I look up, my body uncurls and lifts. Together, as we follow His lead, we can form a body that angles upward in worship and moves outward in service. —SHARON HINCK

FAITH STEP: *Exercise today and notice how the parts of the body work together. Ask Jesus for ways to work well with other parts of His body today.*

Wednesday, June 3

---

*Christ made us right with God; he made us pure and holy,
and he freed us from sin.* 1 Corinthians 1:30 *(NLT)*

"You're such a perfectionist!" my younger sister remarked. To prove her observation, she added, "You cried when you didn't get a perfect score in Spanish," referring to a language class I took in college. I didn't recall the crying incident she was talking about, but I admit that I took my studies seriously. I wouldn't cut classes. I spent extra hours in the library poring over books. I fulfilled any assignment given to me by group mates for a group project. I tried to be a good student. But perfect? No. In fact, I had to enroll in a remedial math class to develop core skills.

It's hard to be a perfect student. It's even more impossible to be a person without fault in *all* areas of life. There isn't one person who is good enough to merit praise from Jesus. His standard for righteousness is so high none of us can meet it. But Jesus, the Perfect One, made a way for us to have relationship with Him. I am blown away at the thought of sinless Jesus sacrificing Himself on the cross to pay the penalty for my sins and to make me acceptable. But I'm humbled and so grateful that He did, for without His perfect sacrifice, there would be no other way for us to one day appear before His Father, spotless and blameless. Jesus Christ made us right with God by meeting all the requirements to save us from sin. That makes Him our Perfect Savior. —Marlene Legaspi-Munar

---

Faith Step: *Because of our failures, it might be hard to believe that through Jesus's death and resurrection, our sins are dealt with. Meditate on 1 Corinthians 1:30 until its truth becomes alive in you. Thank Jesus for being your Perfect Savior and freeing you from sin.*

THURSDAY, JUNE 4

I no longer live, but Christ lives in me. Galatians 2:20 (NIV)

IF YOU THINK ABOUT IT, Paul makes a bold statement here. He's claiming oneness with Jesus so intimate that the lines between the two are blurred. Paul's saying, essentially, that he is dead. No longer there. But in place of Paul, Jesus lives.

I was thinking about this the other day when I felt a great deal of anxiety about something I believe God wants me to do. I was leading music in front of my church, and I just started feeling sick. My hands were shaking, which was a problem, since I was playing the piano. I felt like Peter when he got out of the boat and tried to walk toward Jesus. He was doing it, but then he started to sink.

Did Peter doubt Jesus? Is that what made him sink? Or was he just doubting himself? Because when I'm doing music, I don't feel as if I'm doubting Jesus. But I definitely doubt myself. I wonder if I can really do it, if I'm good enough. I hate for people to be depending on me, looking at me, judging me. But if I no longer live, and Christ lives in me, what difference does it make? It's not about me anymore, so I must be doubting Him.

Those lines are blurry. But if I understand Paul correctly, doubting myself when it's something I believe Jesus has called me to do—it's the same thing as doubting Him. He's called me. He's in me. He's the One doing the work. As with Peter, all I have to do is keep my eyes on Him. That's it. Not worry how I sound, what others are thinking, whether I'll fail. I have to just keep putting one foot in front of the other, trusting Jesus. —GWEN FORD FAULKENBERRY

FAITH STEP: *What does getting out of the boat look like today? It can be just getting out of bed or out of the house. Whatever it is, get out of your comfort zone today and start trusting Jesus. It's not about us.*

FRIDAY, JUNE 5

Give your burdens to the LORD, and he will take care of you.
He will not permit the godly to slip and fall. Psalm 55:22 (NLT)

MY SON AND HIS FAMILY live on the southwestern tip of Vancouver Island, British Columbia. My husband and I wanted to show them our sailboat shortly after we bought it, so we headed their direction by sea. Thankfully the winds and waves were gentle. Nonetheless, we rocked and rolled for two full days and one night.

Our daughter-in-law invited us to sleep in their home rather than on our boat in a nearby marina, and we accepted. That night while getting ready for bed, I stood on one leg to remove my jeans. To my shock, I suddenly keeled over sideways and hit the floor. *What in the world caused that?* I wondered as I picked myself up, grateful no one had witnessed my tumble.

A seasoned fisherman later told me that constant sea motion forces our brains and bodies to compensate so we can stand upright on a boat. Returning to land requires our bodies to readjust. Until they do, we may feel tipsy or lose our balance.

Becoming aware of this helped me remember to look for ways to steady myself onshore after other voyages—walk while holding my husband's arm or stand near a counter. It also made me more appreciative of Bible promises like today's key verse. Its application is short but oh, so sweet: our life's experiences can sometimes upset our emotional, mental, or spiritual equilibrium, but nothing throws Jesus off balance. He steadies us, and He will never let us slip and fall. —GRACE FOX

FAITH STEP: *Write today's verse on a recipe card. Add Psalm 16:8 (NLT) beneath it—"I know the LORD is always with me. I will not be shaken, for he is right beside me."*

SATURDAY, JUNE 6

---

*Jesus answered, "I am the way and the truth and the life.
No one comes to the Father except through me." John 14:6 (NIV)*

MINI GOLF IS A FUNNY place to think about Jesus, but that's what I found myself doing. Club in hand, each member of our family took turns aiming the ball toward tiny holes in fake barns or used advanced geometry to compute bank shots. As I watched, I saw similarities to the unique routes each of us chose for our faith journeys.

Though our goals were identical, we all attacked the challenge differently. My son-in-law studied the various traps and used great care for each shot, a reflection of the thoughtful way he lives his faith. My daughter kidded around until the moment she swung the club; then she concentrated on the shot. Secure as she is in her place with Jesus, her joy is infectious, her witness focused and effective. My husband seemed to follow the longest route to the hole, as if on purpose. He relishes every moment with the Lord, spending valuable time in the Bible and serving others daily.

I just whacked the ball and hoped. For years I've relied on Jesus to direct me past the tricky anthills and blind shots of life, trusting in Him to guide me along the way. Even if I smack the ball completely off the course, He always lets me back in the game.

The eighteenth hole was simple—one stroke. Each of our balls circled the hole and then disappeared. Like the variances in how we live out our faith, we all acknowledge there are many ways to Jesus—but only one way to the Father. Jesus. Our hole in One.
—HEIDI GAUL

FAITH STEP: *Play a game of mini golf with friends. Watch the different techniques each one uses and consider the freedom we have following Christ to the Father— our inevitable, magnificent goal.*

SUNDAY, JUNE 7

There is therefore now no condemnation for those who are in Christ Jesus.
Romans 8:1 (ESV)

A FRIEND, FACING A THICKET of seemingly random yet serious problems with her family, asked me, "Is God punishing me? What else could account for this persistent mess?"

The fact is, life this side of heaven is broken. Sometimes things go wrong for no reason, apart from the fall that marred paradise. Other times, we suffer the consequences *of*, not punishment *for*, our actions. It's not Jesus wagging His finger in dismay. He lovingly allows us our free will, the freedom to choose our actions.

My friend had made it a practice to critique various family members' life choices, unsolicited, then discussed her views with others. Eventually word got around and the pressure cooker popped. Consequences. Brought before Jesus, our consequences can be priceless growth opportunities that mature us and point us back to the infallibility of Scripture. Once we repent and make amends to those harmed, Jesus will pour out His grace. He can use what seems like a mistake to greatly bless us and others (Romans 8:28).

I'm in the midst of the predictable and hard consequences of what now seems like a flawed and carnal decision. I don't know the ultimate outcome, but Jesus has already used it to dramatically shape, guide, and yes, bless me in unexpected ways. Jesus's intent is always love. If I look for love in consequences, I'll see Jesus.
—ISABELLA YOSUICO

FAITH STEP: *If you're feeling punished or condemned, meditate on Romans 8:1.*

MONDAY, JUNE 8

"He will wipe every tear from their eyes, and there will be no more death or sorrow or crying or pain. All these things are gone forever." And the one sitting on the throne said, "Look, I am making everything new!"
Revelation 21:4–5 (NLT)

ONE OF MY FAVORITE MOVIE lines comes from the *The Best Exotic Marigold Hotel*. Patel is a young man struggling to revive his family's dilapidated hotel. Whenever something doesn't work out or a problem arises, he tells the other person, "In India, we have a saying: 'Everything will be all right in the end. So if it is not all right, it is not yet the end.'" Some people scoff at what they see as Patel's blind optimism, but guess what? By the end of the movie, things do turn out all right.

Maybe I need to hear Patel's favorite saying every day. Don't get me wrong—I understand that we live in a world broken by sin. I know that Jesus told us to expect troubles in this earthly life. Yet still I look for the fairy-tale ending. I grow impatient waiting for loose ends to be wrapped up in a neat, tidy way. I want to see wrongs righted, broken relationships restored, and evil conquered by good.

Although there are many things I don't fully understand in the book of Revelation, I'm so glad it lets us know that one day we'll witness the ending we long for. Jesus will lead an army in the final battle to eradicate evil. All things will be made new. We will live with Jesus forever and no longer experience suffering, heartache, pain, or death. In the meantime, when a problem arises, or things don't seem to be working out, I need to remember that's because "…it is not yet the end." —DIANNE NEAL MATTHEWS

FAITH STEP: *What is discouraging you today? Remind yourself that all earthly things will pass away. Thank Jesus that one day He will make all things right.*

Tuesday, June 9

I am the true grapevine, and my Father is the gardener . . . . Remain in me, and I will remain in you. For a branch cannot produce fruit if it is severed from the vine, and you cannot be fruitful unless you remain in me.
John 15:1, 4 (NLT)

A FRIEND WHO WORKED OVERSEAS in the Middle East recently returned home. When he visited our family, he gave us a box of dates—those sweet brown, fleshy fruits of the palm tree. They were delicious.

Fruit has always been a refreshing and desirable staple in the Middle East. But in Jesus's day, a tree full of fruit was a blessing and a sign of prosperity. The purpose of the tree was to provide its owner with sustenance, wealth, and the ability to plant more trees. When Jesus was hungry and saw a fig tree by the side of the road, He was more than frustrated when He couldn't find any fruit. The fig tree was not fulfilling its purpose. It was a disappointment. What use is a tree without any fruit? Not much. It is the same when it comes to us bearing spiritual fruit.

Jesus's purpose for me is to bear spiritual fruit—to become an outpouring of His love to those around me. When I remain in Jesus, when I depend on Him daily and rely on His grace, I'm able to serve people using the spiritual gifts, talents, and abilities that He's given me. I can be Jesus's instrument of healing to those who are hurting. I can refresh others who are in need. Instead of being a fruitless disappointment, I can encourage others. As I allow Jesus to work in and through me, I should bear fruit naturally. I want to abide in Jesus, the vine, so I can be fruitful and useful, bringing life to all those around me. —MARLENE LEGASPI-MUNAR

FAITH STEP: *List your talents, skills, and expertise. Identify ways you can use them to help your community or serve in your church. When you see an opportunity, offer to help.*

WEDNESDAY, JUNE 10

Why are you in despair, O my soul? And why have you become restless and disturbed within me? Hope in God and wait expectantly for Him, for I shall again praise Him for the help of His presence. Psalm 42:5 (AMP)

IT'S ALMOST SUMMER AND "THE living" is supposed to be "easy," according to the George Gershwin song "Summertime." But sometimes it's not so easy. I'm off work every summer, and every summer I have a battle in my mind. In the last few weeks several famous people have committed suicide. Every time I hear about suicide, I am reminded of my teenage and young-adult years when I longed to die. I was hopeless. It wasn't until Jesus came into my life at the age of twenty-six that I began to look at life through a lens of hope.

Having Jesus as my Savior, knowing He is with me and that He cares for me, gives me strength. His presence helps me fight when my mind wants to focus on regrets, failures, shortcomings, and all manner of negativity. Those negative thoughts trouble me the most when I am not working. That's why it's necessary for me to be even more vigilant about focusing on the words of Jesus during the summer. I have to find a way to stay busy. So this summer I'm delighted to have the chance to write. It gives me purpose and draws me closer to Him.

It is a humbling and awesome honor to be able to refocus negative thoughts into hopeful thoughts in Jesus. I think of His goodness toward me and His promises to me. I begin to praise Him for His help and His presence. Because Jesus lives, I have hope for the future, and I can face the summer. Words cannot express my gratitude to Jesus for giving me *hope*! —TRACY ELDRIDGE

FAITH STEP: *When you feel hopeless, turn to Jesus and His Word for encouragement, so your hope can be restored. Allow your mind to focus on His goodness, His mercy, and His grace toward you. Watch your hope rise.*

THURSDAY, JUNE 11

A voice cries: "In the wilderness prepare the way of the LORD,
Make straight in the desert a highway for our God." Isaiah 40:3 (RSV)

WHO LIKES BEING CRITICIZED? I sure don't. Except by my friend Jen!
Jen has this way of pointing out my faults that takes the sting out
of it. She'll laugh when she hears about something I've done and
say, "You are a piece of work!" or she'll say with a genuine grin, "You
should come with a warning label!"

This is her way of letting me know that I've done something that's
more brazen or confrontational than I realized at the time. The key is
the *love* in her response. It's what comes through first. Her eyes smile
when she's giving me this feedback. Hers is an honest response to my
honest way of being. This blend of honesty, love, and lightheartedness
is probably why I can take the critique. Instead of triggering
defensiveness, it gives me an opportunity to ponder my actions and
wonder if I might try a different approach in the future.

As Christians, we're familiar with the concept of "preparing the
way of the Lord." Jen's affectionate perspective prepares me to see
something about myself that I wouldn't otherwise be open to seeing. Jen's strategy has taught me that when it comes to growth and
change, love prepares the way.

And I know that Jesus is preparing our way with love all the
time! In every moment, Jesus's response to us is love. Nothing
but love. When I allow myself to feel that love, I soften and open
to the growth and change that Jesus is gently preparing me for.
—ELIZABETH BERNE DEGEAR

FAITH STEP: *Next time you have to critique someone you love, spend some time
with the "love" part first. Ask Jesus to help.*

FRIDAY, JUNE 12

Your people will rebuild the ancient ruins and will raise up the age-old foundations; you will be called Repairer of Broken Walls, Restorer of Streets with Dwellings. Isaiah 58:12 (NIV)

MY HUBBY AND I HAVE remodeled three homes, some with true fixer-upper needs. In our current home, we've knocked out walls, gutted the kitchen, and finished the basement. Last year, we tackled the downstairs bathroom. For me, the first scary part of remodeling is the point where everything is ripped out, and I wonder if we'll ever finish the project. The other scary part is discovering what hides behind the facades. When my hubby tore out the Sheetrock of the basement bathroom, he discovered mice nests, wasp nests, decay, and mold.

Have you ever had a season of life when you felt the entire building of your life had been ripped down to the studs? Perhaps the job you served for years is torn away. Perhaps the person you trusted most betrayed you. Perhaps a ministry you've invested years of time and energy has fallen apart.

Sometimes when life seems to be tearing us apart, it reveals problems hidden deep in our being. When a project I'd poured my heart into ended, I saw how much of my identity had gotten wrapped up in the work, instead of my role as a humble child beloved by our Savior. The situation became an opportunity for Jesus to clean out nests of pride and scrub away the mold of self-reliance.

There may be times we feel as broken as the decimated ruins Isaiah described. But Jesus doesn't leave us in that scary place. He is our Builder and Restorer. He delights in converting our fixer-upper lives into a beautiful home where His Spirit can dwell. —SHARON HINCK

FAITH STEP: *Identify one place in your life that could use a remodel: a relationship, an attitude, a habit, a role. Ask Jesus to renovate your heart.*

SATURDAY, JUNE 13

And I heard a sound from heaven like the roar of rushing waters and like a loud peal of thunder. The sound I heard was like that of harpists playing their harps. Revelation 14:2 (NIV)

MY FIRST VACATION TO CANADA'S Niagara Falls was a wonder to my soul. I remember that the white rushing falls roared like thunder and crashed without ceasing into the blue Niagara River. Dressed in rain gear on a boat with other tourists, my husband and I held tightly to the railing as the staggering vessel sailed through blinding sheets of water and we passed very close to the falls.

I took several pictures of the Niagara Falls. Only when I returned home and had an opportunity to sit with the pictures did I understand the messages and the metaphors represented in my vacation slideshow. Like the Niagara Falls and their crushing waters that roll without ceasing, Jesus is forever my power source and strength. He is my overflow and abundance. And like the tranquil roaring of the falls, Jesus is my peace. The psalmist sings, "Deep calls to deep in the roar of your waterfalls; all your waves and breakers have swept over me" (Psalm 42:7, NIV).

While waterfalls can provide a measure of power and electricity, we know that Jesus is mightier than the waters He created. All of nature is merely a limited expression of His supreme majesty, and here is some good news. Nobody has to go on vacation to see the natural wonder of the Lord's glory. We see Him in the stars, a rose petal, and a butterfly. We see the Lord's face in the morning sun.
—ALICE THOMPSON

FAITH STEP: *Celebrate Jesus's majesty today by sitting outdoors to marvel at the flowers, trees, and sky.*

SUNDAY, JUNE 14

"Come," he said. Then Peter got down out of the boat, walked on water and came toward Jesus. But when he saw the wind, he was afraid and, beginning to sink, cried out, "Lord, save me!" Matthew 14:29–30 (NIV)

LIKE PETER, I WORRY WHEN I am faced with the storms of life. Too often, when life gets wild, I forget to stay focused on Jesus. We all have storms in our lives, but Jesus is there for us. A day at the lake with my boys when they were small brought this truth home to me.

My husband, Clay, and I were enjoying a day of fishing with our six-year-old twin sons, Jeremy and Joshua. After a few hours, I noticed a little bit of water in the back of the boat and mentioned it to my husband. "Don't worry," he said, "the boat is fine. It's just a small leak. It'll be all right. We'll be leaving soon."

A few minutes later, I turned and looked at Joshua. He had his little arms stretched out as far as they could go. He was holding on to both sides of the boat so tight his knuckles were white. I tried to encourage him. "Come, fish! They're really biting." I looked a few minutes later, and he was still holding the sides. "Why aren't you fishing?"

"I can't!" he said.

"Come on, Joshua. See if you can catch another fish."

He sat there, clenching his teeth, still holding to the edges of the boat. "I can't," he replied. "I'm holding up the boat!"

How often do we think that it is up to us to hold up the boat? Just like Joshua, we are giving it all we've got. But Jesus is asking us to let go and trust Him. When we put our trust in Jesus, He will always come through for us. He sustains us and gives us peace.
—KATIE MINTER JONES

FAITH STEP: *Don't look at the storms of life, but look to Jesus and He will rescue you.*

MONDAY, JUNE 15

For we do not have a high priest who is unable to empathize with our weaknesses, but we have one who has been tempted in every way, just as we are—yet he did not sin. Hebrews 4:15 (NIV)

THIS WEEKEND I VISITED A shipwreck on Oregon's coast. The massive sailing vessel, the *Peter Iredale*, ran aground over a century ago on an otherwise uneventful journey from Mexico. It had almost reached its destination when unforeseen strong winds drove it ashore.

Lately I've been on my own journey of sorts. I've been watching my diet and exercising, trying to take off a few pounds. My diligence is beginning to pay off. At home, I make low-calorie meals and when meeting friends for lunch, I order a salad. I ignore dessert menus and drink lots of water. I'm prepared for temptation, blocking it before it snares me. It's the unexpected enticements I struggle with, the tasty samples offered at the grocery store, the cookies my neighbor brings over. At times like those, I'm as wrecked as that ship. Temptation hits full on, sending me off course, as vulnerable as a child's newspaper boat on a blustery day.

Jesus faced every temptation known to man yet didn't sin. And in His love for us, He left directions to keep us out of trouble. Believers can pray not to be led into temptation, but to be delivered from evil (Matthew 6:13), using the words Jesus taught us. And we should stay alert, as He instructed the disciples in Matthew 26.

Jesus Himself, when tempted by the devil in the desert, fought back by speaking the Word itself. There is no stronger defense. I plan to use it, not just with my food choices but in all of life's temptations.
—HEIDI GAUL

FAITH STEP: *Ask Jesus to direct you to Scripture for when you're tempted. Memorize the verses for the next time the enemy attacks. Prepare for victory.*

TUESDAY, JUNE 16

And God dealt well with the midwives; and the people multiplied and became very strong. And it came to pass, because the midwives feared God, that he made them houses. Exodus 1:20–21 (DARBY)

I NEEDED A PLACE TO write for a few days—someplace that nurtured my devotion to God so that I could help others tap into their devotion. Lovely friends of mine have a bungalow by the ocean, just the sort of nurturing environment I knew I needed. So I dared to ask if I could stay there during the work week while they were in the city. They said, "Yes!" I felt lucky and grateful and blessed.

But when I arrived at the beach house, I was overcome with unworthiness and guilt. Had I forced their hand? Did I deserve to be so generously received into their home? I quickly busied myself with writing, hoping that I could somehow earn the invitation extended to me.

Several hours later the vast calm of the ocean and the nurturing spirit of my friends' home had begun to ease my tension. I closed my writing journal and took a deep breath. That's when it dawned on me: the journal I had been furiously writing in had been given to me as a thank-you gift a few months before. I had welcomed a friend's parents to stay in my home for a few days so they could attend their grandson's baptism. It had been a pleasure.

In that instance I had been host, and here at the beach I was now guest. In both I was part of a network of love and generosity, and there was nothing to be ashamed of. I wondered about my sense of unworthiness. How often has Jesus extended invitations to me that I have been too self-conscious to accept? —ELIZABETH BERNE DEGEAR

FAITH STEP: *Today, accept someone else's generosity without unworthiness. Imagine they are midwives helping to bring Jesus's kingdom into the world and by receiving you are participating in that glorious birth.*

WEDNESDAY, JUNE 17

Blessed are those who mourn, for they will be comforted. Matthew 5:4 (NIV)

A MAN IN MY NEIGHBORHOOD was robbed and beaten to death. I saw the report on the evening news. While I did not recognize the man's name or face, I grieved the loss of his life. I grieved for my city that is plagued with high rates of unemployment, poverty, and crime. I have considered packing up and moving to another neighborhood or another city and state. Each time I make this proposal to my husband, he reminds me that unemployment, poverty, and crime are problems across the nation. He is right.

There is nowhere to run from these problems. My protection or safekeeping is not a place. My protection is a person, and His name is Jesus. Gospel artists sing, "Jesus is a fence!" And what is considered the *Psalm of Protection* says, "Whoever dwells in the shelter of the Most High will rest in the shadow of the Almighty. I will say of the LORD, 'He is my refuge and my fortress, my God, in whom I trust'" (Psalm 91:1–2, NIV).

Newspaper headlines make it clear that no city is without the presence of evil. While school students engage in community service and volunteer work, school shootings are at an all-time high. While police officers serve and protect, incidents of police brutality also occur with saddening regularity. In life, we have a myriad of reasons to mourn, and by all means, let us freely mourn because there is a promise in our tears. When our hearts are heavy, Jesus comes quickly to comfort us. His arms embrace us. He is our safe harbor and rock for all the ages. —ALICE THOMPSON

FAITH STEP: *Throughout the day, softly say the name of Jesus. Feel the power of His name seal you in His peace and protection.*

THURSDAY, JUNE 18

The Spirit of the Lord GOD is upon Me, Because the LORD has anointed Me . . . To console those who mourn in Zion, To give them beauty for ashes, The oil of joy for mourning, The garment of praise for the spirit of heaviness.
Isaiah 61:1, 3 (NKJV)

FATHER'S DAY IS IN A few days. My dad passed away in February 2013, and I think about him every day. We grew closer during the last twenty years of his life. He would often share his life stories, joys, disappointments, and sorrows with me. It was during those conversations that I realized that emotionally, we were alike. We were both sensitive souls who could be easily wounded. He became my best friend, someone who didn't judge or criticize me. On my toughest days I long to hear his voice because sometimes that was enough for me.

In the days after he passed away, it was Jesus whom I cried out to for comfort. As I sang praise songs and fell to my knees, I could feel Jesus's arms around me, holding me up. When I woke in the middle of the night and remembered that my father was gone, Jesus would rock me back to sleep as tears soaked my pillow.

It was during this time that I learned that Jesus was my joy and my comfort in the time of sorrow. Now, when I buy a sympathy card for someone, I write inside, "May you find comfort and peace in the loving arms of Jesus." I want them to know Jesus will hold them in His arms. Jesus will calm your heart while you grieve your loved one. —TRACY ELDRIDGE

FAITH STEP: *If you have lost someone close to you, and you find the pain unbearable, look to Jesus for comfort. He will give you the "garment of praise," "beauty for ashes," and the "oil of joy" in your mourning (Isaiah 61:3, NKJV).*

FRIDAY, JUNE 19

The seed that fell on good soil are those who hear the word and commit themselves to it with a good and upright heart. Luke 8:15 (CEB)

I'M A MINIMALIST GARDENER. My husband built raised beds, so I don't have to bend over. I mulch with environmentally friendly black fabric so I don't have to weed. But I do appreciate the harvest—fresh vegetables, beautiful flowers.

The day I had free to plant the garden this year was perfect for planting. Soon after, a gentle rain fell. Mixed days of warm sun and refreshing rain followed—ideal conditions for a new garden.

With hanging baskets of flowers and herbs planted and thriving, I discovered a leftover basket in which I planted unused seed packets and hung the basket on the deck rail. It hung close to the deck floor, but I planned to move it as the flowers grew.

Nothing sprouted. Ever. The chipmunks found the basket just the right height for a seed buffet table.

One of the parables Jesus told that farmers and gardeners—even minimalist gardeners—understand is the one about of the sower. In Luke 8:4–15, my extra flower basket was like the seed that fell on the path that birds snatched up. In my case, furry little thirteen-striped "birds."

I love the end of that parable, about those who respond to Jesus's invitation to follow Him. They "commit themselves to [the Word] with a good and upright heart. Through their resolve, they bear fruit" (Luke 8:15, CEB).

Jesus, we're resolved to bear fruit, vegetables, flowers. We're committed to Your Word. —CYNTHIA RUCHTI

FAITH STEP: *Keep a seed packet or potted plant to remind you that commitment, plus a good, upright heart, watered with resolve, produces the kind of harvest Jesus expects.*

SATURDAY, JUNE 20

Jesus Christ is the same yesterday, today, and forever. Hebrews 13:8 (TLB)

YESTERDAY, MY FITNESS TRAINER ASKED me about my summer plans. I was pleased to tell him I am finally doing something I have been dreaming of for the past twenty years—writing. Then I described the type of writing I am doing and explained to him why I am so thrilled to have the opportunity to write. I told my trainer that the dream started years ago after Jesus saved me and I became aware of the fact that Jesus loved me unconditionally. It was such a life-changing revelation for me that I felt the need to let everybody know. I started writing about the love of Jesus, adding Scriptures to my writings so I could show anybody who didn't know that His love was real, unconditional, and transformative.

A few years after the love affair with Jesus started, my world was rocked when the Lord denied a specific prayer request I had prayed. Still immature in spiritual matters, I blamed myself for my request being denied. My shortcomings became my focus. I couldn't see Jesus's love for me, and I stopped writing about His love. Thankfully Jesus's love, just like Him, is the same yesterday, today, and forever, regardless of what happens in our lives. As the storm lifted, I realized that His love is what buoyed me and carried me through one of the lowest moments in life. Over the past fifteen years, I have been repeatedly awed and overwhelmed by the steadfastness of Jesus's love. The fact that this current writing opportunity has been placed in my life now is a tremendous testament to the everlasting and unchanging love and purpose of Jesus. —TRACY ELDRIDGE

FAITH STEP: *Write down the times in your life when you couldn't feel the love of Jesus. Then write about how He showed you love during those times, even though you didn't immediately see it.*

FATHER'S DAY, SUNDAY, JUNE 21

*The eternal God is your dwelling place, and underneath
are the everlasting arms. Deuteronomy 33:27 (ESV)*

BEFORE MY SPINAL SURGERY IN 2018, I made the house patient-friendly. There would be limitations on my movements, so I arranged items I use on a daily basis within easy reach. I bought a grabber stick so I could pick up things for myself. The doctor's office advised having help at home the first few weeks. But my husband had to return to work a few days after my surgery, and we had no family nearby.

I reminded myself how "tough" I was. While our children were growing up, we'd never had family near us, and my husband worked long hours. Twice in recent years, he'd moved across the country for a new job and left me behind in an area where we were still newcomers. Once I drove myself to the emergency room at 3:30 a.m.

After the surgery, the worst pain came when I stood up. I learned to push on my thighs to help raise myself. Often my husband walked into the room as I started to get up from the couch where I spent the first week. He'd put his arms under my shoulders and lift me up. I worried about my weight straining his back, but it was a relief to sink into his arms and avoid the pain!

During my recuperation, I often thought about Jesus and His arms. *How much pain do I needlessly suffer because of prideful independence?* Jesus wants to carry my burdens, but first I have to let them go. Instead of relying on my own strength, I can depend on the strong, loving arms of Jesus to bear me up. —DIANNE NEAL MATTHEWS

FAITH STEP: *Is something in your life causing you pain or making you feel weak today? Imagine sinking into Jesus's arms and allowing Him to support you.*

MONDAY, JUNE 22

Jesus Christ the same yesterday, and to day, and for ever.
Hebrews 13:8 (KJV)

IT'S A ROUGH PATCH FOR me as a mom. My oldest daughter, Grace, is spending the summer at a camp for the top students in our state. It's an honor for her to be there. She's having a great time, meeting neat people, learning a lot. Blah, blah, blah.

I'm happy for her. I really am. She was excited as we entered the college campus and friendly to everyone as we moved her into her dorm. She was adorable as she skipped away from us toward her first meeting, leaving me standing on the sidewalk staring after her like a lost puppy. On the drive home, my heart ached.

That was a week ago. Yesterday, we picked her up and brought her home for church and Father's Day lunch. Later I drove her back to camp, ninety miles away. After she was safe in her dorm, I sat in the parking lot and sobbed. Then I drove home alone.

I called my mom. "It was my dream being a mom and having all my kids at home. Now that's all changing." (Pause for nose blowing and tear wiping.) "We're going on vacation this summer without her, and next year she'll go to college and move out for good."

My mom was her usual patient self. She told me she'd felt the same way when I grew up. Then she said something profound. "There's so much joy in life, mingled with great sorrow. The one thing that never changes is that Jesus is with us through it all."

What a comfort that no matter what season of life we're in, we're not alone. Whether our hearts burst with joy or break with sadness, Jesus is with us. A support, a steady presence, a faithful friend.

—GWEN FORD FAULKENBERRY

FAITH STEP: *Memorize today's verse. Life changes, but Jesus never will.*

TUESDAY, JUNE 23

Instead, we will speak the truth in love, growing in every way more and more like Christ, who is the head of his body, the church. He makes the whole body fit together perfectly. As each part does its own special work, it helps the other parts grow, so that the whole body is healthy and growing and full of love. Ephesians 4:15–16 (NLT)

MY HUSBAND AND I LEAD short-term mission teams to Eastern Europe every summer. The teams' mix of personalities and giftedness always makes us smile.

Peggy B. has participated in our evangelistic family camps in Poland nine times. She'd been our daughters' preschool teacher, and she loves kids, so we knew the children's program would be in good hands.

Some volunteers coordinate crafts. Others teach workshops about marriage or parenting. Some lead games, and others serve in worship.

Some find joy serving behind the scenes—organizing supplies, babysitting infants so the parents can participate in Bible study, or connecting with campers one-on-one. They see unmet needs and quietly fill those gaps.

North Americans who speak fluent German have joined us as well, and used their language skills to connect with German families.

Jesus is the ultimate team coordinator. He knows the skills and personalities needed to host these cross-cultural camps, and He puts each team together accordingly. When everyone does their own special work, His purposes are accomplished. His love is communicated through word and deed, and lives are changed. —GRACE FOX

FAITH STEP: *Meditate on today's verse. How can you join with others to do His special work?*

WEDNESDAY, JUNE 24

At dawn Jesus was standing on the beach, but the disciples couldn't see who he was. John 21:4 (NLT)

SUNRISE AT THE BEACH IS my favorite place to worship and fully experience Jesus; I'm overwhelmed by His presence there. His majesty is displayed in the splendor of the sunrise as the rays paint the sky with beautiful shades of color. The roar of the waves proclaims His might. The smell of the salt in the air, the feel of the soft sand beneath my feet, and the cool mist all refresh me.

When Jesus was on earth, He must have loved the sea also. The Bible tells several stories where He's on the sea or at the beach. Jesus was walking by the Sea of Galilee when He called two fisherman, Peter and Andrew, to be His disciples, making them fishers of men. In Matthew 8:24–27, Jesus was on the boat asleep when the disciples became afraid and woke him. A storm was threatening to sink the boat, and Jesus calmed the wind and the waves, unleashing His power on the sea. Jesus didn't stop there . . . He walked on the water. And after Jesus was resurrected, He stood on the beach at dawn, but the disciples did not recognize Him. They had been out all night, fishing without a single catch. He told them to cast their nets to the right side of the boat, and their nets became full. A miracle on the beach! Time after time, Jesus uses the backdrop of the sea to reveal His love to humanity.

The Bible describes His love for us as being deeper than the ocean. The beach proclaims His majesty, His presence, and the depth of His love. Let the vastness of the ocean and the beauty of His creation remind you again today that His love for you is fathomless.
—KATIE MINTER JONES

FAITH STEP: *Look up pictures of the ocean. Remind yourself of the amazing depths of love that He has for you and praise Him.*

THURSDAY, JUNE 25

The LORD himself goes before you and will be with you; he will never leave you nor forsake you. Do not be afraid; do not be discouraged.
Deuteronomy 31:8 (NIV)

WEDDINGS ARE JOYFUL OCCASIONS. AT least they're supposed to be. Recently I was talking with friends at a wedding reception. We were laughing so hard I didn't hear the DJ's announcement. Suddenly the spotlight was on the dance floor. A familiar song started playing. The father of the bride took his daughter by the hand and led her to the dance floor. He held her in his arms for the father-daughter dance. My joy turned to sorrow.

Holding back tears, I smiled faintly, quickly excused myself, and headed to the bathroom. Thoughts of my father filled my mind. He'd left me as an infant. When I met him at fourteen, he told me, "Please don't call me daddy. I'm an elected official and the voters don't know about you." I rarely saw him after that first painful meeting. I never heard him say, "I love you." "Jesus, why?" I cried. "Wasn't I worthy?"

Regaining my composure, I freshened up at the sink. A framed Bible verse sat near the mirror. The verse was Deuteronomy 31:8 (NIV), "He will never leave you nor forsake you." In that moment I realized that my heavenly Father had always been there for me. My true Dad had never left me or forsaken me.

I smiled, thanking Jesus for His love. He promised that He'd be a father to the fatherless (Psalms 68:5). One day I will meet my heavenly Father and have the father-daughter dance I've always wanted.
—KATIE MINTER JONES

FAITH STEP: *Reread Deuteronomy 31:8. Know that you are His child and that Jesus will never leave you or forsake you.*

FRIDAY, JUNE 26

Jesus said, "Let the little children come to me, and do not hinder them, for the kingdom of heaven belongs to such as these." Matthew 19:14 (NIV)

WE RECENTLY SENT MY SON off to our church's weeklong sleepover camp. Pierce was uncharacteristically anxious and looking for reasons not to go. At first, we were prayerfully clear about our decision to send him, but then my husband and I started to worry a little.

My husband and I talked and prayed with Pierce about it, naming his utterly normal fears. We asked Jesus for peace, reassurance, maybe a familiar face, and above all, a life-changing time with Jesus. By the time we pulled into the church parking lot, he was ready to go.

As we made our way toward the church, his basketball coach emerged with a smile of recognition and warm greeting. He'd just dropped off his son, Tre, Pierce's teammate, who would be on the same camp team. Then Pierce saw another familiar face. Then the familiar faces soon connected with their other buddies and Pierce seemed lost. I hung around, uncertain. The fear crept back.

Then it dawned on me. I was hovering, hindering Pierce from connecting—either with friends or with Jesus. Instead of trusting Jesus to care for Pierce, I was in the way. I hugged Pierce and left.

We couldn't communicate with Pierce while he was away, but I dismissed my anxious thoughts and continued to pray. Five days later, Pierce returned on fire for Jesus, eager to take his faith to the next level: getting baptized. He'd come to Jesus unhindered by a worried mom. Just as I gave my life to Jesus for safekeeping, I can entrust my kids—and others—to Jesus's loving care. —ISABELLA YOSUICO

FAITH STEP: *Is there an area in which you're hovering over a child, youngster or adult? Ask God to help you to entrust him to His loving care so he can come to Jesus unhindered.*

SATURDAY, JUNE 27

For he is our peace. Ephesians 2:14 (KJV)

MY WRITING DESK TODAY IS a patio table in the screen house on the deck. Our quiet neighborhood seems especially silent today because the road in front of our house is closed to through traffic while the county resurfaces the asphalt a few miles to the north. A soft breeze is blowing. The only conflict within sight is a war between two cardinals and a blue jay. The cardinals are winning.

It is a place of peace. The garden's growing at a pace I can almost hear. My Bible's open in front of me. Peace.

But I might not recognize the external serenity if it weren't for my internal serenity. Despite deadlines, projects waiting for me, family health needs yet unresolved—more than a few pockets of uncertainty—peace reigns in my soul because the Word of God is true: Jesus *is* our peace.

That thought will never cease to amaze me. It's an "anyway" peace. And that's what amazes others too.

"Why aren't you rattled? Have you been listening to the news?"

"Peace anyway."

"How can you be so calm? You must be in denial about what's happening."

"No. Peace anyway. I have Jesus. I have peace."

It's not a trite saying. Ask a person of faith who has weathered a crisis without collapsing. Ask a caregiver who keeps pressing on in love. Ask someone who's followed Jesus a lifetime—a lifetime that's drawing to an end. Peace anyway. Because He is our peace. —CYNTHIA RUCHTI

FAITH STEP: *Find a spot today—inside or outside—that represents peace. Capture the image and make it the wallpaper for your phone or the screen saver on your computer. Sketch the scene as a reminder that Jesus is our "anyway" peace.*

SUNDAY, JUNE 28

When the disciples James and John saw this, they said, "Lord, do you want us to call fire down from heaven to consume them?" Luke 9:54 (CEB)

MY FRIEND RECENTLY SUFFERED A serious rejection. My heart broke for her. It was unfair, uncalled for, and put her in a difficult position for her near-future plans. To increase the distress, she'd worked hard the past several years to heal from words that had shredded her soul. Now this.

My heart ached as if it had happened to me, but then I realized what I felt on her behalf could be little more than a shadow of what she was experiencing. The above verse came to mind and lingered. But only for a moment. It's a good thing I remembered the words that follow them in the Bible.

Jesus and His disciples had been rejected by a whole town. He'd sent messengers ahead of the team to find a place to stay on the long trip to Jerusalem. Their path led through a Samaritan village. But the village "refused to welcome him because he was determined to go to Jerusalem" (Luke 9:53, CEB).

James and John must have been humiliated, angry, and hurt for their Friend, but when they asked Him if they should obliterate them with fire from above, Jesus "turned and spoke sternly to them [James and John], and they went on to another village" (vv. 55–56, CEB).

James and John sounded a little like superheroes overly-impressed with their own power. Or friends bent on revenge. Jesus, who really did have the power to call down fire from heaven, didn't. He moved on.

My friend is moving on. She's a Jesus follower. That's what Jesus followers do when they listen to Him. —CYNTHIA RUCHTI

FAITH STEP: *Has someone you love been hurt or rejected? Is a fire burning within you, a need for revenge, and it seems justifiable? Hear the voice of Jesus calling. Douse the flames and keep traveling the path with Him.*

MONDAY, JUNE 29

Yet, the strength of those who wait with hope in the LORD will be renewed. They will soar on wings like eagles. They will run and won't become weary. They will walk and won't grow tired. Isaiah 40:31 (GW)

WAITING IS AN UNAVOIDABLE PART of life, isn't it? This morning, I waited for the leak in our brand-new air-conditioning unit to be fixed. All week I'd hoped to hear the results of my grandson's MRI and news of my teenage granddaughter's first trip to camp. Meanwhile, my daughter sat in the ER, waiting to learn if her foot was broken.

My husband and I have endured our share of long waits. We've waited for job offers during times of unemployment. We've waited for homes to sell, and we've waited to hear if offers on homes we wanted to buy were accepted. I'm still awaiting answers to prayers for some of my deepest longings.

The Bible gives extreme examples of waiting. Jacob waited seven years to marry Rachel, the woman of his dreams. Abraham waited twenty-five years for his promised son and heir. Due to disobedience, the Israelites wandered in the wilderness forty years before entering the Promised Land. The world waited centuries for the promised Messiah.

I'm sure that Jacob, Abraham, and the Israelites felt like what they received was worth the wait. But sometimes it doesn't happen that way. Remembering that Jesus controls my life helps me be more patient when I have to wait. Trusting that He's working everything out for ultimate good (Romans 8:28) makes it easier when I feel as though the waiting ended in less than the desired results.
—DIANNE NEAL MATTHEWS

FAITH STEP: *In what area of your life is Jesus asking you to wait patiently?*

TUESDAY, JUNE 30

For everything that was written in the past was written to teach us,
so that through the endurance taught in the Scriptures and the
encouragement they provide we might have hope. Romans 15:4 (NIV)

A FRIEND AND I WERE talking about our grown children, and our longing for stronger and deeper relationships with them. I shared that the last time one of my boys stayed with us, I imagined the great conversations we would have. Instead, he was busy and away most of the time, and I had few interactions with him. My friend and I realized that when we set our hopes on our own plans and prescriptions for how things should unfold, we are often disappointed. That disappointment can even lead us to give up on improved communication ever happening. Have you ever felt that sense of hopelessness, the temptation to believe things will never change?

We encouraged each other to instead invite Jesus to create opportunities in ways we may not expect and to help us be available to His prompting when those moments come. We decided to keep praying in faith that He is working in our children's lives and our relationships with them. We won't give up hope, but we'll stop measuring our hope by our own expectations.

Right after our conversation, my friend received a daily Bible verse email: Romans 15:4. I love when Jesus joins in to the conversation that way. He reminded us that the Scriptures will encourage us and that He *does* want us to keep hoping for all good things.

When we expect specific outcomes we're often disappointed, but when we watch expectantly for Jesus, we'll never be disappointed.
—SHARON HINCK

FAITH STEP: *Ask Jesus for the endurance to keep praying, keep watching for Him to act, and keep hoping.*

WEDNESDAY, JULY 1

His life is the light that shines through the darkness. John 1:5 (TLB)

THIS SUMMER I VACATIONED WITH my family to South Dakota's Black Hills and the Rocky Mountains in Colorado. We drove our RV and ended up having a great time, but the first few days were rough for me. I struggled to stay in the moment and appreciate what I had because I felt overwhelmed by what—who—was missing. Our oldest had chosen a really neat opportunity that was offered to her for the summer and therefore wasn't with us. It was the first time we'd ever been on vacation without one of our kids. It stank.

To make matters worse, the other three weren't getting along. They all wanted to look at screens instead of scenery, and when they weren't looking at screens, they were fighting. The balance of different personalities and ages seemed to be thrown off by the absence of Grace. I felt like I was nagging them all the time. I began to feel hopeless and lost.

One morning in an RV park at the foot of Crazy Horse Memorial, as rain fell on the roof of the RV, I got up early and made a pot of coffee. I opened my Bible to the book of John, the place I go when I'm out of ideas. There's a reason I do this, I was reminded immediately. As I read the words, light began to shine in my darkness.

I don't have a deep theological insight to share from those moments. Nothing new was revealed. The only explanation I can give is that it centered me. The Word, the Light, Jesus—shone in my heart and everything else seemed to gather around that light. I could see my way through the darkness and walk on. —GWEN FORD FAULKENBERRY

FAITH STEP: *What is the ritual that centers you? If you don't have one, try reading the entire first chapter of John. And don't pray anything fancy. Just say the name: Jesus.*

THURSDAY, JULY 2

For I hold you by your right hand—I, the LORD your God. And I say to you, "Don't be afraid. I am here to help you." Isaiah 41:13 (NLT)

I GLANCED AT THE DOOR of the bank, eager to step inside so I could make a bank transaction before the end of the day. Then I saw a gray-haired man, wobbling and straining to reach for something firm to hold on to as he made his way unsteadily toward the bank.

I rushed to the old man and extended my right hand. He beamed, pleasantly surprised by the gesture. Then he muttered, "This arthritis . . . it's hard for me to move because of it."

As I held his wrinkled hand to support him, I felt his thick, hard palm and gnarled fingers. He explained how difficult it was for him to move around and even apologized for being elderly. He repeatedly thanked me, grateful for the sudden but much-needed help.

I tried to imagine how that man must have felt while staggering his way into the bank. *Was he afraid of tripping and hurting his fragile self? Did he pity himself for being weak and alone, without a family member to support him?* I would have wanted someone to help me if I was in his shoes. We all need a helping hand. I'm grateful that Jesus helps us most of all.

Jesus reached out His hand to Peter as he began to sink after his brief walk on the water. Even though Peter doubted when he saw the strong waves, Jesus immediately rescued him. When fear, doubt, and worry cause us to quiver and tremble, the strong hands of Jesus will protect and comfort us, just as they did Peter.
—MARLENE LEGASPI-MUNAR

FAITH STEP: *Visit an elderly person today and extend any help that he or she might need, just as Jesus would. Spend some time and provide good cheer.*

FRIDAY, JULY 3

But we do not want you to be uninformed, brothers, about those who are asleep, that you may not grieve as others do who have no hope. For since we believe that Jesus died and rose again, even so, through Jesus, God will bring with him those who have fallen asleep. 1 Thessalonians 4:13–14 (ESV)

THIS MORNING AT 2:00 A.M. my husband and daughter climbed into the rented moving truck and set out for Nashville. My girl is moving across the country for a job with a company she loves. I'm thrilled for her opportunity and her courage. But here's the thing. She's our youngest of four, and the one who still lived in town. She would come over each week to do laundry, have a meal, and watch a cooking show with us (which we'd always save for her). On holidays when none of the other children could make it home, she was the gentle and constant presence that we appreciated so much.

So, while I'm happy for her, I'm also grieving. To cheer me, my husband reminded me that after a writer's conference where I'll be teaching next summer we will be halfway to her new home. He suggested that after the conference we take a left on the map and go visit her. Anticipating that visit is definitely helping.

As followers of Jesus, we aren't immune from loss and grief. Circumstances may move us far from our family and friends. Even more painful, those we are close to may go to heaven. We miss them, and it hurts. But Jesus reminds us that these partings are temporary. In the face of eternity together, these times of separation are brief. We may grieve, but not as those who have no hope. We'll be able to join Jesus and our loved ones soon. What a reunion that will be! —SHARON HINCK

FAITH STEP: *Think of the family and friends you are missing today, whether because they have moved away or graduated to heaven. Thank Jesus for the coming reunion.*

SATURDAY, JULY 4

I will lie down and fall asleep in peace because you alone, LORD,
let me live in safety. Psalm 4:8 (CEB)

MY GRANDKIDS WERE THRILLED ABOUT the big Fourth of July cel-ebration in their new town. They wore patriotic clothes and bought red, white, and blue "glow" glasses and light-up sticks. My three-year-old granddaughter, Lilah, enjoyed dancing to the music of the live band. Finally the sky grew dark; the big moment had arrived. The first screeching rocket burst into bright colors with a loud boom. I glanced at Lilah to see her reaction. Her beaming smile had been replaced by a grimace and she had both hands over her ears. I had to put my ear next to her mouth to hear her cries, "It's too loud! It's too loud!"

This is bad! I thought. *The car's so far away, and it would take forever to maneuver through this crowd.* I looked at Lilah again. She had gone to her daddy for comfort, her head laid on his chest as he reclined on the quilt. Within moments, she was fast asleep—oblivious of the loud noises from the fireworks and cheering all around her.

I wondered if the secret to Lilah's ability to rest during the fire-works was being close to her dad's heart. Could she hear or sense his heartbeat? Then I thought about how we can stay close to our heavenly Father's heart through prayer and reading His Word. And by spending time with the One who revealed the Father's heart of love, compassion, and understanding

Since we know Jesus as our Lord and Protector, we can draw close to Him at the first hint of danger. Then we will feel as safe and secure as a beloved child with her head against her daddy's chest.
—DIANNE NEAL MATTHEWS

FAITH STEP: *As you prepare for sleep this evening, imagine resting your head against Jesus as He guards and protects you all through the night.*

SUNDAY, JULY 5

"Come," he said. Then Peter got down out of the boat, walked on the water and came toward Jesus. But when he saw the wind, he was afraid and, beginning to sink, cried out, "Lord, save me!" Immediately Jesus reached out his hand and caught him. "You of little faith," he said, "why did you doubt?" Matthew 14:29–31 (NIV)

I'M ROUTINELY AMAZED AT HOW Jesus reveals Himself through real-life experiences, particularly when I include Him in the process.

My son, Isaac, has Down syndrome, and loving him has blessed and grown me in unexpected ways. Isaac has inspired me to be a better person and face many fears. One recent example was advocating for Isaac in making changes to his IEP (Individualized Educational Program).

My husband and I had a vision for Isaac, but even after doing extensive research, praying, and seeking expert counsel, I was full of doubt and fear. Was this plan best for Isaac? Could I make my case? What if I was wrong? Eventually I had to step out of the boat. I had to take the risk of trusting my gut, of pushing hard, of making a mistake, and then leave the outcome to Jesus.

Now, a year after the major changes I demanded on Isaac's behalf, I marvel at the fruits of that arduous process. Pressing on produced incredible results, far exceeding what I imagined.

Since then I've faced other challenges that trigger the same fear and uncertainty—there have been many situations wrapped in that familiar invitation to answer Jesus's call *to come. Will I follow, entrusting the results to Him who loves me?* My Savior is a trustworthy counselor and advocate (John 16:7). —ISABELLA YOSUICO

FAITH STEP: *Are you struggling with a dilemma fraught with fear? Recall a time when you struggled with a difficult decision and could later see Jesus's hand.*

MONDAY, JULY 6

Look! I stand at the door and knock. If you hear my voice and open the door, I will come in, and we will share a meal together as friends. Revelation 3:20 (NLT)

I'D JUST ACCEPTED A NEW research project and needed a millennial perspective, so I texted my daughter to ask her what FOMO (Fear of Missing Out) meant to her. FOMO is all over social media these days.

"It's when you see your friends' posts of weddings, a new baby, a new job, or exotic vacations, and you feel depressed or left out," my daughter wrote back. One article I read described the FOMO mind-set as "social envy" or "social anxiety."

But when I thought about it more, I realized that people have always struggled with feeling left out—long before social media ever existed or the term FOMO was coined.

The Bible says it's not wise to compare ourselves to others (Galatians 6:4), but we do it anyway. We feel envious and want what others have, forgetting that God's created blessings just for us. We worry about missing out on important social activities. We make the wrong choices while others seem to succeed. But as I make time for Jesus and become more intimate with my Perfect Friend—Jesus Himself—He assures me that I'm not missing out. The more time I spend with Jesus, the more my heart knows there's no worldly thing that could ever compete with Him. He reminds me not to worry (Matthew 6:34), to be grateful for what I have (Philippians 4:12–13), and to trust His plans for me (Jeremiah 29:11). Spending time with Jesus is one thing I wouldn't miss for the world—nothing compares to hanging out with Him. —MARLENE LEGASPI-MUNAR

FAITH STEP: *If you carve out time to abide in Him, you'll realize you're not missing out on anything. Set two places at your table and dine with Jesus today.*

TUESDAY, JULY 7

Samuel was ministering before the LORD, a boy wearing a linen ephod.
His mother used to make for him a little robe and take it to him each year.
1 Samuel 2:18–19 (NRSV)

"MOM, SHOULD I TAKE THIS robe?" My about-to-be-a-teenager daughter is holding out her pink fleece robe as we pack for sleepaway camp. It comforts me to imagine her snuggled in the soft robe during a cold night when she is far from home. I want to wrap my arms around her and say, "Every time you feel like you need me, put on this robe, and I'll be hugging you tight!" But I know she would shrug me off. These days she wants a hug from me only sometimes and on *her* terms.

This tug between letting our children go off to live their lives and pulling them in tight to hold on to them is as old as the human heart. My Old Testament hero, Hannah, lived that tension in such a poignant way. God granted her the child she so desperately wanted, and then she granted that same child, Samuel, to service to God.

As we finish packing the trunk I realize I'm the one who needs a hug. Silently I ask Jesus to wrap me in His love so that I can send my child off with grace.

In the Scripture above, we learn that each year Hannah would weave Samuel a robe and bring it to him during her annual visit to the temple. The Bible doesn't give us the details, but we know them, don't we? We can imagine her choosing the colors with such care, planning the size of the robe to allow for his growth over the course of that year, and weaving her love into every thread. Each night as she fell asleep, she knew her child, far away, was wrapped in that weave of her love. I am so grateful that no matter where my children are, I know Jesus's loving embrace surrounds them. —ELIZABETH BERNE DEGEAR

FAITH STEP: *Imagine yourself wrapped in the weave of Jesus's love.*

WEDNESDAY, JULY 8

And lo, I am with you always [remaining with you perpetually—regardless of circumstance, and on every occasion], even to the end of the age.
Matthew 28:20 (AMP)

WHENEVER I AM IN A multistory building, I take the stairs as much as I can. This week I am staying in a hotel to attend our church conference. Today while walking up the stairs to my hotel room, I breathlessly reached the top of the fourth floor where my room was, grabbed the card key out of my back pocket, and dropped it. But instead of just falling onto the top stair, the card literally slid to the bottom stair four flights below. With much aggravation, I walked back down the stairs to get the card, saying to myself, "Just when you reach the summit of achievement, something tries to bring you down."

Sometimes life is just like that. Several years ago, I had finally reached a point in my life where I was moving up financially, so I bought a new car. One year later I was laid off and it took me eight months to find another full-time job. I was stunned, hurt, and confused, but during those eight months I knew I had to trust Jesus. Even with my money running low, crying tears of discouragement because no one was calling me back for a job, I knew Jesus was with me. Since my new position paid less than I made before, I felt as if I was starting all over again, but I realized I just had to keep climbing to get back to the top! And that's something we all have to do. When situations knock you down, get back up and start climbing again, knowing that Jesus is with you. It won't always be easy, but as long as you keep climbing, trusting Jesus all the way, you will reach the top again. —TRACY ELDRIDGE

FAITH STEP: *Look back to the times in your life when a challenge, sickness, or tragedy sent you sliding down and you felt alone. When you recall the situation now, can you see that Jesus was with you all the while?*

THURSDAY, JULY 9

I say to myself, "The LORD is my portion; therefore I will wait for him."
Lamentations 3:24 (NIV)

MY FATHER WAS A GIFTED talker who relished sharing life lessons and telling jokes. At family or social events, a crowd of attentive listeners would gather at his feet. He wasn't a writer, but he could weave oratorical yarns that would make you laugh out loud.

One day I visited my father in his new home with shiny new appliances and a new car in the driveway, and he made it clear that he had no inheritance for me. "Before I leave here," he said, slapping a stack of bills against his marble table, "I intend to spend every dollar I ever made."

This was my father talking, the jokester, so I assumed he was kidding. After all, by the time he took ill, Daddy was a God-fearing Bible-thumper who could quote Scripture from memory from Genesis to Revelation. He knew Proverbs 13:22: "A good man leaves an inheritance to his children's children." (NKJV)

Ha! It was *no* joke. When he died, he left just enough money to bury him and pay for the repast. I expected a house, a car, or a sizable check, but his shiny new possessions were returned to his creditors. And when the executor of my father's estate said there was nothing for me, I was angry. After I'd stewed for several weeks, Jesus spoke to my heart from Lamentations 3:24. I realized that the Lord is my portion and having a relationship with Him surpasses any gift that could come from man. I came to understand that Jesus is my inheritance. My abundance is in Him. —ALICE THOMPSON

FAITH STEP: *What heirloom do you want to leave to a loved one? Don't delay. Share it today.*

FRIDAY, JULY 10

"What should we do?" the king of Israel cried out. "The LORD has brought the three of us here to let the king of Moab defeat us." But King Jehoshaphat of Judah asked, "Is there no prophet of the LORD with us? If there is, we can ask the LORD what to do through him." 2 Kings 3:10–11 (NLT)

MOUTHS PARCHED, STUMBLING FROM HEAT and exhaustion, both kings floundered in the wilderness with their armies. What started as a bold campaign to reclaim Moab's tax now looked grim. Because of their roundabout route, the kings ran into a problem: no water. The reaction of the two leaders caught my attention. The king of Israel accused God. They'd both made decisions that led them here, but now that the situation grew difficult, he blamed God.

Sadly, I can relate to that impulse. Moving ahead with a choice, I often encounter unexpected problems. If I'm fearful, like Israel's king, I may begin to doubt the goodness of the Lord. The lie says that since He's all powerful, then maybe He's out to get me.

When I catch myself flailing against Christ in my prayers, I know it's time to stand against those lies and remember the truth of His love. I'm encouraged by the example of the King of Judah. His response when encountering an insurmountable obstacle is to remind himself and others, "Let's ask the Lord what to do."

Last week a friend shared her deep discouragement and confusion about her career. I admitted similar doubts and fears. We reminded each other of the marvelous resource available to us: Jesus invites us to ask Him for guidance and help. The next day she told me about a new direction that she planned to pursue. Inspired by her Shepherd, she felt enthusiasm and hope again. —SHARON HINCK

FAITH STEP: *Next time you feel the temptation to blame Jesus for a struggle, stop and kneel. Quietly ask Him to show you how to respond to the problem.*

SATURDAY, JULY 11

Jesus said, "Let the little children come to me, and do not hinder them, for the kingdom of heaven belongs to such as these." Matthew 19:14 (NIV)

EVERY SUMMER OUR CHURCH OPENS its doors to the community by hosting a VBS (Vacation Bible School.) This year, a group of older children stood at the back of the registration line. These rowdy kids had attended before, but now they were older and rowdier. One of the teachers whispered, "I thought we weren't accepting kids over twelve." The director responded, "All are welcome! Everyone needs Jesus." So we smiled, prayed for the best, and signed them up.

The older kids kept us on our toes that week. They weren't bad kids, they just tested their limits. And ours. Every night, I prayed for Jesus to touch the children, but the night it was my turn to teach the older ones, I prayed for guidance. Lots of it.

The next day I took a deep breath and talked about creation. "What's the opposite of beginning?" They answered, "The end." "Did you know that just as this world began, it'll end? Jesus will come back." They were captivated. The room was quiet. "The Bible shows us signs, and the time is near." The room erupted with questions. Several children stayed after class and asked about salvation. These kids were reaching out for Jesus.

Jesus is always asking us to extend ourselves to those on the fringes... to children, to the elderly, to those who are unruly and unwanted. He always invites "the least of these" to experience His love and grace and wants us to do the same. —KATIE MINTER JONES

FAITH STEP: *In the spirit of Jesus, look for an opportunity to minister to children in your church or neighborhood.*

SUNDAY, JULY 12

For if you forgive other people when they sin against you, your heavenly Father will also forgive you. But if you do not forgive others their sins, your Father will not forgive your sins. Matthew 6:14–15 (NIV)

GROWING UP IN A CHILDREN's home and foster care left me with bad memories. For years I was haunted by nightmares about abusive caregivers. One night after a bad nightmare, I couldn't go back to sleep. *Jesus, please give me peace*, I prayed as I slid closer to my husband who was sleeping soundly. *They can't hurt you anymore*, I thought. But they were hurting me. I was still angry and bitter.

I walked to the living room as thoughts drifted back to my childhood. Overwhelming anger washed over me. The reality of the past was worse than the nightmares. Trying to shift my focus, I thanked Jesus for blessing me with a wonderful husband, precious children, grandchildren, many friends, and my church. Still no peace. I tuned the television to a Christian station. A pastor was speaking about forgiveness. I'd heard such sermons, but that night the message was different. "Jesus forgave you when you didn't deserve to be forgiven. You must forgive others to have peace."

So I prayed, handing over to Jesus years of anger and pain. That night, Jesus filled me with a sense of peace like I'd never experienced. The past finally had no control over me. Forgiveness didn't change my past, but it brought the nightmares to an end. I had peace.

Jesus wants us to experience His peace and hope; even when faced with tragedy or cruelty. When we ask Jesus to help us forgive, He opens the door to healing. —KATIE MINTER JONES

FAITH STEP: *Ask Jesus to help you forgive those who have wronged you and let Him usher His peace and hope into your heart.*

MONDAY, JULY 13

But understand this, that in the last days there will come times of difficulty. For people will be lovers of self, lovers of money, proud, arrogant, abusive, disobedient to their parents, ungrateful, unholy.
2 Timothy 3:1–2 (ESV)

PHOTOS ARE PRECIOUS, BUT SOCIAL media has distorted the time-honored tradition of memory making for me. At some point I started to feel as if I were staging my life rather than living it.

Getting the family to all look at the camera for a few vacation pictures felt like a professional photo shoot. Relocating our fun a few feet to the left. Or having the kids strike a once-spontaneous pose for the fourth time. Or actually interrupting a magical moment to make sure I caught it with my smartphone. Ick. Let's not even talk about posting or answering comments. It had to stop.

Most of our family, including our older kids, live a distance away, so social media does help us keep in touch, but I want to be *present* for the memories. Undistracted.

I've learned that no matter how many "likes" a post gets, my true audience of close friends and family is pretty small. They know me and like me, post or not, but ultimately, mine is an audience of One, who knows the hearts and stories behind the pictures intimately, without my having to post a single one.

Today, I still snap photos but not as many and not as staged. And I only post a few times a week, no more 24-7 newsreel. Best of all, the people I love still love me. Just like Jesus. —ISABELLA YOSUICO

FAITH STEP: *Meditate on Matthew 6:33. Reorder your priorities and "seek first the kingdom of God . . . , and all these things will be added to you." (ESV)*

TUESDAY, JULY 14

*Every good and perfect gift is from above, coming down from the
Father of the heavenly lights, who does not change like shifting shadows.*
James 1:17 (NIV)

EIGHT MONTHS AGO, OUR FAMILY of five moved from a four-bedroom, two-bath rental home to a nine-hundred-square-foot, two-bedroom, one-bath rental home. It squeezed us in more ways than one. We lost a bathroom in the process, and bathrooms are important. There have been harsh words exchanged over who gets the bathroom first and discussions over how long a shower needs to be. (Both are followed by pounding on the bathroom door). We have struggled with the loss. *Don't we deserve two bathrooms?*

Really, we have more than we deserve. Over two billion people in the world don't have basic sanitation. One bathroom is over-the-top living. This small home has been an eye-opener and a reminder of how easily we take for granted the extravagances of modern life. Not only has Jesus provided us with eternal life, but He's provided for our physical needs here on earth. From the electricity that lights up our homes to the food on our table. He gives us so much. Often, we take it as if we deserve it. Like rich kids who don't recognize their dad's generosity. In the presence of Jesus's daily abundance, we easily feel entitled and forget how truly blessed we are. But we don't have to forget. We can choose to move away from an attitude of entitlement and embrace an attitude of gratitude. Jesus has blessed our socks off. Let's decide to live with open hearts, full of thankfulness, for every good and perfect gift that Jesus has sent our way. —SUSANNA FOTH AUGHTMON

FAITH STEP: *Write a list of ten things you're grateful for and put it on your fridge. Each time you open your fridge today, read the list aloud and thank Jesus.*

WEDNESDAY, JULY 15

His master replied, "Well done, good and faithful servant!"
Matthew 25:23 (NIV)

THIS SPRING, I MADE A new friend, Steven Batchelor, at one of my workshops. After class he told me about his ongoing fight with cancer and went on to mention a book he'd written called *Don't Miss Love*. Sadly he passed away shortly thereafter. As I read his book, I was struck by its theme—spreading Jesus's love any way we can with everyone we encounter. Steven's determination to use every single one of his God-given talents to glorify Christ touched me deeply.

I spent some time thinking about this quiet, gentle man of God, now resting in Jesus's peace. Steven left behind a legacy of caring and a life well-lived. Beyond his family, he bestowed blessings on his readers, so we may live out the life he suggested.

My mind drifted to Jesus and His parable of the talents (Matthew 25:14–25) and to the way He'd lived. Everything He did reflected perfect love. He buried none of His talents. Was it too late to uncover the talents I'd buried in fear and turn them into glory for Jesus?

Losing a friend is a wake-up call, a chance to assess where we've been and where we're heading. Sometimes it's a source of joy as we discover the wisdom in another's life. Learning how they used the gifts the Lord gave them—their time, their money, and their hearts—changes us. We want to live as Jesus did, sharing all, sparing nothing. —HEIDI GAUL

FAITH STEPS: *How can you influence others with your love? Grow your legacy to glorify Jesus.*

THURSDAY, JULY 16

[Jesus said] "My purpose is to give life in all its fullness." John 10:10 (TLB)

ONE AFTERNOON, MY HUSBAND ATTACHED our new license plates to the backs of our vehicles. I joked about ordering a custom plate containing some profound words for the front end of my car. "Well, I'll probably put *Live, Love, Laugh* on mine," he said.

Richard was being sarcastic. For some reason, he dislikes plaques and home décor objects with words on them (although he waited forty years to tell me). He especially makes fun of the popular quote "Live well, laugh often, love much," which is on everything from coasters to pillows and doormats. When we visited our daughter's house and found that quote hanging on her living room wall, the whole family teased Richard about wanting to buy one just like it.

The first two words of that adage remind me that Jesus calls me to live a rich, abundant life filled with meaning and purpose. Living a full life doesn't mean that I'll have everything I want. It doesn't mean that I won't go through hardship and trials. But if I accept His love and forgiveness, allow Him to guide me daily, and imitate His life of holiness, then my life will rise above the ordinary.

Jesus didn't come to earth, suffer, and die so that we can merely exist; He came for us to live abundantly. The best way to live well is to honor and obey Jesus's Word. Then life will overflow with things that satisfy the soul. And if that's the case, we'll also laugh often and love much. —DIANNE NEAL MATTHEWS

FAITH STEP: *Ask Jesus to show you any habits, attitudes, or behaviors that hold you back from living the full life He wants you to enjoy.*

FRIDAY, JULY 17

Whoever serves me must follow me; and where I am, my servant also will be. My Father will honor the one who serves me. John 12:26 (NIV)

"THE HALIBUT, PLEASE." I FOLDED the menu shut and smiled at the server. My husband and I sat at a small table at an outdoor café in Mexico. "I'm sorry, we're out of halibut tonight." The waiter glanced downward before handing the menu back to me.

I blocked its return. "That's okay. I'll have the crab instead."

"We just served our last one, Señora."

"Okay...the tilapia?"

"No more today. Sorry."

"What's left?" At this point, the situation seemed laughable.

He bowed his shoulders and shook his head, as if at a loss for words. "I have an idea. I'm in a rut, always wanting the same things. Ask the chef to surprise me. I'm sure I'll like whatever he comes up with." Straightening, he raced back to the kitchen. When my dinner arrived, it was a feast, better than anything I could have imagined. I left more than satisfied, knowing I'd been blessed.

Jesus often surprises me, turning my focus in a direction quite different from the one I'd planned. As I follow Him, He seasons my dreams and goals, switching them up to meet His standards. And when I serve others according to His will, even with unfamiliar tasks, I feel fulfilled, nourished from the inside out. I'm free to be what He wants me to be and my faith increases as I obey.

Jesus knows what's best for me. He's never disappointed me and never will. I only need to trust in whatever He cooks up for me! —HEIDI GAUL

FAITH STEP: *Be brave and follow a new recipe, adding spices you wouldn't usually choose. As you sit to enjoy your meal, ask Jesus to lead you to exciting new opportunities to serve Him.*

SATURDAY, JULY 18

Be kind to one another, tenderhearted, forgiving one another,
as God in Christ forgave you. Ephesians 4:32 (ESV)

JUDY HAD NOT SPOKEN TO her sister in thirty years. One night as she added the usual "Bless Mary Beth" to her prayers, she sensed a clear message: *That's not good enough. You need to go ask her for forgiveness.* Judy felt shocked. *"Ask her* for forgiveness?" But she flew out to visit Mary Beth, who was in poor health. When Mary Beth said she didn't feel like she could be forgiven for the life she'd led, Judy shared the love of Jesus and then mailed her a Bible. Two months later, Mary Beth was found dead. Nearby the Bible lay, open to a psalm.

As Judy shared her story in Bible study, a thought nagged Gayle: *I've made a mistake.* Gayle and her own sister had not communicated much through the years due to various reasons. Now Sandy was recovering from a stroke. Gayle drove two hours to Sandy's house and spent the evening talking. The door opened to a close and loving relationship.

Refusing to forgive someone is like getting trapped in a maze of bitterness and resentment that stunts our spiritual growth and infects all areas of our life. Even simply neglecting a family relationship can steal our joy and peace. If we sense a prompting to take the first step toward reconciliation, it's a gift from God. Yes, we'll feel awkward or fearful reaching out, wondering if our efforts will be rebuffed. Yes, we do risk getting hurt. But Jesus will give us the ability to forgive if we ask for His help. And who knows what chain reaction of grace our obedience might set off? —DIANNE NEAL MATTHEWS

FAITH STEP: *Ask Jesus to reveal anyone you need to reach out to for reconciliation. Trust Him to give you the courage to take the first step and the wisdom to speak the right words.*

SUNDAY, JULY 19

While Peter was talking, a bright cloud covered them. A voice came from the cloud and said, "This is my Son, whom I love, and I am very pleased with him. Listen to him!" Matthew 17:5 (NCV)

ALONG WITH JAMES AND JOHN, Peter received a special revelation. Jesus briefly revealed His glory to these three disciples on a mountaintop, His clothing and face glowed with a supernatural brightness. Suddenly the two greatest Old Testament prophets appeared and talked with Jesus. Peter may have been thinking about the Feast of Tabernacles when he offered to put up three shelters for Jesus, Moses, and Elijah. But before Peter finished speaking, God interrupted him with praise for His Son and instructions to listen to Him.

I often feel a kinship with Peter, and sometimes forget that a big part of prayer is listening. Sometimes I pray while I'm driving, walking, or doing household chores. Other times I enjoy a dedicated time of quiet, concentrated prayer. Even then I often focus on making sure I include all the right elements: Did I offer praise and thanksgiving? Confess everything? Include all my requests and needs? A more important question: Did I spend time listening for Jesus's voice?

Prayer is a two-way conversation, not a monologue. Jesus wants to speak to us and calm our fears, offer guidance, and assure us of His loving presence. We can miss His voice if we're solely focused on our own agenda. But Jesus knows me intimately; He also knows what my day holds. So when it comes to prayer, I should be glad to let Him dominate the conversation. —DIANNE NEAL MATTHEWS

FAITH STEP: *Pray and ask Jesus what He wants to say to you. Listen for His voice.*

MONDAY, JULY 20

---

*One day soon afterward Jesus went up on a mountain to pray,
and he prayed to God all night. Luke 6:12 (NLT)*

MY FRIEND RECENTLY CLIMBED MOUNT St. Helens and reached the summit. She said, "It was a very challenging climb but truly rewarding." Friends congratulated her for the feat, since she was in her fifties. She'd also climbed the peak in chilly, windy weather. "I had to push myself to reach the summit," she said. With jubilation, she added, "Thank You, Lord, for giving me the determination to complete the climb!"

I also know other people who love to hike in the mountains. Aside from getting good exercise and reaping its health benefits, being close to nature has a calming effect on one's soul. Reaching the summit gives one the opportunity to experience an awesome view. But I also sense that being in an isolated place like the mountains makes us more sensitive to Jesus. Alone with Jesus, surrounded by His creation and away from the noisy crowd, we can become more in tune with Him.

Jesus would often go to a mountain by Himself or with His disciples to pray to His Father. When His disciples got too busy, He urged them to go to a secluded place where they could rest. I sense that call too. So every morning I step out of the house and breathe in deep gulps of fresh air. I take in the lush scenery as I look at the trees. Then I spend quiet time with Jesus, hearing Him speak as I read the Bible. It's a refreshing experience to be in touch with Him.

—MARLENE LEGASPI-MUNAR

FAITH STEP: *Find a quiet place where you can pray regularly. Consider scheduling a personal retreat this year in a place surrounded by nature.*

TUESDAY, JULY 21

Stop and consider God's wonders. Do you know how God controls the clouds and makes his lightning flash? Do you know how the clouds hang poised, those wonders of him who has perfect knowledge? You who swelter in your clothes when the land lies hushed under the south wind, can you join him in spreading out the skies...? Job 37:14–18 (NIV)

IT'S THE MIDDLE OF SUMMER, and last week the weather forecast called for rain for ten days. Invitations to summer fun fell like dominoes, parties canceled, outdoor activities postponed.

And then—you guessed it—it turned out that the forecast was gloomier than the reality. On most days, rain has been brief or hasn't come at all. This morning—at the dawn of the weekend of so many canceled events—the sun is bright, the birds chirping.

We're told that forewarned is forearmed, and there's wisdom in that. But I'm thinking about how Jesus came to preach good news—the kind of news that is radically different from what people expect from the world. That's the forecast I want to hear and follow!

Technology seems to be "enhancing" our lives by increasing the amount of information at our fingertips so that we can make better decisions. But all that data distracts and deceives us. It keeps us from remembering Jesus is in control, not us.

Meanwhile, Jesus is here with us, right now, sharing a very different forecast. It's as if Jesus is saying, "I have planted the answers in your heart, and you'll grow into them in time." In prayer with Jesus, we can let ourselves breathe, let go of our predictions, and ask Him to share some good news with us. —ELIZABETH BERNE DEGEAR

FAITH STEP: *Do you spend more time using technology than you spend in prayer?*

WEDNESDAY, JULY 22

Now to him who is able to strengthen you according to my gospel and the preaching of Jesus Christ, according to the revelation of the mystery that was kept secret for long ages . . . Romans 16:25 (ESV)

A BOUT WITH PNEUMONIA—MIDSUMMER, OF all things—sapped my strength. I'd had such plans. The weather was beautiful. I couldn't get off the couch. I had meaningful, soul-refreshing work to do. It waited, untouched. I had to cancel a speaking engagement.

Even after I started to feel better, pneumonia's "tailings," its lingering aftereffects, reminded me that strength is nothing to . . . pardon the pun . . . sneeze at.

The day I swept the kitchen floor felt like a major victory in the healing process. One day earlier, I wouldn't have had the strength.

The Bible tells us that the gospel of Jesus Christ—the good news of who He is and of the forgiveness and eternal life He offers us—is strength-building. He doesn't just save our souls. He infuses us with strength for the day-to-day spiritual, relational, emotional, and mental challenges we face.

That news—that Jesus is not only faithful to save us but faithful to sustain and strengthen us—forms a base of operations for His followers. It's a truth to which we can return when our strength is flagging. Focusing our thoughts on the gospel of Jesus Christ makes us stronger than we were the day before. Remembering what He's done and is doing increases our strength for all that lies between here and heaven. —CYNTHIA RUCHTI

FAITH STEP: *Find a before-and-after picture of someone who worked hard at strength training and has well-defined muscles that were once weak. Use it as a reminder that Jesus uses His good news to accomplish a similar strengthening within you—spiritual biceps.*

THURSDAY, JULY 23

Show me the right path, O LORD; point out the right road for me to follow.
Lead me by your truth and teach me, for you are the God who saves me.
All day long I put my hope in you. Psalm 25:4—5 (NLT)

MY HUSBAND AND I RECENTLY explored Portland Island, a provincial park in the southern Gulf Islands off British Columbia's coast. It features more than six miles of hiking trails. At the start of the trail system stands a map that shows optional destinations.

Gene and I chose an hour-long walk to a sheltered cove on the opposite side of the island. The path led us through dense woods and intersected with other trails several times. We could easily have followed any of them and been misled. Thankfully the park caretakers had gone before us and posted little wooden signs with arrows and smaller maps.

Where the forest thinned and allowed sunshine to warm the ground, the path disappeared into a meadow of soft grasses covered with delicate yellow flowers. *Which way should we go now?* we wondered. We searched the meadow's perimeter for a few minutes and, sure enough, found another sign pointing us toward the cove.

Whenever I face a major decision, I ask Jesus to guide my path. He is the way, the truth, and the life, and I count on Him to direct me. He always gives markers to point me in the right direction—Bible verses that speak to me, the Holy Spirit's whispers, other people's wisdom, and circumstances.

My confidence in Jesus's ability to guide me to His desired destination for me has increased exponentially over time and through experience. I never fear taking the wrong path. He's too loving and faithful to allow me to be misled. —GRACE FOX

FAITH STEP: *Draw a picture of an arrow-shaped sign. Write a prayer of thanksgiving to Jesus for His promise to guide you in every decision you make.*

FRIDAY, JULY 24

And let us consider how we may spur one another on toward love and good deeds, not giving up meeting together, as some are in the habit of doing, but encouraging one another—and all the more as you see the Day approaching. Hebrews 10:24—25 (NIV)

MY THIRTEEN-YEAR-OLD SON, PIERCE, IS a natural athlete. As his bookish mom I've had a lot to learn. Initially going to practices and games was purely a labor of love, though I enjoyed watching my son enjoy himself. Over time, I've come to appreciate sports much more, and I have a newfound respect for the deeper values sports teach, including the power of positive encouragement. Perhaps nowhere is this more evident than in baseball.

The batter swings and misses, the crowd screams, "Good cut." A play is a disaster of errors. Parents holler, "Shake it off!" The batter hits a foul ball. Viewers shout, "Good contact!" praising the fact that the bat hit the ball at all. This isn't always the case, but many coaches, parents, and fans find a way to discern the positive in even the worst performance, knowing that if the players lose confidence or get negative, their performance will decline.

Likewise, Jesus's interactions with even the "worst" of sinners always sought to lovingly restore them, even as He confronted their sin. The woman at the well, the adulteress, the apostles, and Peter in particular…Jesus's endgame was never to condemn, but to lovingly correct and instruct. He'd have been a great coach. Like Jesus, I cannot only seek to affirm others, but must do the same for myself, extending loving encouragement as Jesus did. —ISABELLA YOSUICO

FAITH STEP: *Try to identify the positive in something apparently negative. If someone makes a mistake, share words of encouragement, in the spirit of Jesus.*

SATURDAY, JULY 25

*Taste and see that the LORD is good; blessed is the one
who takes refuge in him. Psalm 34:8 (NIV)*

MY HUSBAND AND I TOOK our granddaughter to a local museum.
They were hosting a special "girls in science" day with many hands-
on activities. Instead of viewing paintings and sculptures from a
distance or displays of taxidermy animals and pottery shards under
glass, she got to explore rooms featuring math, weather, and medicine. She created a lava lamp with oil and food coloring. She painted
a coffee filter and watched the colors spread while learning about
chromatography. In the weather area, she watched a machine create
a tornado and reached in to touch it. In the medical science exhibit,
she performed an ablation surgery on a pig's heart.

Watching her play and learn, I thought about how much we
absorb through tangible interaction, and the verse from the Psalms
came to mind. Jesus invites us to do more than observe the walk of
faith from a distance. He calls us to enter in. To taste and see what
kingdom life is all about.

He gave His disciples opportunities to go out and preach and heal
those in need. They sat at His feet and listened, but they also experienced the journey of faith in tangible ways. Jesus continues to invite us
to learn from Him in tangible ways. He gives us the waters of baptism
and His body and blood in the sacraments. And He calls us to carry out
His work of feeding the hungry, visiting the lonely, bringing hope to
the hurting. Being a disciple of Jesus isn't about viewing His life from a
distance, like an exhibit under glass. It's about joining Him in washing
feet, wiping away tears, and breaking bread. —SHARON HINCK

FAITH STEP: *Ask Jesus to show you a hands-on way to share His love today.
Taste and see His goodness as you serve.*

SUNDAY, JULY 26

---

*HONOR [esteem, value as precious] YOUR FATHER AND YOUR
MOTHER [and be respectful to them]—this is the first commandment with a
promise—SO THAT IT MAY BE WELL WITH YOU, AND THAT YOU MAY HAVE A
LONG LIFE ON THE EARTH. Ephesians 6:2—3 (AMP)*

JESUS OPENED MY EYES TO the importance of honoring my mother
and father. As a teenager I was disrespectful toward my mother.
When my parents were going through their divorce, I was experiencing my own lonely descent into low self-esteem and depression. I was hurting; consequently I lashed out at the person who
was closest to me, my mother. I couldn't empathize with her pain,
and I didn't think she cared about mine. Once I was saved, Jesus
showed me how to honor my parents. Jesus respected His earthly
parents even though He was their Savior. He followed their commandments and was accountable to them. Jesus didn't say to honor
your parents unless they hurt you, He simply said to honor them.

Understanding that honoring my parents is meaningful to Jesus
helped me to be more respectful toward my mother, even when we
disagreed. Today, we enjoy a close relationship. I honor her for all
the sacrifices she made and continues to make for me.

As He was agonizingly stretched out on the cross at the crucifixion, Jesus made sure His mother, Mary, would be cared for. Jesus
told John and His mother, "Dear woman, here is your son." And he
said to his disciple, "Here is your mother" (John 19:26–27, NLT).
John took her to his home. Even in His most distressing time, Jesus
honored His mother. In honoring our parents, we follow in the
footsteps of Jesus and His love. —TRACY ELDRIDGE

FAITH STEP: *If you're estranged from family, ask Jesus to help you forgive them
and ask them for forgiveness. Allow restoration to begin.*

MONDAY, JULY 27

"Again I tell you, it is easier for a camel to go through the eye of a needle than for someone who is rich to enter the kingdom of God." When the disciples heard this, they were greatly astonished and asked, "Who then can be saved?" Jesus looked at them and said, "With man this is impossible, but with God all things are possible." Matthew 19:24–26 (NIV)

I SYMPATHIZE WITH THE DISCIPLES. God's commandments felt overwhelming, and they wanted encouragement. Perhaps a pat on the back and "At least you're trying your best." Instead, Jesus said disruptive things like "It's worse than you thought. To meet God's standards, it's not enough to avoid killing a man, you can't even call him a fool (Matthew 5:22). Even the rich and powerful can't find an easy entry into the kingdom of God (Matthew 19:24)." Was Jesus making salvation seem impossible? In a way, yes.

At the end of the day, I'm tempted to calculate my virtue, decide I've done a bit more good than bad, and congratulate myself for achieving a bit of "righteousness." We humans are prone to rely on ourselves, believing we can solve our own problems. Jesus turns that thinking upside down and reminds us that we are helpless to reach the kingdom of God by our own efforts. But then Jesus continues with the Good News: with God, all things are possible. Eternal salvation is possible through Christ.

Since Jesus has solved the unsolvable problem of sin and granted the way of salvation through His sacrifice, then all our other unsolvable problems are also safe in His care. —SHARON HINCK

FAITH STEP: *Think of one problem. Thank Jesus that in Him all things are possible.*

TUESDAY, JULY 28

But he said to me, "My grace is sufficient for you, for my power is made perfect in weakness." Therefore I will boast all the more gladly about my weaknesses, so that Christ's power may rest on me. 2 Corinthians 12:8–9 (NIV)

I USED TO DISQUALIFY MYSELF from ministry or job opportunities because of my weaknesses that seemed too glaring, too great. Yes, I disqualified *myself*. Even when an opportunity came to me or I was assured of my suitability.

I'd tell myself that I wasn't (fill in the blank) enough to do a particular task, or face a particular challenge. My own perception of my weakness prevented me from doing something I might have even really wanted to do. But I eventually learned that believing in my own weakness was a self-fulfilling prophecy.

Truly by the grace of God, I now know better. Christ's grace is *truly* sufficient. His unfathomable power is *truly* perfected in my weakness. As I decrease, He increases (John 3:30). Apart from Him, I can do nothing (John 15:5). In Him, I can do all things He calls me to do (Philippians 4:13). I have found there are a couple of important caveats. First, recognizing my powerlessness, and second, the task being something that Christ has called me to.

Today, when a daunting opportunity shows up I first ask Jesus if it's from Him and wait for an answer. Then I prepare appropriately, continually turning to Him for power and relaxing in the certainty of His sufficiency. —ISABELLA YOSUICO

FAITH STEP: *Is there something you've felt called to do but hesitate because of your weakness? Consider and claim the assurance of Paul's assertion. The degree to which you are weak is the degree to which Jesus's power shows up! If God called you to it, He'll get you through it.*

WEDNESDAY, JULY 29

May you experience the love of Christ, though it is too great to understand fully. Then you will be filled with all the fullness of life and power that comes from God. Ephesians 3:19 (NLT)

WHEN MY ELDEST DAUGHTER, STEPHANIE, was born with hydrocephalus—water on the brain—at a mission hospital in Nepal in 1985, she needed lifesaving surgery, but limited resources meant surgeons couldn't perform the operation there. As a result, my husband returned to North America with her when she was three days old. Doctors said Stephanie would require ongoing care, so returning to Nepal was impossible.

Stephanie grew up longing to visit her birthplace, so she and her husband saved enough money to fulfill her dream on her thirty-third birthday. They invited me and Gene to join them.

Stephanie's birthday dawned with breakfast at the mission hospital guesthouse. I was talking with a Nepalese woman working in the kitchen. Within seconds, she exclaimed, "I remember you! You left due to a medical emergency, right?"

"Yes," I said. I motioned toward Stephanie. "There she is."

The woman's jaw dropped. She hugged Stephanie tight. "I prayed for you!" she said. "Look at how God has answered!"

Stephanie's eyes filled with tears. Growing up, her physical challenges occasionally left her wondering if Jesus loved her as much as He loved others. Realizing that He'd burdened a stranger half a world away to pray for her erased all doubts.

The opportunity for Steph to see her birthplace and hear a stranger's affirmation was a glorious birthday gift from Jesus, chosen especially for her because He knew it would meet her heart's unique needs. My finite mind can't comprehend such love. —GRACE FOX

FAITH STEP: *List three ways you may have taken Christ's love for granted.*

THURSDAY, JULY 30

"For I know the plans I have for you," declares the LORD, "plans to prosper you and not to harm you, plans to give you hope and a future. Jeremiah 29:11 (NIV)

WHEN I WAS FOUR YEARS old, I traveled with my church to a youth convention in Texas. We lodged at a Dallas motel with a pool. I was the "baby" in our group. The remaining youth were college students. While my mother read a novel in our motel room, the college kids promised to watch me at the pool. They assured my mother, "We will take care of Alice." My three attendants splashed in the shallow water. They were not swimmers and neither was I. When no one was looking, I raced up the diving board ladder above the ten-foot-deep section of the pool. I yelled, "Look at *me*!"

The Bible warns, "Folly is bound up in the heart of a child" (Proverbs 22:15, NIV).

No lifeguard was on duty and a sign warned, Swim at Your Own Risk.

"Alice!" screamed one college kid. "Get down from there!"

I was unaware of the danger and bounced on the diving board as the college kids yelled my name. Just as I can't say why I foolishly climbed that ladder, I can't say why I didn't jump but darted down and returned poolside. The college kids should have scolded me or carried me to my mother for a punishment. Instead, they showed me mercy and grace, circling me in a huddle of hugs.

At fifty years old, I understand with perfect hindsight that there are times we don't make the right choices. And yet the love of Jesus protects us from our personal folly. He pulls us close and reminds us that we are forgiven. Yes, we are loved. —ALICE THOMPSON

FAITH STEP: *Recall a time you were protected from your own unwise choices. This morning, ask Jesus for wisdom and guidance in all your decisions today.*

FRIDAY, JULY 31

Don't worry about anything, but in all your prayers ask God for what you need, always asking him with a thankful heart. And God's peace, which is far beyond human understanding, will keep your hearts and minds safe in union with Christ Jesus. Philippians 4:6–7 (GNT)

IN ONE MORE MONTH, I will be at a new school. I will have to learn new names and new surroundings and face new challenges. It's an opportunity for me to start over with a new attitude to help affect positive change. A part of me is anxious because of all the newness and the unknown. For years I used to suffer frightening anxiety attacks. As I grow in my relationship with Christ, I use the promising words of Jesus in this Scripture to soothe my nerves.

As I approach this new school year, I am confessing that it will be the best year I have ever experienced in my career. I am thanking the Lord for the opportunity and for the ability to do the job with excellence. As I pray these things, I feel the peace of Jesus beginning to calm me.

Some anxiety is normal, but for some people it can be debilitating. The fact that we can confidently go to Jesus in prayer when we are feeling anxious can positively alter our outlook on life. While we are awaiting the manifestation of whatever we have prayed for, the peace of Jesus is there to help us wait patiently. That kind of peace is humanly incomprehensible. The peace of Jesus is so incredible that in times of trouble or uncertainty, we can experience sweet peace instead of making ourselves sick with anxiety. When we offer Jesus our worries and fears, He replaces them with His amazing peace. —TRACY ELDRIDGE

FAITH STEP: *The next time anxiety comes along to steal your peace, close your eyes, ask the Lord to fix the problem, and thank Him for His answer. Repeat, repeat, repeat, until you feel the peace of Jesus that surpasses all understanding.*

SATURDAY, AUGUST 1

Jesus Christ is the same yesterday, today, and forever. Hebrews 13:8 (NLT)

IN 1997, MY HUSBAND AND I playfully discussed the possibility of living on a sailboat someday. That conversation turned serious in August 2017, when we both sensed Jesus say, *Now's the time to act.*

We knew this would be a significant transition. We asked Jesus to guard us from making decisions based on emotion and to lead us to the boat of His choice. We asked Him to go before us and open all the necessary doors to make this happen, and He answered.

Every detail fell into place. Within six months, we'd joined the ranks of official "live aboards" in a Vancouver marina and faced more changes than I can mention here.

For example, limited cupboard space means buying smaller quantities of food and going grocery shopping more often than in the past. Having no washer or dryer means using the marina's laundromat. The fridge and freezer open from the top rather than the front. Our V-shaped beds require altered sheets and practically doing gymnastics to change them. The toilets flush differently than those in a house. I have no yard in which to find privacy if I sit outdoors. I've had to learn how to avoid blowing fuses accidentally. And my husband now commutes two hours for work as opposed to running a flight of stairs from home to office as he did for three years prior.

Whenever newness threatens to overwhelm me, I focus on the One who led us to make the transition. I pray, "Jesus, be my rock. Hold me steadfast," and He answers, replacing my angst with His peace. —GRACE FOX

FAITH STEP: *Transition provides opportunity to experience Christ's faithfulness in new ways. What changes have you recently experienced? List three ways in which those changes have deepened your relationship with Jesus.*

SUNDAY, AUGUST 2

Think about the things of heaven, not the things of earth. For you died to this life, and your real life is hidden with Christ in God. Colossians 3:2–3 (NLT)

PREPARING TO MOVE ABOARD A sailboat meant purging nearly all our earthly belongings. The only other option was to rent a storage unit nearby, but that seemed like unwise stewardship. "It's cheaper to replace those belongings when we return to shore than to pay storage fees for several years," Gene assured me.

I sorted through closets, cupboards, and drawers. I donated and sold clothing, appliances, books, home décor, and furniture. Parting with my possessions came more easily than I'd expected with the exception of two items—our mattress and my favorite leather love seat.

The mattress was less than three years old and one of the best purchases we'd ever made. Its firmness helped me sleep well every night. The love seat was my sacred space—it's where I enjoyed my quiet time with Jesus, wrote my devotional blogs, and cuddled my grandbabies. It represented my "home sweet home" after each overseas ministry trip.

The anticipation of parting with these items pained me until Jesus whispered, *Am I not enough for you?* His words, gently spoken, challenged my perspective. He'd given His life for my sake. Could I not give up a mattress and love seat for Him? Sure, these things had brought me deep satisfaction, but would I not experience even greater satisfaction in knowing my obedience brought Jesus pleasure?

"Yes, Jesus. You are enough," I whispered. "Thank you for loaning me these gifts and for the joy they've brought. Now I give them back to you." —GRACE FOX

FAITH STEP: *Look around your home. What possessions bring you joy? Consider giving away one of these beloved items as an act of worship or a demonstration of your willingness to share with others the blessings Jesus has given you.*

MONDAY, AUGUST 3

If you love your father or mother more than you love me, you are not worthy of being mine; or if you love your son or daughter more than me, you are not worthy of being mine. If you refuse to take up your cross and follow me, you are not worthy of being mine. Matthew 10:37–38 (NLT)

MOVING ONTO A SAILBOAT HAD many ramifications. Besides having us purge our possessions and planting us in a new environment, it meant no longer having space to host all our kids and grand-children overnight. Family time brings me great joy, so that reality grieved me.

Knowing this transition would have an impact on our family, we brought our kids into the conversation within days of sensing God say, *Now.* We assured them that we valued their opinions, and asked them to pray as we continued to seek the Lord's direction.

Our kids understood that Christmas and Thanksgiving at Mom and Dad's would no longer happen, but they supported us anyway. I suspect that's because, from their childhood, we'd taught them that loving and obeying Jesus is of utmost importance. Obedience despite personal cost or inconvenience proves our love for Him. It also shows our willingness to trust Him with our lives even when we haven't got a clue about the outcome.

Having our kids' blessing made saying yes to Jesus easier than had they disapproved. But if they'd objected, our responsibility would've been to obey Jesus rather than comply with their wishes. Being His disciples means giving Him full allegiance. —GRACE FOX

FAITH STEP: *Today's key verse teaches that following Jesus requires sacrifice. Write down three reasons why He deserves our wholehearted love and obedience.*

TUESDAY, AUGUST 4

No one lights a lamp and then puts it under a basket. Instead, a lamp is placed on a stand, where it gives light to everyone in the house. In the same way, let your good deeds shine out for all to see, so that everyone will praise your heavenly Father. Matthew 5:15–16 (NLT)

FIVE MONTHS AFTER WE MOVED into the marina, an eleven-month-old puppy belonging to one of our neighbors broke its leg. The neighbor, unemployed at the time, managed to take the dog to a vet. Surgery was necessary.

"I don't know what to do," the neighbor said, sprinkling his conversation with expletives. "I don't have the money." He was in anguish; his dog was his sole companion, his best friend.

Weeks prior, my husband and I had prayed for God to give us creative ways to help people in need. When the thought of hosting a GoFundMe campaign to raise money for the vet bills popped into my head, I knew He'd answered.

Within three days of launching the campaign, donations exceeded the total needed and the puppy had surgery. Kindness paved the way for spiritual talk with our neighbor. "I'm going to give God the credit," he said.

"Good idea," I replied. "He's pursuing you, my friend, and He's using this situation to show you that He cares about you."

Kindness transformed our marina community into a true neighborhood and put me and my husband on the radar. We're certain they've pegged us as "religious," but we're praying that our good deed for the dog will shine a light and point people to Jesus.
—GRACE FOX

FAITH STEP: *Ask Jesus to show you a need and give you creative ideas so you can shine a light that points to Jesus.*

WEDNESDAY, AUGUST 5

When Jesus came by, he looked up at Zacchaeus and called him by name. "Zacchaeus!" he said. "Quick, come down! I must be a guest in your home today." Luke 19:5 (NLT)

OUR MARINA IS AN ENVIRONMENT unlike anything I've ever known. My former neighborhoods had families with young children and people who shared my beliefs and values. But it's different here.

About fifteen permanent residents live along our dock. Only three are women, myself included. One says, "You have to be slightly eccentric to live here." All but one of the male residents is single, and alcohol and marijuana play a significant role in their lives. More men and a few women live nearby on boats and vessels undergoing repairs onshore. I've yet to find another Jesus follower in this mix.

Gene and I believe God placed us here to reflect His light in the darkness. In an effort to build relationships, we stroll the docks to meet other residents and talk to people in the marina laundromat. But we love to invite neighbors to share a meal.

Four men came, booze in hand, the first time we did this. Obscenities, off-color humor, and a heated debate about politics marked their conversation during the meal. *I wonder if this resembles Jesus's evening with Zacchaeus, the rich tax collector,* I thought. *If so, then I'm in good company.*

Following Jesus's approach to evangelism means being intentional about developing friendships with people radically different than myself. It stretches me beyond my comfort zone, but it's worth it.
—GRACE FOX

FAITH STEP: *Ask Jesus to show you how He'd seek to build a friendship with a "Zacchaeus," (someone who is different than you.) Trust Him for the courage to obey.*

THURSDAY, AUGUST 6

Jesus was sleeping at the back of the boat with his head on a cushion.
The disciples woke him up, shouting, "Teacher, don't you care that
we're going to drown?" Mark 4:38 (NLT)

SOON AFTER MOVING ABOARD, WE set aside a Saturday to sail with friends and family. The weathermen predicted strong winds—the kind on which experienced sailors thrive.

As we motored down the Fraser River, we ran into howling winds. I felt queasy. Two guests became seasick, but there was no turning back—it was too late to go against the tide. Our only option was to keep going until the tide changed direction in about six hours.

I couldn't wait for the tidal change, but not everyone agreed. This was Gene and our-son-law's idea of a perfect day.

What was the difference between them and the rest of us? They understood sailing and how to capture the wind for our advantage. We imagined the worst and hung on for dear life. Their skill and knowledge gave them confidence. Our lack thereof created fear.

I relate to the disciples' response, but I also understand Jesus's: "Why are you afraid?" (Mark 4:40, NIV). "Where's your faith?" (Luke 8:25, NIV).

Gene could have asked me a similar question: "Haven't I been sailing for decades in extreme weather? Am I not cautious? Why are you afraid?"

If I'd focused on Gene's relaxed demeanor rather than the wind and the waves, I would've known that everything was going to be fine, just as the disciples would've known that everything was okay if they'd focused on Jesus rather than the storm. —GRACE FOX

FAITH STEP: *Close your eyes, and thank Jesus for being in control of the emotional winds and waves in your life.*

FRIDAY, AUGUST 7

"My sheep listen to my voice. I know them and they follow me." John 10:27 (CEB)

MY GRANDDAUGHTER'S DOG KNOWS MY voice. And my name. All dog lovers will understand. I don't see Sadie very often, but she "knows" that I'm family.

If my daughter says, "Sadie, Grammie's coming," the dog will run to the door, sit, and wait for me. My daughter has learned not to say, "Grammie's coming next Thursday." Too long a wait for a dog.

When Sadie sees me climbing the steps toward the house, she starts a wiggle pattern that won't stop until long after I've greeted her, rubbed her belly, picked her up, and snuggled her like a baby.

It was no flippant choice of wording Jesus used to answer the always oppositional Jewish leaders who surrounded Him in the temple, badgering Him to tell them once and for all if He was the Messiah. Jesus said, "I have told you, but you don't believe.... because you don't belong to my sheep. My sheep listen to my voice. I know them and they follow me" (John 10:25–27, CEB).

Jesus not only understood that the opposition couldn't grasp the truth, but that those who *did* grasp the truth about Him would have an automatic response. At the sound of His voice, they would follow. That's the expectation and the longing of Jesus's heart.

We know Him because He revealed Himself to us. We've heard His voice, and we follow, matching our stride and pace with His.
—CYNTHIA RUCHTI

FAITH STEP: *Are you a distracted or a devoted follower of Jesus? Call to Him. Ask for His help in planting your feet in the footprints He leaves so the evidence of where you've been is evidence of where He's been.*

SATURDAY, AUGUST 8

But godliness with contentment is great gain. For we brought nothing into the world, and we can take nothing out of it. But if we have food and clothing, we will be content with that. 1 Timothy 6:6–12 (NIV)

AUGUST IN FLORIDA. SIGH. UNLESS you live on the equator, you haven't felt heat like this until you've been here in summertime. I grew up in suburban Baltimore and saw my share of hot summers, but this is altogether different. The humidity is like being in a hot-dog steamer.

I was born in southern California and spent many childhood summers in coastal Italy with family, so I'm a warm weather, sun-loving girl. But even I sometimes start to groan when I step out into the hot and heavy Florida heat.

Then come fall and winter. No kaleidoscope of leaves, but weather so perfect you can't imagine. Brisk mornings and evenings. Beach-worthy days. Relentless sunshine.

By January though, the cold days linger. There are a few gray days, and I'm indignant, bundled in my fluffy down coat. The same one I wore in twenty-degree days up north. The very first year we moved here, I complained bitterly about two weeks of unreasonable cold.

How very fickle and changeable I am. How very, very spoiled.

Today, my spiritual aim is to relish today, hot or cold. To be content and grateful.

Thank You, Jesus, for all these blessings. —ISABELLA YOSUICO

FAITH STEP: *Pick a recent grievance—whether weather, job, relative, or home—and write ten positive things about it. Then thank Jesus.*

SUNDAY, AUGUST 9

Then Jesus spoke to them again, saying, "I am the light of the world.
He who follows Me shall not walk in darkness, but have the light of life."
John 8:12 (NKJV)

I LOVE LIGHTHOUSES! WHENEVER I go on vacation and there is a lighthouse nearby, I try my best to find it. Last summer, I was excited to finally get a chance to take a tour inside a lighthouse in Biloxi, Mississippi. The lighthouse was a magnificent white towering presence in the center of town. After climbing the long, spiral staircase to the small opening at the top of the lighthouse where the beacon is located, I was rewarded with the most amazing view of the ocean and the town. My joy and excitement were almost uncontainable. According to Britannica.com, a lighthouse's purpose is to aid in navigation, warn of hazards, and guide maritime vessels to their destinations using various shapes or colors with lights and patterns of radio signals.

As I stood there, I imagined the ships that were guided by the Biloxi Lighthouse during tumultuous tides. There were historical documents in the lighthouse that provided information about ships that were able to avoid maritime disasters when the lighthouse was in use. While listening to our tour guide, I thought about Jesus as a lighthouse. He aids us in our daily lives. He warns of us danger that may be lurking near us. He guides us daily in the way we should go. He helps us navigate the murky, dark, and dangerous waters we sometimes face in life, and brings us to a place of safety. When we follow Jesus, we walk in His light. —TRACY ELDRIDGE

FAITH STEP: *The next time you feel as if the dark waters of heartache, fear, or pain are threatening to overtake you, look to Jesus, your lighthouse, to navigate you to safe, calm waters.*

MONDAY, AUGUST 10

*I sought the LORD, and he answered me; he delivered me
from all my fears. Psalm 34:4 (NIV)*

*I'M USUALLY LATE FOR THIS meeting but for once I'm early. Thank You,
Jesus!* I thought as I was driving. I pondered the route I should take.
*The bridge over the railroad tracks really terrifies me, so I'll just go
through town and cross the tracks.*

As I got closer to the train tracks, the traffic stopped. A train
was blocking the intersection. *It's okay. I still have time.* A few cars
started turning around to go to the overpass. *The train will move
soon,* I tried to reassure myself. *It won't be long.*

A few minutes passed, and more cars started turning around. Several
people had gotten out of their cars. A truck driver walked past my
car and said, "It's going to be about thirty minutes, try the overpass."

My tongue let loose, "That bridge really scares me!"

The man encouraged me, "Just ask Jesus to help you. He'll protect you." Reluctantly I turned around. I knew I had to face my fear.

As I neared the bridge, I gripped the steering wheel. *Jesus,* I prayed.
*Please protect me. I know the bridge is safe, but I am afraid. You protected
David when he faced Goliath. You protected Daniel in the lions' den, and
You protected the three men in the fiery furnace.* I began to focus on
remembering the names of Shadrach, Meshach, and Abednego. In
moments, Jesus had calmed my fear and I'd crossed the bridge.

Jesus doesn't want us paralyzed by fear. He wants us to live
courageously. When we're afraid and ask Jesus to help us, He does,
and He reminds us of His love. His perfect love casts out all fear.
—KATIE MINTER JONES

FAITH STEP: *If fear has you in its grip, call out to Jesus for His help and protection.*

TUESDAY, AUGUST 11

Weeping may stay for the night, but rejoicing comes in the morning.
Psalm 30:5 (NIV)

TODAY I AM GOING TO meet my sister, Jenny, for coffee and a pedicure. We have lived within thirty miles of each other for the past fourteen years. In three weeks...she and her family will be moving to Colorado. I have known the day of Jenny's departure is coming. I have been crying a lot. This is the unraveling of my heart, the loosening of the bond that ties me to Jenny. When they drive away, I want to send her off to her new adventure with joy, shouting, "Go with God!" instead of "Stay with me!"

My sorrow comes from knowing we will never be the same. We have shared the goodness of our closeness. That part of our relationship is ending. I will miss her with my whole heart. Sorrow is a heavy, deep thing. But love is the thing that buoys us up: the love of family and friends and mostly...Jesus. *Weeping may endure for the night, but joy comes in the morning.* We don't always understand why life takes the twists and turns that it does. But His love makes a way for us to look past the present sorrow and know that joy will come again.

Jesus is close to the brokenhearted. He is close to those of us who are experiencing loss in a million different ways. He is pulling us into His arms, filling us with strength, inviting us to look beyond what we are feeling and recognize who He is. He is the lifter of our heads. His love will lift us up. And that is where the joy comes in.

—SUSANNA FOTH AUGHTMON

FAITH STEP: *Whatever state your heart is in right now, tell yourself who Jesus is. He is love. Sit in His presence and let His great love surround you in this moment.*

WEDNESDAY, AUGUST 12

Take heed that ye despise not one of these little ones; for I say unto you, That in heaven their angels do always behold the face of my Father which is in heaven. Matthew 18:10 (KJV)

MY DADDY FATHERED AN ILLEGITIMATE child. This betrayal is one of many things that led to my parents' divorce. Sound crushing? It was. To make matters worse, as my baby brother grew up, doctors discovered he had a learning disability. My father enrolled my brother in special classes to support his academic development. And at my father's request, my brother would visit with my mother, who was a successful reading teacher. During his visits, she helped Junior complete school projects that eluded my father's impatience.

To watch my mother embrace my little brother with such tenderness and care was a demonstration in love's ability to redeem a soul and set it free. Because my mother forgave my father his transgressions, he was free to seek her help for his young son. Mother helping Junior also inspired me to love him and accept him completely as my brother. We never use the word *half.*

Today my brother is a college graduate and works as a computer programmer. He has overcome his learning challenges. Reading is his favorite pastime. And when I look back over the distant years, I understand now what my mother understood when Junior was born. While she could no longer depend on my father's fidelity, my baby brother deserved her attention and help because Jesus loves little children. He loves every one of them—no matter what.
—ALICE THOMPSON

FAITH STEP: *Every newborn child is precious in the eyes of Jesus. Pray today for the protection and care of all children in our nation and across the world.*

THURSDAY, AUGUST 13

Let the wise hear and increase in learning, and the one who understands obtain guidance. Proverbs 1:5 (ESV)

A FEW YEARS AGO, MY mother requested an iPad, so my siblings and I pitched in to buy her one. With the help of her computer-savvy grandson, she eagerly learned how to use it. My mother retired years ago, and has been out of school even longer, but she continues to learn new technology and use it to her advantage. She's on Facebook every day—chatting with her children who live in different places, reconnecting with her childhood friends, watching sermons on YouTube, and learning life hacks from viral videos.

I'm happy that my mother has not stopped learning, in spite of her age. At seventy-five years old, she uses social media to keep her mind busy and sharp. She still attends church small groups and prayer meetings. And like me, she still enjoys traveling. Her curiosity and desire to learn are inspiring. My mother shows me that a willingness to learn is a trademark of a disciple of Jesus.

Jesus is calling me as His disciple to keep learning, particularly from Him. He praised Mary for sitting at His feet, listening to Him teach. He gave the two disciples on the road to Emmaus a crash course in Old Testament studies and Christology. If I keep an open mind and a humble heart, I can learn a lot from Jesus. He's telling me, "Learn from me, for I am gentle and lowly in heart" (Matthew 11:29, ESV). With Jesus as my Teacher, I'll grow wiser. I'll know Him better and gain a deeper understanding of His loving character. Who wouldn't want such a teacher? —MARLENE LEGASPI-MUNAR

FAITH STEP: *What new insights have you gained from your relationship with Jesus?*

FRIDAY, AUGUST 14

A scribe then approached and said, "Teacher, I will follow you wherever you go." And Jesus said to him, "Foxes have holes, and birds of the air have nests; but the Son of Man has nowhere to lay his head."
Matthew 8:19–20 (NRSV)

FOR A YOUNG WOMAN WHO "woke up to Jesus" in my mid- to late-twenties, these words were among the first that really jumped out at me when I started reading the Bible. In my case one thing was clear: following Jesus meant waking up—the opposite of putting your head down. Jesus was giving me the ability to be aware as I went through every life experience, but this meant I could no longer dodge difficult truths by being in denial or avoid confrontation by going along with something that I knew in my heart was not right.

Today, many years after I first woke up, I hear something else too. I'm getting ready for a road trip visiting friends, as I make my way through beautiful New England. The images of the fox burrowing in his hole and the bird settling into her cozy nest remind me that I will miss how easy it is to fall asleep in my own bed. On the road, sleep itself is part of the adventure; going to bed at night has an uncertain quality to it. For me it doesn't always translate into a good night's sleep.

But I am more than willing to give up this comfort of home as I head out on my travels. Jesus is saying, "Follow Me," and I'm ready to go! As I spend time in nature, encounter new experiences, and reconnect with treasured friends, I hope to be awake to whatever graces and truths Jesus wishes to bestow upon me. —ELIZABETH BERNE DEGEAR

FAITH STEP: *Take some time to ask yourself: Is there some area of my life where I still hide from Jesus? Is that part of me ready to wake up and follow Him?*

SATURDAY, AUGUST 15

"Love the Lord your God with all your heart and with all your soul and with all your mind and with all your strength." The second is this: "Love your neighbor as yourself." There is no commandment greater than these. Mark 12:30–31 (NIV)

MY HUSBAND AND I STOLE away for a weekend at the coast. Along the way, we stopped at a picnic area above the Columbia River. Below was an island, a teardrop of forested land, punctuated with meadows and small structures. I was intrigued. On a whim, we detoured, taking a ferry along the river to the island's shore. Driving across the land, sparsely settled with historic houses, I wondered about the rugged individuals who called this place home. How did they live in such isolation?

When we passed an old church, its clapboard siding glowing in the sunlight, its lot crowded with vehicles, I wondered if I'd found my answer. Was this small community rooted in faith? Were the residents living out Jesus's great commandments?

My world isn't as small as the group of people living on that island. I don't depend on others the way the islanders might lean on each other for support. But as with those believers, my love is refined when I focus my heart, soul, mind, and strength on the Lord. And it's complete when I love my neighbor as I love myself.

I'm taking Jesus's words to heart. I want to love my neighbors, no matter what, and remember we're *all* neighbors. I pray I can love others with the same understanding I afford myself. A love born of Jesus's love for me. —HEIDI GAUL

FAITH STEP: *How can you offer neighbors your love? Bake them a treat, help them in the yard, or offer to pray for them.*

SUNDAY, AUGUST 16

---

*And let the peace (soul harmony which comes) from Christ rule
(act as umpire continually) in your hearts [deciding and settling with
finality all questions that arise in your minds, in that peaceful state]
to which as [members of Christ's] one body you were also called [to live].
And be thankful (appreciative), [giving praise to God always].*
Colossians 3:15 (AMPC)

MY THIRTEEN-YEAR-OLD SON, PIERCE, PLAYS baseball (among other sports), and now this nonathlete, writer mom is enriching her writing with lots of handy sports metaphors. In baseball, the umpire is in charge. He's the all-powerful referee. He starts and ends the game, enforces the rules, etc. Boy, talk about effective imagery!

Colossians 3:15 is crystal clear and so practical, particularly in the Amplified Bible. Let Christ's peace be the controlling factor in our decision-making. It's a great feeling to make decisions with that deep sense of supernatural serenity. Yet sometimes prayerful, peace-filled decisions lead us to unexpected places that seem anything but peaceful. Think of Moses, Jonah, the virgin Mary, or just anybody who answered God's call, "feeling" peaceful or not. I have made some decisions in life, full of peace, that went on to be extraordinarily challenging, but rich with spiritual fruit for me and for others.

In Little League, you'll sometimes have an umpire who makes downright bad calls; calls that everyone agrees are wrong. With Christ as our utterly perfect Umpire, we can rest in perfect peace, whether our fickle feelings say "peace" or not. Because of Jesus, we have the assurance of an eternal resolution to every bad call in eternity, and access to the transcendent serenity this side of heaven. —ISABELLA YOSUICO

FAITH STEP: *How can peace be the umpire of a situation you're facing today? Ask Jesus to help give you His peace that surpasses understanding (Philippians 4:7).*

MONDAY, AUGUST 17

To everything there is a season. Ecclesiastes 3:1 (KJV)

THIS PAST WEEKEND I VISITED a town in northwest Arkansas where one of my best friends lives. She invited my girls and me to join her at her house on Beaver Lake, where we rode on her boat, swam, and relaxed. As we always do, we reminisced about the years I lived down the street from her, when we first became friends.

I asked about people I'd known in those days and she gave me updates on their lives—how they're doing, if they have kids, still have the same jobs, etc. Driving home, I thought about them all, which led me to think about other people I've known who aren't a part of my life anymore. This is a relief with a few people, but mostly it makes me feel a little sad. It's weird when you realize there are people you once shared important things with who are practically strangers now.

The writer of Ecclesiastes tells us there's a season for everything, and we see that truth reflected in the life of Jesus. Even in His short thirty-three years, He had different types of relationships, and people moved in and out of His life. Peter, James, and John were His inner circle, and then the twelve, although one of them betrayed Him. Mary, Martha, His mother, Mary, and Mary Magdalene were the women most prominent in His life. Then there were onetime encounters with individuals, as well as the multitudes He fed.

Relationships vary with seasons and stages of our lives. Sometimes we have control, but often we don't. Living in the moment, appreciating what has been, and trusting Jesus for the future is where peace lies. —GWEN FORD FAULKENBERRY

FAITH STEP: *Meditate on the fact that like a tree, your roots are tapped into Jesus. He will nourish and sustain you through every season.*

TUESDAY, AUGUST 18

Such things were written in the Scriptures long ago to teach us. And the Scriptures give us hope and encouragement as we wait patiently for God's promises to be fulfilled. Romans 15:4 (NLT)

I LOVE TO TRAVEL, BY myself or with my family. This summer, my husband and our two grown children took a twelve-hour overnight bus trip to reach a mountain tourist destination. After enjoying our time there, we left for another city, but this time we had to endure a grueling six-hour trip across zig-zagging roads. While my head was whirling with dizziness, a thought saddened me. *I would love to see more places. But I may not be able to do that as I get older. I might not be able to endure long trips.* I brushed away that negative thought and thanked Jesus instead for the many beautiful excursions I've experienced thus far.

Three days after our trip, I was empowered and encouraged as I read a passage in my bible. Eighty-five-year-old Caleb declared, "I am as strong now as I was when Moses sent me on that journey, and I can still travel and fight as well as I could then" (Joshua 14:11, NLT). How liberating! My heart leapt with the possibility of living energetically, going to different places, and continuing to travel and learn, even in old age. If it was possible for Caleb, I'm willing to trust Jesus to make it possible for me too.

Jesus was right when He said that we will know the truth and the truth will set us free. As I read the Bible, Jesus sets me free from false teachings, enslaving thoughts, and limiting ideas. With Jesus, the possibilities go far beyond what I can imagine. —MARLENE LEGASPI-MUNAR

FAITH STEP: *What thoughts have been discouraging you? Consider the promise of Jesus that He will always be with you to help you, comfort you, and strengthen you. Let that truth empower you to overcome what's bothering you.*

WEDNESDAY, AUGUST 19

*For we are God's handiwork, created in Christ Jesus to do good works,
which God prepared in advance for us to do. Ephesians 2:10 (NIV)*

WHENEVER I FEEL INADEQUATE OR feel I don't have the ability
to accomplish something, I remember a lady I once met when I
applied for a job. She was the receptionist and her desk was located
behind a wall with a sliding glass window. When I tapped on the
window, she smiled and asked, "How may I help you?"

I told her I was applying for a job, and then stood amazed as I
got a better look at her. The sleeves of her blouse were sewn up at
the shoulders because she had no arms. She slid open the window
with her foot and gave me an application. She turned to me again
and smiled. "Do you need anything else?" she asked. "Yes, ma'am, I
forgot my pen." She *handed* me a pen.

While completing my application, I couldn't help glancing up at
her. She typed, filed, answered the phone, and performed all of her
tasks with her feet. She was smiling, and seemed polite and friendly.
I quickly looked down every time she turned my direction. I didn't
want to stare, but it was difficult not to. I was in awe.

I didn't get the job, but when I think of that lady I am still in awe.
She was a testament of good stewardship. The receptionist used the
gifts the Lord gave her with grace and dignity.

Jesus wants us to use our gifts and talents to the best of our abilities.
We might not think that we have much to offer the world, but Jesus
has good works for each of us to accomplish, using our specific set of
gifts. If we use our gifts and talents well, our lives can leave a lasting
mark and inspire others for years and years. —KATIE MINTER JONES

FAITH STEP: *Thank Jesus for your abilities and gifts today. Know that He has
prepared good works, in advance, for you to accomplish.*

THURSDAY, AUGUST 20

I have good plans for you, not plans to hurt you. I will give you hope and a good future. Jeremiah 29:11 (NCV)

BY THE TIME I DUG my phone out of my purse, I'd missed a call from my sister-in-law, Julie. We rarely talk on the phone, so my imagination kicked in and my mind raced. Was my eighty-eight-year-old mom okay? *It must be something really bad—because if Julie's calling, that means my brother is too upset to call. Should I abandon my grocery cart and get ready for the long drive to Tennessee? What about my daughter and grandkids flying in for a visit?*

Unable to reach Julie, I called my brother. Relief filled me as Phillip answered in a normal voice and said the call must've been an accident, since Julie was at work. I explained what I'd been thinking; Phillip assured me he understood. The next day he confirmed that Julie had accidentally called me while looking for another phone number.

Somewhere I read the advice to expect the best but prepare for the worst. Sadly it's much easier for me to expect the worst. After all, Jesus warned that we would have troubles in our earthly life. That means that our fears do sometimes become reality. But Jesus also said that we have nothing to fear if we trust Him. As long as we nurture a close relationship with Him, we'll be prepared to weather the worst of times with His help.

The Bible also makes it clear that God wants to bless us. Jesus came so that we can have a life filled with joy. Since He has our best interests at heart, shouldn't we expect the best? —DIANNE NEAL MATTHEWS

FAITH STEP: *Are you having a hard time believing a positive outcome for a situation you're facing? Memorize Jeremiah 29:11. Thank Jesus that He has good plans for your life.*

FRIDAY, AUGUST 21

But when you pray, go into your room, close the door and pray to your Father, who is unseen. Then your Father, who sees what is done in secret, will reward you. Matthew 6:6 (NIV)

DURING A RECENT WEEKEND TRIP to the coast, my husband and I stayed in a motel at a marina. Sailboats and fishing vessels lined up, cozy as eggs in a carton. We sat on our balcony that evening, talking.

The next morning, I woke early. I tiptoed to the balcony so as not to wake my husband. As I watched the boats bobbing softly, black water lapping at their hulls, a sensation of deep peace poured over me. I was alone with Jesus. I didn't have to be anywhere or do anything. I had time to enjoy His presence. I wasn't in a room with the door shut, but I was by myself and centered on Him.

Praying during sunrise, I felt satisfaction filling my heart, and I realized how much I missed these precious uninterrupted moments with Jesus. When had life become too busy? Yes, I prayed to Him several times daily. But I'd stopped setting aside enough time to listen for His answers and to simply rest in Him.

I'm home now, and the bustle of a happy life continues to crowd my waking moments. But a desire as real as hunger has grown in me. The stillness of those intimate minutes with the Lord beckon.

Tomorrow, I'm going to rise before daybreak and steal away to the rocker on my porch. I won't have boats to watch or seagulls. But I'll have my Comforter, Friend, and Savior. And He's all I need.
—HEIDI GAUL

FAITH STEP: *Take a few minutes at dawn or dusk and rest in the Lord. Pray your deepest personal thoughts, knowing that Jesus is with you and He's listening.*

SATURDAY, AUGUST 22

Return to us, God Almighty! Look down from heaven and see!
Watch over this vine, the root your right hand has planted, the son
you have raised up for yourself. Psalm 80:14–15 (NIV)

THE ROAD TWISTED THROUGH SWITCHBACKS, making its way up the mountain. My husband, daughter, and I were driving to a family reunion in Colorado. Cliffs loomed over the road. Signs warned of avalanches and rock slides. The terrain was beautiful but forbidding.

Out of the harsh ground, pine trees stretched toward the sky. I marveled that they could cling to the steep slopes. At first, I pictured the trees desperately straining and grasping to hold on to their safe place. But then I changed my perspective and thought about the firm ground of the mountain securing the root system—and the towering pines—in place. If their roots weren't being firmly held by the mountain, they would tumble and crash into the valley below.

When Jesus tells us He is the vine, He's not telling us that it's all on our shoulders to strain and struggle and cling to Him as treacherous slopes try to pull us away. He is the strong, mature, nurturing vine that secures us, even when life feels steep and difficult. He reminds us to embrace that connection. As we spend time with Jesus each day, our roots stretch more deeply into Him, and we learn to trust that we are held by Him, woven into Him, a part of Him that He won't abandon.

When our life is shaken by storms or we feel as if rocks are tumbling down on us, it's easy to fear we'll lose our grip. What a comfort to know that Jesus will never lose His grip on us. —SHARON HINCK

FAITH STEP: *Find a picture of trees growing out of steep mountains and thank Jesus for holding you firm in the difficult places of life.*

SUNDAY, AUGUST 23

What do you think? If a man owns a hundred sheep, and one of them wanders away, will he not leave the ninety-nine on the hills and go to look for the one that wandered off? And if he finds it, truly I tell you, he is happier about that one sheep than about the ninety-nine that did not wander off. Matthew 18:12–13 (NIV)

"HEIDI! HEIDI!" I YELLED, STANDING at the edge of the woods. Heidi, one of our four dogs, was lost. I had already looked for her down by the pond and all around our yard. *Please help me find her,* I asked Jesus. I had driven around the neighborhood hoping to see her. Some neighborhood kids offered to help look. *Heidi is going to be in trouble when I find her. That crazy dog.* I had looked every place I could think of.

Jesus, please help me find her and don't let her be hurt. Then I thought, *What if she is hurt? What if we never see her again?* As these panicky thoughts filled my mind, I started crying and headed to my neighbor's backyard because sometimes our dogs played together. I was hoping Heidi had found her way there. While I was standing there crying, my neighbor's dog, Sandy, kept rubbing against my leg. "Quit, Sandy, I'm busy," I said. She put her paw on my leg. I looked down and saw that it was Heidi! "Heidi!" I yelled with joy. All thoughts of punishing her flew out the window. In that moment, all I wanted to do was hold her tight and love her.

Jesus feels exactly the same way when one of His sheep is lost. He wants us found. He adores each and every one of us. He can't stand to be separated from us. He yells for joy when one of His lost sheep comes home. —KATIE MINTER JONES

FAITH STEP: *Pray for those you love who are lost, that they would come to know the amazing love of Jesus.*

MONDAY, AUGUST 24

So you also are complete through your union with Christ, who is the head over every ruler and authority. Colossians 2:10 (NLT)

WHO DOESN'T REMEMBER THE SCENE in the movie *Jerry Maguire* when the Tom Cruise character realizes that Renée Zellweger *is* in fact the love of his life? He bursts into a room full of bitter divorcées and declares to a teary Renée, "You complete me."

Last night, I watched a documentary about the relentless pursuit of extreme wealth. The excesses were at once pitiful and repellant: Women buying fifteen-thousand-dollar handbags in every color. Former Wall Street tycoons had crossed the line and now live in exile on the Most Wanted list. A common refrain from those profiled is that getting more only led to wanting more.

I pursed my lips in judgmental disgust. But then I realized I've done the same. I still struggle to seek fulfillment in people and things instead of Jesus. My husband, professional achievement, cash, and yes, handbags of the thirty-dollar variety. For me too, it's never enough.

Many Bible translations use the word *fullness* instead of *complete*. In Ephesians Paul reminds us of the fullness we have in Christ. In Jesus, I am filled with all good things. The very fullness of God is my re-birthright. I can be satisfied and content. In Him I am complete.

Jesus, please help me to experience the fullness and contentment available only in you. —ISABELLA YOSUICO

FAITH STEP: *Pray the prayers in Ephesians 1:16–23 and Ephesians 3:16–19 in first person.*

TUESDAY, AUGUST 25

When Jesus spoke again to the people, he said, "I am the light of the world. Whoever follows me will never walk in darkness, but will have the light of life." John 8:12 (NIV)

THE HALLWAY WAS PITCH-BLACK. I'D awakened in the middle of the night to the sound of my cats squabbling in the living room. Coming out of a deep sleep, I hadn't been alert enough to flip the light switch as I raced past. Now I stood, disoriented and groggy, not sure how far I'd sleepwalked and if I was about to collide with furniture or trip on a pet. I reached for the walls, blind and uncertain. By now the caterwauling had stopped, so I couldn't even rely on my sense of hearing.

Frozen in place, I felt my eyes slowly adjusting to the darkness surrounding me. First, I could distinguish picture frames hanging a few feet ahead and then the outline of the couch. As my vision turned from black to shades of gray, two lumps on the floor transformed into the rascals that had interrupted my rest. By now they'd forgotten their argument and sat primping. *Cats.*

Sometimes I get lost in the shadowy spots of daily life. I run headlong into places I have no business entering and have no idea how to go forward or turn back. I freeze. Without Jesus, I'm blind to my situation and see no escape.

When I'm confused and unable to find my way, the Lord guides and returns me to where I belong. I trust Jesus to give me His peace. I can reach for Him in prayer, and He leads me back to His holy Light. —HEIDI GAUL

FAITH STEP: *Close your eyes and take a few steps. Be careful and take it slow. Open your eyes. Then pray for Jesus's light to shine on obstacles you're dodging as you walk with Him.*

WEDNESDAY, AUGUST 26

Then I heard the voice of the LORD saying, "Whom shall I send? And who will go for us?" And I said, "Here am I. Send me!" Isaiah 6:8 (NIV)

REVEREND WILLIS VISITED THE NEIGHBORHOOD gym every day. We spoke to each other when I found myself walking next to him on the treadmill. He was a blind preacher whose wife drove him to and from the gym. Besides that, I knew nothing about his life.

One morning I walked into the fitness room to find Reverend Willis walking on his favorite treadmill and listening to music piped in over the gym speakers. The Lord spoke to me and moved me to inquire about his transportation for the day. The blind preacher replied that his wife's car was in the shop. The Lord then moved me to offer him a ride home. I obeyed the Spirit and immediately Reverend Willis stopped the treadmill to clap his hands with delight. He said, "I've been on this machine talking to God and praying for a ride."

My encounter with Reverend Willis was proof that Jesus speaks. By His spirit, He speaks to each of us in prayer. He also speaks to us through Bible readings, sermons, friends, and His still, small voice that whispers to the soul. The Gospel of John says that the Lord's sheep know His voice (John 10:4). Clearly Jesus aims to be in direct communication with us because there is service for others that He requires us to do.

Are you listening for His voice? Jesus is speaking to you today. Learning to hear Him takes practice. Rising to respond to His call takes courage. What is the voice of the Lord saying to you?
—ALICE THOMPSON

FAITH STEP: *As an ambassador for Jesus Christ, ask Him to speak with you today and fill your heart with the courage to meet His every request.*

THURSDAY, AUGUST 27

But blessed is the man who trusts in the LORD and has made the LORD his hope and confidence. He is like a tree planted along a riverbank, with its roots reaching deep into the water—a tree not bothered by the heat nor worried by long months of drought. Its leaves stay green, and it goes right on producing all its luscious fruit. Jeremiah 17:7—8 (TLB)

I LOVE LOOKING AT THE big, tall trees on the riverbank by the Mississippi River. I also appreciate their shade while I stroll on the bank, gazing at the muddy waters in the river. The roots of those trees go deep down in the river, which lets me know they have been there a long time. In my lifetime, there have been several floods that sent the river waters over the riverbank. The water completely covered the park area and the parking lot. Yet, after the water returned to the river, the trees on the riverbank were still standing tall. They have managed to thrive in other harsh conditions as well. Even in extreme heat, their leaves remain green.

In Psalm 1:1–3, David compared the person who delights in the Lord and meditates daily on His Word to a tree planted by the riverbank. The last line of the Scripture states that this person will be successful. I desire to be like a tree planted by the riverbank with my roots in the water, confident I will always be watered and nourished. As we learn to trust in the Lord, our hope and faith in Jesus will continuously fill us with confidence, helping us stand strong even when the conditions around us are hot and dry. If we stay rooted and grounded in His Word, we will be as trees planted by the riverbank. —TRACY ELDRIDGE

FAITH STEP: *Look at pictures of the roots of trees on a riverbank. Notice how deep they are and picture yourself as a tree with your faith rooted and grounded in Christ.*

FRIDAY, AUGUST 28

And he didn't send me to [tell about him] with a lot of fancy rhetoric of my own, lest the powerful action at the center—Christ on the Cross—be trivialized into mere words. 1 Corinthians 1:17 (MSG)

FOR YEARS, A LOCAL RADIO station conducted an all-day Bible trivia contest and invited teams and individuals to compete for prizes. Our church team fared well and worked hard to keep our competitive nature secondary to the fun and tidbits of Bible knowledge we learned in the process.

The trivia contest changed with the arrival of high-speed internet. No longer were we poring over research books, maps, concordances, and Bibles. Within seconds, we could find the answer online and soon the contest was about who had the fastest internet rather than who knew God's Word or how to dig for answers. Despite the fun we used to have on Trivia Contest Day, none of us would've wanted to trivialize the message of the Bible.

When writing to the Jesus followers at Corinth, Paul expressed a similar thought. He preached Jesus. Just Jesus. He didn't use fancy words or the day's popular circular logic. Clever rhetoric would have drawn attention to the words themselves, turning the focus away from the message's true heart—Christ on the cross.

Despite all the sermons preached, the articles written, the books published, none of it means more than the simple truth of Jesus conquering sin and death on the cross. —CYNTHIA RUCHTI

FAITH STEP: *In a prominent place, write "Christ on the cross." Let that guide your thoughts and decisions today.*

SATURDAY, AUGUST 29

*Enter through the narrow gate. For wide is the gate and broad is the
road that leads to destruction, and many enter through it. But small
is the gate and narrow the road that leads to life, and only a few find it.*
Matthew 7:13–14 (NIV)

LIKE PORTS WORLDWIDE, TAMPA BAY has a carefully charted narrow shipping channel—the National Oceanic and Atmospheric Association (NOAA) chartbook leaves no guesswork for a boater, whether a day sailor or a freighter captain.

My husband once went sailing on the Chesapeake Bay with a friend, running aground in shallows, only to be towed off the sandbar hours later by the coast guard.

In 1980, a ship drifted off course in a blinding storm and plowed into the Tampa Bay's Sunshine Skyway Bridge; thirty-five people died. Drifting is dangerous. Sometimes fatal. The perils are detailed and documented. Go outside the lines and you may get stuck on a sandbar, or worse.

Even as a Christian, I admit I've caught myself drifting outside Christ's channel, sometimes even openly defying God's chartbook, the Bible. I've run aground, harmed another, or been damaged as a result. Now I can see how I ignored Jesus's gentle nudge or other early warnings that would've averted trouble. When going my own way became too painful, Jesus was there waiting to welcome me back, His grace gently steering me to safe waters and healing me from harm. Jesus's ways, like the shipping channel, guide me to my destination in the best way possible.

When we drift, Jesus lovingly welcomes us back.

—ISABELLA YOSUICO

FAITH STEP: *Are you drifting spiritually? Ask Jesus to steer your ship back on track.*

SUNDAY, AUGUST 30

Come to me, all you who are weary and burdened, and I will give you rest.
Matthew 11:28 (NIV)

TWO YEARS AGO, MY HUSBAND bought me an adult tricycle. It's blue and beautiful. I love it. That first year I rode until the weather turned. Last year, not strong enough to ride, I fought back and joined a gym. I rode a stationary bike, then followed up with weights.

Months passed. Spring's rains ended, replaced by sun-filled days rich with possibility. Still I avoided the trike. I lied to myself, "No time." Busywork crowded my mind, sapping my energy and souring my perspective. How could I play when there was so much to do? The house should be cleaner. There was always something.

Beautiful days flew by, I avoided the trike, and felt tired and discouraged. Then one day I saw a sign: Don't Give Up Your Daydream. Not your day job, your daydream. I'd forgotten how. I recognized Jesus's whisper. Or was He yelling? He gave me life, a gift worthy of joy, not dread. He grants me rest. So last night, I placed my troubles in His capable hands.

This morning I climbed on my trike and took off. Crisp air ruffled my hair as I zipped along. Flowers fragranced my world. My body came alive, leg muscles pumping, oxygen clearing my thoughts. I was refreshed. If I'd stayed home, I'd have finished the dishes and swept the floor.

Instead, I heard children laughing, watched sunlight play through the clouds, and sensed Jesus smiling. I found rest. —HEIDI GAUL

FAITH STEP: *Do something spontaneous today, especially if you're busy. Look for glimpses of the joy Jesus has planted in your life. Daydream.*

MONDAY, AUGUST 31

But I tell you that I am going to do what is best for you. That is why
I am going away. The Holy Spirit cannot come to help you until I leave.
But after I am gone, I will send the Spirit to you. John 16:7 (CEV)

I REMEMBER A PARTICULAR WEEK when people close to me were either moving up, moving out, or moving on. My son was moving up to college. Our neighbors—a married couple with five girls—were moving out of their apartment. And a friend confided to me that she finally had closure with her ex-husband and was ready to move on.

That week, I had mixed feelings because everyone was moving. I was sad, yet I was also glad. A college education was expensive, but it would give my son a better chance to qualify for work. It was sad to part ways with kind neighbors, but it gave both our families the opportunity to meet new friends. It was painful for my friend to let her ex-husband go, but this paved the way for her to have a fresh start.

Jesus told His disciples that it would be for their benefit that He was going away. He was referring to His nearing ascension to heaven after His death and resurrection. He would no longer be with the disciples physically, but He would be with every believer through the Holy Spirit. Jesus never thought of leaving us alone and He has no intention of moving out of our lives once we have welcomed Him into our hearts. We don't see Him physically, but surely He dwells in us as He said He would, when we believe.
—MARLENE LEGASPI-MUNAR

FAITH STEP: *Be aware that Jesus is with you every minute. Pray for insight into how Jesus is very much present in your daily life and how He works to make all things work together for your own good and His glory.*

TUESDAY, SEPTEMBER 1

For God has not given us a spirit of fear and timidity, but of power, love, and self-discipline. 2 Timothy 1:7 (NLT)

FEAR IS A DREAM KILLER. Fear makes me think of all the negative outcomes that could happen if I do something out of my comfort zone: *Somebody might not like it. I don't know how to do it. People will talk about me. Or… it might not work.* I weary myself listening to the naysaying in my head and talk myself out of trying to do anything new. Or if I start a project, fear keeps me from finishing it. Eventually I allow my dreams to be killed by fear.

Lately as I have been studying the Scriptures, spending time with Jesus, and listening to my pastor's sermons, I am giving faith a try. I am fighting fear with faith in Jesus. Instead of focusing on the negative and unknown, I am trying to train my mind to simply trust Jesus. Last school year I took a faith step by asking to chair a school program. Putting the program together was not a smooth project. In my mind, all I could see was failure. Nevertheless, I stayed committed because I didn't want to give up. Ultimately the program was a success, and the students did an amazing job.

Faith in Jesus Christ will give us power over fear. In Matthew 8:23–26, Jesus was asleep on the boat when the wind and the waves rocked the boat and frightened the disciples. They cried out to Jesus to save them, and He asked them why they feared, telling them they had little faith. Then He calmed the wind and waves. He can do the same for us. Jesus is right here with us, ready to calm our fears when we place our faith in Him. —TRACY ELDRIDGE

FAITH STEP: *Hebrews 12:2 (KJV) states that Jesus is "the author and finisher of our faith." If you have something on your heart you want to try, step out in faith, trust Jesus, and kill the fear.*

WEDNESDAY, SEPTEMBER 2

You are the salt of the earth.... the light of the world. Matthew 5:13–14 (NIV)

MY SON, STAR QUARTERBACK IN junior high, is now the newbie on the high school team. He's learning to navigate bigger defensive players, bigger stakes, and bigger egos. Instead of being the team leader, he's playing behind a senior All-State quarterback who, thankfully, is also a friend.

One thing he's noticed is that the biggest guy on the team messes with people in a way that's not always nice. It's surprised him that the others allow it. We've been talking about ways to handle that.

The other day in practice the big guy kept mouthing off at the quarterback. Apparently this happens a lot, but usually the quarterback just tunes it out in order to keep the peace. I guess this time he'd had enough. He turned to the guy and yelled, "Shut up! You're the biggest jerk I've ever played football with!"

My son said the team fell silent. The big guy stood staring in shock. Before he could speak, the coach said, "Get back to work," but the point had been made. The quarterback was a hero.

This story made me think about different ways to be salt and light. Jesus was as gentle as a lamb. But He was also a lion. Sometimes He used shocking words like "brood of vipers" to provoke understanding—but always from a place of love. Glorifying God was the endgame.

Sometimes it's easier to be a lamb than a lion. It feels less risky. But Jesus was not one-dimensional in how He related to others. He did whatever the situation called for. And so must we.
—GWEN FORD FAULKENBERRY

FAITH STEP: *Who or what are "big guys" in your life? The next time you feel Jesus nudge you to speak up for truth, don't be afraid.*

THURSDAY, SEPTEMBER 3

*May Jesus himself and God our Father, who reached out in love
and surprised you with gifts of unending help and confidence,
put a fresh heart in you, invigorate your work, enliven your speech.*
2 Thessalonians 2:16–17 (MSG)

AMONG MY DAY-TO-DAY ACTIVITIES, I'M tasked with evaluating manuscripts for their publication potential. In a way, I'm a quality-control specialist in a story factory. I examine an author's writing with the literary equivalent of a "tuning fork." If it doesn't sing, it's removed from the conveyor belt. I test its integrity. If it doesn't pass that test, off it comes.

Without fail, two factors will make an author's submission suspect before I get to the manuscript—if the author's résumé or cover letter is overconfident or underconfident.

What am I looking for? What is Jesus looking for in His followers? Those who understand the value of appreciating the gifts of "unending help and confidence" that can invigorate a work.

Overconfidence—boasting, puffing up a résumé or using lofty descriptions of self—shows the author is dependent on his or her talent. But amazingly the overconfident are often the least talented.

Underconfidence—apologetic language, minimizing the worth of the work, self-shame—reveals a neglect to tap into and receive the gift of "unending help and confidence" with which Jesus generously blesses those who follow Him.

No matter what our line of work or the divine assignments we've been given or the service opportunities to which we're assigned, the offer is there—Christ confidence. It passes all the tests. —CYNTHIA RUCHTI

FAITH STEP: *Today, believe that the Lord will send His help and confidence for every situation.*

FRIDAY, SEPTEMBER 4

*About noon as I came near Damascus, suddenly a bright light
from heaven flashed around me. Acts 22:6 (NIV)*

MY THIRTEEN-YEAR-OLD JUST STARTED SEVENTH grade. I periodically grab him by the shoulders, look him in the eye and firmly command, "Stop growing!" Seriously, what happened this summer? My little boy mysteriously became more man-like seemingly overnight. I'm not sure I'm ready.

To be frank, I've almost never been ready for the major changes in my life. Being told I'd have a child with Down syndrome. Finishing two degrees after years of study. My parents dying; one suddenly, the other, after ailing a long time. Stepping off the corporate ladder. Moving to Florida quickly, after years of contemplating.

I didn't think I was ready. God said I was. In *His* strength.

The apostle Paul's life seemed settled. He was an elite Jewish Pharisee, one who persecuted Christians with self-acclaimed zeal. A sudden flash from heaven blinded Paul, leaving him helpless while God continued His transforming work.

Yet in Galatians, Paul proclaimed, "God...set me apart from my mother's womb and called me by his grace...to reveal his Son" (1:15–16, NIV). Before Paul was born, God had another plan for him. And He has a plan for you and for me.

God's purpose in my life was established before time, no matter how "suddenly" things seem to happen from my perspective. As I navigate another major course correction in my life, waiting on God, I can restfully anticipate His faithful purpose, knowing that suddenly is actually right on time. —ISABELLA YOSUICO

FAITH STEP: *Write down the many ways Jesus has worked suddenly in your life.*

SATURDAY, SEPTEMBER 5

My God will use his glorious riches to give you everything you need.
He will do this through Christ Jesus. Philippians 4:19 (ERV)

EARLY ONE SATURDAY MORNING, I asked the Lord to guide me in all that I do. Immediately I thought of going to the wet market to buy fresh fish. In Asia, a typical wet market has stalls for fish, poultry, fruits, and vegetables. Vendors store fish in makeshift tanks or ice-boxes, which makes the market slightly wet. I don't usually go to the wet market on Saturday, preferring the grocery store instead, but since my son and daughter were home for the weekend, I thought I'd prepare a special dish for them.

I was planning to buy ordinary fish to make a sour stew, but to my surprise, I found salmon heads, which are rarely sold in the neighborhood wet market. I bought about two pounds and cooked them in miso. That day, our family enjoyed delicious salmon soup.

Seeing those salmon heads brought to mind a story of Jesus and Peter. When Peter needed money to pay the disciples' taxes, Jesus told Peter to throw a fishing line into the lake and grab the first fish he caught. Jesus said that in its mouth, Peter would find a coin to pay for their taxes (Matthew 17:24–27). All that Jesus said would happen came to pass. He was constantly meeting the needs of the disciples in unique and wonderful ways.

That Saturday, I didn't hear Jesus's audible voice telling me to go to the wet market or that I would find salmon heads, but I was very delighted that Jesus provided for our needs. Whether it's money to pay for taxes or salmon for lunch, Jesus provides for us. —MARLENE LEGASPI-MUNAR

FAITH STEP: *What is it that you need? Pray for Jesus's leading about what to do. Mention, one by one, all the things that you need and thank Him in advance for how He will provide for you.*

SUNDAY, SEPTEMBER 6

So Peter seeing him said to Jesus, "Lord, and what about this man?"
Jesus said to him, "If I want him to remain until I come, what is that to you?
You follow Me!" John 21:21–22 (NASB)

I JUST LOVE PETER, DON'T you? I'm certain his character is central to the story of Jesus because he *is* most of us. We might read the story and admire John, see Jesus as the hero and Judas as the villain, but without Peter, I wouldn't relate to it nearly as well. He's the one whose passions too often control him, who means well but is always messing up, the one who so clearly represents our weaknesses. If he's not getting in Jesus's way, he's cutting off someone's ear. If he's not asking the hard questions, he's denying he ever knew Jesus. And yet he's still the one who got out of the boat. The one Jesus called His rock. Here at the end of John, we have another classic Peter moment.

John, disgustingly sweet, perfect John, is buttering up Jesus as always. But today it's just more than Peter can take. They don't have much longer with Jesus. And Peter is afraid Jesus won't have enough attention for him, enough work for him to do. He's comparing himself—and it feels like he doesn't measure up. *What about John?* really means *what about me?*

I love Jesus's response. *What's it to you?* There's a rebuke here, but it's not unkind. It's meant to recalibrate Peter. Pull him back into what matters. *Don't worry about anyone else. You follow Me!*

We cannot follow Jesus if our eyes are looking around at everyone else. His directions for Peter are the same for us. *What others are doing is none of your business. You follow Me.* —GWEN FORD FAULKENBERRY

FAITH STEP: *When you are tempted to compare yourself to others today, remember this story. Practice willing yourself back into what matters, every time moving toward comparison to Jesus. The habit of comparison will die if not fed.*

Labor Day, Monday, September 7

Being strengthened with all power, according to his glorious might,
for all endurance and patience with joy. Colossians 1:11 (ESV)

WITH MANY YEARS OF INTENSIVE training, I've learned to wait in many situations. The lines, the traffic jams, and waiting rooms of life don't faze me. I can sit or stand serenely. I can do this mostly without toe-tapping or grumbling.

But the weightier waits... they can still churn me up, though I see progress. At the heart of it is the unknown, the uncertain outcome, and the big question mark. Waiting for relief from my pain and fear to subside those first few months after my son Isaac was born with Down syndrome. Waiting to see if we could sell our home to relocate to Florida. Waiting for the results of my lymph node biopsy. Waiting now, with hopeful curiosity, to see what Jesus has planned for my career with so many treasured balls aloft. Hard waits.

Yet this is the heart of faith: entrusting unanswered questions and unknown outcomes to a knowing God. There's no faith in waiting for slow-changing lights or my name being called or a new roll of register tape. Jesus is found in those cliff-hanger moments of waiting.

There can be sweet freedom, joy, and peace (Jesus things!) in waiting. In Psalm 27, David isn't waiting on his pound of turkey breast or an oil change. Concluding with verse 14, David reminds me that if Jesus is the object of my wait, I can wait with thanks and praise on my lips, even with a little mortal toe-tapping on the way to hope-filled rest. —ISABELLA YOSUICO

FAITH STEP: *Read all of Psalm 27 and be blessed. Journal about three instances when you waited for something and how you saw the goodness of the Lord.*

TUESDAY, SEPTEMBER 8

With the tongue we praise our Lord and Father, and with it we curse human beings, who have been made in God's likeness. Out of the same mouth come praise and cursing. My brothers and sisters, this should not be. Can both fresh water and salt water come from the same spring? James 3:9—11 (NIV)

I WAS IN A STORE looking at furniture when I was interrupted by a storm of profanity coming from an office near where I was standing. A man was yelling and cursing. A few minutes later he stepped out of the office into the showroom. Unaware that I had overheard him, he smiled and greeted me: "Hello. How are you today?" I immediately recognized him from a friend's church. He was a member of the praise team and sang every Sunday. "Have a blessed day," he called out as I was leaving the store.

On the way to my car, I thought about what I'd just experienced. *How can a Christian talk and act that way? What a hypocrite,* I thought. Then I felt Jesus talking to me, *How do you talk when you're angry?* That thought hit home. I knew I said things when I was angry that I shouldn't. *How can I profess to be a Christian and then blurt out profanities? How does that affect my witness? Are others confused when my actions contradict what I profess?* I had to admit I was just as guilty as the man in the store. Sometimes my language did not reflect Christ-like behavior. Jesus had used this man's behavior to convict me of my own.

Jesus longs for His goodness to flow from our lives. This includes the words that flow from our mouths. We can honor Him with the way we live our lives and the way we interact with others. When our words are uplifting and encouraging, we sound like Him. It doesn't get much better than that. —KATIE MINTER JONES

FAITH STEP: *Ask Jesus to help you refrain from language that will affect your witness to others.*

WEDNESDAY, SEPTEMBER 9

Since you are precious to me, you are honored and I love you.
Isaiah 43:4 (GW)

YEARS AGO, I WATCHED A show that featured people who brought in old stuff to have it appraised by experts. Naturally everyone hoped to hear exciting news about their vase, painting, article of furniture, or whatever. Many people left disappointed, but some were shocked to learn that their object was a valuable antique. For a while I attended garage sales and flea markets with one persistent thought: what if I discovered a valuable treasure among someone's discarded junk?

Sad to say, I occasionally witness someone looking at a person as though he or she is discarded junk with little value. That unkempt man holding a cardboard sign by the highway. The woman with dementia mumbling to herself in the park. The special-needs child causing a disturbance in a store. In those moments, I remind myself that God is the True Appraiser, the One who determines our value.

No matter who we are, Jesus demonstrated our worth a couple thousand years ago when He died on the cross. The ransom paid for our sins was not "mere gold or silver," but "the precious blood of Christ, the sinless, spotless Lamb of God" (1 Peter 1:18–19, NLT). The forgiveness, love, and grace that flows through Jesus is available to all of us regardless of how our culture might "rank" us. I like to imagine how our society would change if we all treated each other as someone cherished and treasured by Him. And on those days when I look in the mirror and feel like an antique, I need to remember how Jesus has appraised me. —DIANNE NEAL MATTHEWS

FAITH STEP: *Meditate on one of the verses on this page or another one of your choosing to remind yourself how valuable you are in light of Christ's sacrifice.*

THURSDAY, SEPTEMBER 10

Jesus replied, "Foxes have dens and birds have nests, but the Son of Man has no place to lay his head." Matthew 8:20 (NIV)

MY SON AND HIS FAMILY are living with us as he finishes seminary. We've been blessed by seeing them each day, but two households under one roof is a challenge. One Saturday they were longing for time to themselves. So my husband and I decided to stay out of the house all day and give them space and privacy. We hit several yard sales, then visited my mom, went out for lunch, and then to the zoo. It was a fun day, but we grew thirsty, hot, and tired. We finally stopped at a park, and I rested on a bench, thinking how blessed we are to have a home and that our "pilgrim" status was only for a day. Leaving a familiar and comfortable situation even briefly reminded me of the choice Jesus made for us.

He left the most glorious home imaginable—heaven—emptied Himself, and took the form of a servant. Then while on earth, Jesus was willing to forsake all the comforts of home in order to travel from place to place, ministering to hurting people, all because of His compassion and mercy. He often had no place to lay His head.

Whenever I travel—for a day or for longer trips—I miss my own bed, my teapot, my creature comforts. Those hardly compare to the glories of heaven, which Jesus has set aside for us. When I reflect on His sacrifice, I'm overwhelmed by how deep His love is. Everything in me responds: Jesus, make Your home in me. You are welcome in my heart. —SHARON HINCK

FAITH STEP: *Step outside your home and imagine leaving it all behind for the rest of your life. Thank Jesus for what He forsook because of His love for you.*

FRIDAY, SEPTEMBER 11

[Jesus said,] "I am leaving you with a gift—peace of mind and heart!
And the peace I give isn't fragile like the peace the world gives.
So don't be troubled or afraid." John 14:27 (TLB)

MY HUSBAND LIKES TO KEEP the television tuned to a news station a few hours each day. He watches it before work, during his lunch break at home, and in the evenings. Don't get me wrong—I do want to stay informed about what's going on in the world; I need to know how to pray concerning current events. But sometimes the video clips of evil and violent acts being played over and over get to me. I start to feel unsettled and anxious.

During those times it helps to remember some of Christ's final words before His crucifixion. In New Testament times, a typical way to say goodbye was "peace" or "shalom." To the Jews, this meant more than the absence of conflict, stress, or war. It implied the blessings of wholeness, completeness, health, security, joy, and contentment. Peace on the inside, no matter what's going on around us.

Even though the whole world seems to be involved in tension, conflict, and war, we can enjoy the special peace only believers can possess. The kind that Jesus made possible when He rose from the dead, returned to heaven, and sent the Holy Spirit to live inside His followers. The deep, lasting peace that sustains us through any circumstance.

The world around us may be in turmoil—or worse—but thanks to Jesus we can have peace with God, with one another, and within our own spirit. What a matchless gift! —DIANNE NEAL MATTHEWS

FAITH STEP: *Read Philippians 4:6–9 to remind yourself how to experience the peace of God that will guard your mind and heart. Then write John 14:27 on a card and tape it to your bathroom mirror. Each morning read it aloud as you visualize Jesus speaking the words to you.*

SATURDAY, SEPTEMBER 12

Incline your ear, and come unto me: hear, and your soul shall live.
Isaiah 55:3 (KJV)

I SLEEP WITH MY CELL phone on the nightstand beside my bed. The phone serves as my alarm clock. I also use it to pay bills and to communicate by email with my employer, book editors, and members of my writing circle. I use my phone to promote books and book signings on social media. I use it to connect with family and friends who post occasional pictures of sunny vacations, grinning grandbabies, and cake recipes they will never commence to bake.

While the technology makes me especially accessible to my aging mother, I have reached a resounding conclusion. With all its pings, beeps, and ringing notifications, my cell phone is a distraction. The prophet Isaiah said it is in "quietness" that we find our strength (Isaiah 30:15, KJV). So, each day after the alarm rings, I rise from bed. I mute my phone to pray, read a collection of devotionals, meditate on a Bible verse, and then I sit in silence. In silence I commune with my Creator, who owns infinite wisdom about all the things that will concern my day.

Sustained moments of silence before the Lord are as necessary to each morning as washing my face or combing my hair. In the silence, Jesus speaks to my heart, and I obtain clarity of mind. In the silence of the morning, I also remember blessings from the previous day, month or years past, and these precious memories fuel my heart with the strength to face present challenges. We should cloak each morning in a hush of quiet time with the Lord. It is the only way to be completely dressed. —ALICE THOMPSON

FAITH STEP: *Mute your phone this morning for thirty minutes. Sit in silence and ask Jesus to speak with you. Take notes and answer His call.*

SUNDAY, SEPTEMBER 13

He says, "Be still, and know that I am God." Psalm 46:10 (NIV)

JESUS HAS BEEN DEALING WITH me about busyness (and rest) for a while. Or better yet, about not being so busy. I routinely over-schedule myself and my family; overwhelming everyone even with good stuff like sports, church activities, and social events. I see a need—a friend's, at the boys' schools, in the community—and volunteer. It's all good. Or is it? I'm a hard case. I traded His easy yoke for a hard one (Matthew 11:30).

Yet my deeply personal Jesus deals with me on a very personal level. Decidedly type A, I have a hard time discerning what's busyness, what's essential, and what's simply using my gifts to serve others. *Am I not supposed to help people? Don't I need to cultivate my kids' talents? Shouldn't I maximize every day?* This is especially hard during a busy season with small kids at home.

Well, that's where the stillness comes in. If Jesus's still, small voice can't be heard above the din of my life, I'm too busy. If I can't walk the dog without my cell phone, or just sit and listen to the silence, or just while away an hour that doesn't generate production? I'm too busy.

Willing to obey Jesus's persistent promptings, I've made time for stillness, though it's been uncomfortable. I quit some volunteer commitments and now pause to ask Jesus if He wants me to help. I don't double-schedule activities. I seek Jesus's discernment about social connections to pursue. In that deliberately acquired downtime, He has revealed some misguided motives, validated priorities, provided insight, and delivered me from fears. I've found transcendent serenity affirms Jesus's truly sufficient grace (2 Corinthians 12:9). —ISABELLA YOSUICO

FAITH STEP: *Next time you experience that anxious, driven feeling of busyness, find a quiet place and be still. Use this time to talk Jesus.*

MONDAY, SEPTEMBER 14

For by the blood of Christ we are set free, that is, our sins are forgiven.
How great is the grace of God. Ephesians 1:7 (GNT)

THERE ARE DAYS THAT MY students frustrate me mightily. They can't answer questions about material we've covered for several weeks or worse, they don't do their assignments. They forget paper or pencils. They don't write their names on their papers. They daydream and don't pay attention or they talk too much. Sometimes they can be pretty disrespectful. As I was griping about all this one day to a friend, Jesus brought something to my attention. Sometimes I'm guilty of the same behavior. I zone out at professional development meetings. I forget my work tools sometimes. Occasionally I talk in meetings while the presenter is speaking. I laughed because sometimes I can be just as spacey as my students! After that little chastising from Jesus, I decided that I needed to show my students some grace just as Jesus always gives me the gift of His grace.

From the time we wake up in the morning until we lie down at night, we need His grace. Jesus forgives us time after time. It's an amazing show of love. In the Bible, the apostles begin and end their letters to the churches by praying for the Lord to give them grace. Better still, the Bible ends with an offer of grace. The very last line, Revelation 22:21 reads, "The grace of our Lord Jesus Christ *be* with you all. Amen" (NKJV). We are alive by the grace of God through Jesus, so we should be willing to give grace to others when they don't live up to our expectations. We will never live up to Jesus's expectations and that's why we need His grace that abounds for us more and more every day. —TRACY ELDRIDGE

FAITH STEP: *To whom do you need to show grace today? Give that person the same grace that Jesus grants you.*

TUESDAY, SEPTEMBER 15

For of His fullness we have all received, and grace upon grace.
John 1:16 (NASB)

I HAVE A STUDENT IN freshman English who is sixty years old. He told me he joined the army to get the GI Bill, so he could go to college over forty years ago. Instead, he went to Vietnam. When he came home, he said, he was too messed up to start college. He's had a difficult life but never gave up his dream.

For years, he's been haunted by nightmares that drove him to alcohol addiction. His family left him alone on his farm. Finally he got help and learned he has PTSD. Guess what the cure is? Get out of isolation. So now, using his GI Bill, he's in my class.

This guy could focus on everything that's sad about his story. Just listening to it brought me to tears. But instead, he chooses to focus on the new life he's finding after all these years. He brings an enthusiasm to class that encourages me. *An attitude of gratitude,* as the saying goes. What a difference it makes when one approaches life through the lens of grace.

It's by grace, he believes, that he's alive. By grace his family left him because it forced him to get help. He found grace in the VA (Veterans Administration). It's by grace that he found out he has PTSD. And grace that he can do something to help dispel the darkness in his mind.

This story has helped me to remember that grace is everywhere. There's grace for us in everything. And the source of grace is Jesus. Out of His fullness, grace flows freely and abundantly forever.
—GWEN FORD FAULKENBERRY

FAITH STEP: *Pour out a cup of sugar and try to count the individual granules. The number you get? Not even close to how much grace is yours in Jesus.*

WEDNESDAY, SEPTEMBER 16

One who has unreliable friends soon comes to ruin, but there is a friend who sticks closer than a brother. Proverbs 18:24 (NIV)

I MET FRANKLIN IN COLLEGE. He was tall and lean like a championship athlete. However, during our college years, he traded in his high school football cleats for paintbrushes. If a college club needed T-shirt designs, Franklin was the artist for the job. He also painted and framed abstract drawings made of discarded paper and watercolors. Most of us students had not yet developed a keen appreciation for art, but we supported Franklin's local art shows. And in return, Franklin supported his college friends. He owned a big blue truck and was forever loading it up with computers, furniture, and books when a buddy upgraded to new digs off campus.

In the years after college, Franklin sold artwork for thousands of dollars and taught art until his health failed. When he took ill, I did not immediately visit him. I was angry with Franklin for not seeking medical advice earlier. Maybe, if he had been a stickler for going to the doctor, this illness could have been avoided. The longer I stayed away from visiting Franklin, the more I proved to be an unreliable friend. Then I remembered the Golden Rule. Jesus requires me to treat others the way I wish to be treated.

After five weeks avoiding his hospital room, I visited Franklin and I asked him to forgive me for my delay. I asked Jesus to forgive me too. Think about it. Jesus befriended a myriad of people with a myriad of physical and emotional conditions. He loved them and cared for them until they received their wholeness. It is our duty to offer friends this same unconditional love. —ALICE THOMPSON

FAITH STEP: *Jesus was a friend to the sick. Today, visit one who is in the hospital or a care home. Your friendship is a balm of blessings.*

THURSDAY, SEPTEMBER 17

I lift up my eyes to the mountains—where does my help come from? My help comes from the LORD, the Maker of heaven and earth. Psalm 121:1–2 (NIV)

THIS MORNING I WOKE UP to crazy headlines—again. Foreign wars and carnage. Refugees clamoring for safe haven. Political strife. Financial difficulties. Undercurrents of discontentment. I have been feeling as if I should chuck my phone straight out the window. Maybe that would make the crazy go away.

Instead, I have taken to reading the Psalms to still my soul. When it feels as if the world is plummeting like a rock toward the fiery pit, the Psalms always bring me back from the edge. They put everything back into perspective. The world has always been the world. Wild. Unpredictable. And broken. And Jesus has always been Jesus. Steadfast. Faithful. Powerful. The Psalms remind me of what is real. Verses such as "Whoever dwells in the shelter of the Most High will rest in the shadow of the Almighty" (91:1, NIV) and "The angel of the LORD encamps around those who fear him, and he delivers them" (34:7, NIV). The thing is…hope will never be found in the headlines. That is where fear and anger reside. Headlines were made to get us whipped up. They unsettle us, making us doubt the goodness in the world we live in. But the truth of Jesus's Word…His holy truth…is meant to anchor us with peace. To still our beating hearts in the midst of the storm. To lift our heads and get us focused on the One who is *truly good*…and then some. The One who is in charge and loves us most of all. That would be Jesus.
—SUSANNA FOTH AUGHTMON

FAITH STEP: *This morning as you read the day's headlines, take a moment to change them into prayers. Pray for the hope of Jesus to permeate and change our broken world with His love.*

FRIDAY, SEPTEMBER 18

Jesus, remember me when you come into your Kingdom.
Luke 23:42 *(NLT)*

MY PRODUCTIVITY LEVEL WAS SLIPPING. I'd shoved a few too many pieces of paper into the stack "to be filed." Somewhere in that stack was a list of ideas for future devotions. Conference notes. A receipt I need for a rebate. Time to purge and file and organize.

I discovered a piece of paper that had fallen out of my Bible. The paper held names of those for whom I'd been praying regarding their spiritual health. Some had walked a path that took them farther from the footsteps of Jesus. The list needed to be updated, but not as much as I'd wished.

Many were still walking perpendicular to the path Jesus had laid out. They'd turned their backs on Him and showed no signs of changing. Were my prayers ineffective? Had I been unfaithful to communicate the truth to them?

I was caught short by a poignant scene from the Bible—Jesus on His cross with a thief hanging on either side. One cried out for mercy, convinced Jesus was the Son of God. We have no record the other reached out. The Bible's silence on that subject insinuates that he went to his death unbelieving.

Jesus stood between them. As near to one as to the other. One cried out for salvation. The other—to our knowledge—did not.

I slid the slip of paper back into my Bible, determined to be faithful in prayer, but conscious that even the nearness of Christ is not enough to convince some. All we have to do, though, is ask Him to remember us. And He will. —CYNTHIA RUCHTI

FAITH STEP: *Is your concern for a family member or friend straying into guilt? Let Jesus handle it. He well understands the concern.*

SATURDAY, SEPTEMBER 19

He said to his disciples, "The harvest is great, but the workers are few.
So pray to the Lord who is in charge of the harvest; ask him to send
more workers into his fields." Matthew 9:37–38 (NLT)

HAVE YOU EVER MET A stranger, face-to-face, who turned out to be someone you prayed for in the past? During our church prayer meetings, my friends and I pray for people from all nations to know Jesus Christ as their Savior. We pray for persecuted believers to persevere in their faith. Even without going to the mission field to minister to these people ourselves, we continue praying for them.

When I attended an international publishing conference in Brazil, I met one of the people I'd been praying for! He's a Chinese editor who learned about Christ through a lady professor at his university. He became a Christian and began attending one of the many thriving house churches in China. After coming to know the Lord, he decided to use his editing skills to produce materials about Jesus. Indeed, Jesus works in creative and wonderful ways to spread the news of His love. He wants everyone to know Him.

In Matthew 9, when Jesus saw the crowd who was harassed, distressed, and helpless, He told His disciples to pray for laborers to bring the Good News to them. He sees the world today through the same lens of love and care. Today, many people around the world still need to hear that Jesus is the Savior who gives salvation and eternal life—not only in the afterlife—but here and now. With Jesus, we can have a fulfilling life here on earth. Will you be one of Jesus's laborers and spread the news of His love? —MARLENE LEGASPI-MUNAR

FAITH STEP: *Pray for persecuted believers to be strengthened and to be assured of Jesus's love for them. Pray that they would know how to share the gospel effectively amid persecution.*

SUNDAY, SEPTEMBER 20

*And lo a voice from heaven, saying, This is my beloved Son,
in whom I am well pleased. Matthew 3:17 (KJV)*

I LOOKED OVER MY SON's homework as he computed a problem aloud and then wrote the answer on the math sheet.

"That's illegible," I noted.

Without skipping a beat, he pointed his pencil at me, winked, and flashed a winning smile. "That's because I'm an illegible bachelor!"

I wish I could have that kind of confidence and easy sense of humor when I made a mistake or was having difficulty getting my point across! I love that my son feels *eligible*—in the sense that he knows Jesus loves him! My son is truly and delightfully lovable, and he knows it.

Of course I was also pleased that he rewrote his answer so that the teacher could actually read it when he handed it in the next day. But with his quip we both got a good laugh, and, really, I was the one getting help on my "homework." I must keep practicing: knowing that because of Jesus I am lovable in my being, not in my doing.

—ELIZABETH BERNE DEGEAR

FAITH STEP: *In prayer, spend some time thinking about the difference between your "being" in Christ and your "doing" in Christ. Ask Jesus to show you how to rest in His love.*

MONDAY, SEPTEMBER 21

You must warn each other every day, while it is still "today," so that none of you will be deceived by sin and hardened against God. Hebrews 3:13 (NLT)

I SERVE MY COMMUNITY AS a school librarian. The job is more than shelving books. I labor over lesson plans, state testing, and the management of carts and classrooms filled with hundreds of computers. Every morning, students and faculty charge toward my door, seeking computer help. My library buzzes with few quiet moments. Welcome to the twenty-first-century library!

In the middle of one frenzied morning, I looked up toward the ceiling tile and blurted, *"I hate my job!"* A concerned student athlete approached my desk and asked, "How is your day?"

I groaned, "Not good."

He proceeded to tell me about a Scripture he had learned in his youth group—Fellowship of Christian Athletes (FCA). The Bible says, "Work willingly at whatever you do, as though you were working for the Lord rather than for people" (Colossians 3:23, NLT). My student then advised with a smile, "The day will get better, if you change your attitude."

I took his advice and for the rest of that school year, when times turned hectic, I stopped to view each task, each student or coworker through the lens of Colossians 3:23. I invite you to do the same. Every duty is elevated and takes on the glow of a high calling when we realize Jesus is our boss and infinite help. —ALICE THOMPSON

FAITH STEP: *As believers have encouraged you, ask Jesus for opportunities to encourage others.*

TUESDAY, SEPTEMBER 22

But if you do not forgive, neither will your Father in heaven forgive your trespasses. Mark 11:26 (NKJV)

FORGIVENESS IS A BEAUTIFUL THING. It restores relationships and makes things right. But in the real world? It's hard. A few months ago a colleague did something that hurt me professionally. As far as I was concerned, she didn't deserve my forgiveness. Shortly after the incident, I saw her walking down the hallway toward me and wondered, *Should I take the stairs and avoid her entirely? Or do I walk by without speaking, so she'll know how angry I am?* But as we approached one another, I knew what I had to do. I had to forgive, but it was hard. Grudgingly I said, "Hello." I started to feel my anger subside. I felt lighter. Jesus was doing a work in my heart.

Years ago before I knew the Lord, I wouldn't have considered forgiveness. I would've nursed my grudge and worn it like a badge of honor. Thankfully as Jesus helped me to wholly forgive, my heart toward my coworker has changed. I'm not trapped in bitterness and hurt. I'm moving forward in love.

Jesus forgave me of all my sins, paying a horrendous cost for my salvation. In turn, I'm commanded to forgive, so I can receive forgiveness from my heavenly Father. He asks me to forgive for my benefit. The burden of being unwilling to forgive is heavy, but I'm learning that with forgiveness comes freedom and peace. Forgiveness isn't a sign of weakness but love. Jesus's willingness to give His life and forgive my sins is the ultimate act of love. When I forgive others, I'm His love in action. —TRACY ELDRIDGE

FAITH STEP: *Search your heart and think of people whom you've not forgiven. Start calling out their names in prayer and ask Jesus to help you forgive them. Watch your heart fill with love for them.*

WEDNESDAY, SEPTEMBER 23

For I am not ashamed of this Good News about Christ. It is God's powerful method of bringing all who believe it to heaven. Romans 1:16 (TLB)

MY CHILDREN WERE STUDENTS WHEN the "See You at the Pole" movement started in the nineties. Each September on the fourth Wednesday, I dropped them off early to pray with their classmates before school. After our nest emptied, I forgot about the event—until early one September morning when my daughter, Holly, texted me a photo of her little boy Roman, leaning against a flagpole. Roman wasn't just the only kindergartner to show up; he was the only one from the school. But Holly reported that Roman prayed "a sweet prayer" for his school and country.

That photo reminds me that sometimes following Jesus means standing alone—as His disciples learned. It would've been easy to go with the crowd who followed Jesus into Jerusalem, waving palm branches and shouting, "Hosanna!" But when He was arrested, even His inner circle abandoned Him. Three times Peter denied knowing Him.

It takes courage to stand up for Jesus in a setting where He's not popular. If we heard a friend being disparaged, we'd most likely speak up to defend her. Why don't we also do that for our Savior who died for us? Yet, if you're like me, you recall times when you stayed silent. Or blended into the crowd instead of standing out as a Christ follower. I'm not proud of those moments, but it helps to remember that Peter's failure helped him grow into a strong leader. In the meantime, I want to be like that lone little boy praying and standing by a flagpole. —DIANNE NEAL MATTHEWS

FAITH STEP: *Is there an area in your life where you fail to stand for Christ? Ask Him to forgive you and help you remain strong.*

THURSDAY, SEPTEMBER 24

But when they saw him walking on the lake, they thought he was a ghost. They cried out, because they all saw him and were terrified. Immediately he spoke to them and said, "Take courage! It is I. Don't be afraid." Mark 6:49–50 (NIV)

GEPHYROPHOBIA IS A PHOBIA OF bridges. I once had a friend who would have an someone drive her across Maryland's Chesapeake Bay Bridge, a breathtaking four-mile-long, 185-foot-high expanse. Apparently the fear for many is the imagined threat of losing control, careening through the guardrails, and plummeting to the ground below. Someone else driving is reassurance enough to quell the terror.

I don't have a fear of bridges. But fear of losing control? I have that by the bucketful. And yet it's obvious that driving across the bridge of life is risky. The solution for me is the same: let someone else drive. When I gave my life to Christ, I handed Him the keys to my car. Wrestling over who gets to drive hasn't worked so well.

In the past few weeks, Jesus has used a variety of methods to remind me I gave Him the keys. He has the keys. He is the Key. For one thing, I was without a car for a week while my husband's car was in the shop, and we toiled over whether to repair it or get another. Being carless forced me to be still and let Jesus sort out a flurry of concurrent challenges over which I had no control. Sometimes Jesus has to immobilize me—through circumstances I can't control—to encourage me to hand over the keys to my life. Again.

Will I let Him drive over the current bridge, allowing me to simply enjoy the view?

Will I give Him back the keys? —ISABELLA YOSUICO

FAITH STEP: *Are you clinging to something? Take a special trip to a nearby bridge and imagine entrusting the keys to Jesus.*

FRIDAY, SEPTEMBER 25

Anyone who wants to serve me must follow me, because my servants must be where I am. And the Father will honor anyone who serves me. Now my soul is deeply troubled. Should I pray, "Father, save me from this hour"? But this is the very reason I came! Father, bring glory to your name. John 12:26–28 (NLT)

A WOMAN FROM MY COMMUNITY is undergoing a serious health crisis. She fell for no apparent reason three times in a couple of months. The last fall broke her right wrist. As her wrist mended, her right hand turned limp and useless. Pain and swelling set in. Her entire arm soon developed the same symptoms.

The symptoms are now spreading to her lower body. As she and many others pray for a miracle, bewildered doctors try to help by prescribing pain medication. It doesn't begin to touch the pain that racks her day and night.

In the midst of extreme suffering, this woman has chosen to respond by expressing trust in Jesus's sovereignty in her life. "Satan may want to use this situation to discourage or destroy me," she said, "but I won't let him win. I choose to trust Jesus with my life. He loved me enough to suffer for me, so I will invite Him to use my suffering for His glory. I feel honored that He chose me for this assignment."

Following Jesus includes following His example when we suffer. He experienced anguish in His soul as the crucifixion approached, but He acknowledged God's sovereignty and embraced His purposes. My friend is doing the same. We don't know what her future holds, but we know God will somehow honor her for following Jesus's example. —GRACE FOX

FAITH STEP: *Pray for a friend who's ill or suffering in some way. Send her a card saying she's in your thoughts and prayers.*

SATURDAY, SEPTEMBER 26

And we all, who with unveiled faces contemplate the Lord's glory, are being transformed into his image with ever-increasing glory, which comes from the Lord, who is the Spirit. 2 Corinthians 3:18 (NIV)

WHAT A MESS! I'D DROPPED an open jar of spaghetti sauce on the kitchen island. Somehow the glass hadn't broken, but the sloppy red goo was everywhere. Globs spread across the floor, splattered the cabinets, and even sprayed the ceiling. A massive cleanup job filled my immediate future. Grabbing cloths, a mop, and a bucket, I set to work. Soon the splashed portions of the floor, cabinets, and ceiling shone like they hadn't in years.

I discovered a new problem. The untouched areas had seemed fine previously, but now the fresh-cleaned spots made them appear dirty. I'd have to deep-clean the entire room.

As I mature in faith, I sense Jesus doing the same work in me. He's washing impure and self-centered behaviors away. When He finishes with one area of sin, He moves on to another. Some problems require more work on my part than others. And aspects of my personality that seemed acceptable in the past now glare with filth in comparison to attitudes He's already transformed.

That day, as the hours slipped past, I found I couldn't reach one part of the ceiling, even standing on a step stool. For several minutes I struggled, but after it became a clear impossibility, I let the grimy circle remain. I keep it as a reminder that the transformation Jesus continues within me will never be finished this side of heaven. There's plenty more to do. And that's okay. The important thing is that with His help, I'm willing and able to pitch in. —HEIDI GAUL

FAITH STEP: *As you embark on a large cleaning project, let your mind wander to places Jesus is doing work inside you. What is He telling you to do to make the job easier?*

SUNDAY, SEPTEMBER 27

Don't you realize that God's kindness is supposed to lead you to change your heart and life? Romans 2:4 (CEB)

WHILE BROWSING THROUGH OLD PHOTOS, I came across one of my daughter beaming, with her arm around her first-grade teacher. Memories flooded back as I recalled what a wonderful school year Holly had with Mrs. Smith. Each time I volunteered in her classroom, I sensed something different from other classes. The atmosphere seemed more peaceful, the kids more cooperative and positive. I wondered what made the difference.

I found out when I accompanied the class on a field trip. After the bus arrived at our destination, Mrs. Smith stood up. No last-minute instructions, no review of the rules or proper etiquette. Mrs. Smith looked into the children's faces and smiled as she assured them of her confidence in their behavior. "We're going to have fun today. I'm so proud of you. I know you're going to be the best-behaved group of first-graders this museum has ever seen!"

That day I understood why Mrs. Smith's students seemed better behaved than some classes: those boys and girls knew their teacher loved and valued them. They wanted to please her and live up to her expectations. A reminder of her confidence in them reaped greater results than listing a set of rules.

The Bible includes commands, guidelines, and warnings about the consequences of disobedience. It's important for us to heed them. But our primary motivation for living a life that pleases God is our Savior who values us and loved us enough to die for us. How could we not want to make Him even more proud of us? —DIANNE NEAL MATTHEWS

FAITH STEP: *As you begin your day, imagine Jesus smiling and telling you how proud He is of you. Then look for ways to honor Him in all that you do.*

MONDAY, SEPTEMBER 28

And he said to him, "You shall love the Lord your God with all your heart and with all your soul and with all your mind." Matthew 22:37 (ESV)

LIKE MANY OTHER PEOPLE, I enjoy social media, television, reading, and talking on the phone. Until recently, the first thing I did every morning was look at social media and see what was going on with my friends. I enjoyed sending birthday and anniversary greetings. Afterward, I would say my prayers. But I began to I realize, I was spending more time posting on Facebook than talking to Jesus or reading His Word.

The things I enjoy are not sinful. Work, family, relationships, and hobbies are good things. But sin comes creeping in when we make these things a priority over Jesus. The first commandment says for us to have no other gods before Him. I had literally put my entertainment before Jesus. Matthew 6:33 (ESV) instructs us, "But seek first the kingdom of God and his righteousness, and all these things will be added to you."

When I evaluated my time, I realized that *all* of my time was really His time. I rearranged my priorities and put Him first.

Since I have reorganized my priorities, I begin each day by praying and connecting with Jesus. I read my Bible and devotions daily and listen to Christian music while I'm working or driving. Throughout the day, I talk to Jesus. Since Jesus has become first in my life, everything else is falling into place. His peace is filling my heart. I still enjoy Facebook and chatting with friends, but I don't let them rule my life and time. —KATIE MINTER JONES

FAITH STEP: *Evaluate how much time you spend doing other things and if Jesus is your priority.*

TUESDAY, SEPTEMBER 29

This High Priest of ours understands our weaknesses. . . . So let us come boldly to the throne of our gracious God. There we will receive his mercy, and we will find grace to help us when we need it most. Hebrews 4:15–16 (NLT)

MY FATHER COULDN'T JOIN OUR family vacation abroad because of his fear of flying. He was close to tears when my mother, siblings, and nephews were about to leave for the airport, and remained speechless, unable to wish them a safe and happy trip. His physical condition also made it difficult for him to travel. Though our family wanted to take him on the trip, we thought it best he not go, so I stayed home and took care of my father while our family traveled.

A few hours after their departure, my father urged me to check and see if my brother had posted pictures of their trip on Facebook. When I showed my dad the photos, he smiled and commented about my mother, who was wearing a thermal jacket. "Your mother is cold," he said, obviously concerned. But I also sensed loneliness in his voice.

Taking care of my father reminded me that Jesus understands our loneliness and weaknesses. He is with us. When we feel lonely and weak, we can come to Jesus and receive from Him the help that we need. We can also appreciate the people He sends to be with us. As for me, I am thankful that I was able to be with my father in his time of need. I rely on Jesus and allow His grace to fill me, so I can be a caring daughter to my father and others in need.
—MARLENE LEGASPI-MUNAR

FAITH STEP: *What lessons have you learned from taking care of someone? Spend a moment to pray and encourage a caregiver today.*

WEDNESDAY, SEPTEMBER 30

And whoever compels you to go one mile, go with him two.
Matthew 5:41 (NKJV)

HIS BEDROOM DOOR WAS LEFT ajar, so I could help my father right away if he needed anything. "Good morning, Pa! What would you like to have for breakfast?" While moving slowly toward the dining table, he said, "I'd like some tea."

As I prepared his tea, I made a mental list of the things I needed to do. *Wash the dishes. Clean the house. Check if there's a message from Mother, who was on vacation overseas with my siblings.*

Before he took his noon nap, Pa requested pizza. I quickly took a bath but skipped my usual routine. Ordering the pizza was the priority. I didn't want him to wake up hungry and have to wait for his lunch.

Later that day, when I finally had time for myself, I found an online article by a daughter who was caring for her aging parents. She said, "Daughtering for a parent with chronic illness or an aging parent is selfless because there's no glory and no recognition." I agree. But Jesus was and still is the model caregiver. He exemplified selflessness. He often ministered to people without fanfare (Mark 1:40–44). Even when He Himself needed rest, He healed the sick (Matthew 14:13–14). He did not seek glory or recognition for Himself but was and is concerned about our welfare. In every situation, Jesus gives us the best care we could ever receive.
—MARLENE LEGASPI-MUNAR

FAITH STEP: *Ask a caregiver how you can help. If you're a caregiver, don't hesitate to ask for help or prayer.*

THURSDAY, OCTOBER 1

Though one may be overpowered, two can defend themselves. A cord of three strands is not quickly broken. Ecclesiastes 4:12 (NIV)

THE MONTH OF OCTOBER IS bittersweet for me. It is sweet because my mother was born in October. October is bitter because Ray, my godson, died in a one-car accident on the first day of the month. He was twenty-five years old and served our city as a fireman.

Prior to Ray's death, when I was in a slump, his parents, Katrina and Ray Sr., were the two friends that I called for a ready prayer, a quick word of encouragement, or laughter to keep from crying. With their positive outlook and joy for life, Katrina and Ray Sr. offered me sunshine on cloudy days. Our friendship shifted with the passing of their son. It was now my turn to offer them prayer, encouragement, and laughter. It was now my turn to visit them in a posture that was slow to speak and eager to listen, with endless offerings of my mother's famous sweet tea.

An old church song reminds us that "Jesus is a rock in a weary land." I understand that the assurance and refuge we receive from our Lord are the gifts that we must offer to our friends when they face the trials of life. Katrina and Ray Sr. might shed a variety of tears this October. But like Jesus who comforted the disciples and was an ever-present help to the bereaved, I will visit their home and make myself available with a big pitcher of tea and a box of tissue, if it is needed.

We must all emulate our Lord's compassion and be a sturdy shoulder for friends. Sometimes just being present to sit and listen with others is our greatest contribution. —ALICE THOMPSON

FAITH STEP: *On this morning, remember friends who are grieving. Call them today, offer them a listening ear, and end your call in prayer.*

FRIDAY, OCTOBER 2

But seek first his kingdom and his righteousness, and all these things will be given to you as well. Matthew 6:33 (NIV)

WHEN I WAS A YOUNG mother, there was always too much to do and too little time in which to do it. Between working, cleaning the house, running errands, cooking, doing the laundry, taking the children to their activities, and shopping, as well as being a wife and mother, I was always busy. I just didn't have much time for Jesus. I felt like a gerbil running inside a wheel, constantly running but never going anywhere. I was overwhelmed and frustrated. On Sundays, I was either too tired or too busy to go to church.

But as much as I loved my family, friends, and hectic life, I knew there was something missing. One night, feeling tired and empty, I reached out to Jesus. I knew that He needed to be a priority. It was time to make changes in my life. *Dear Jesus, I will put you first. Please give me peace. I can't do this without you,* I prayed. The next morning, I began the day with a prayer. I listened to worship music on the radio. I realized that Jesus wouldn't mind if I was washing dishes, cleaning the house, or driving while I prayed. He just wanted me to talk to Him. I began reading my Bible and devotionals more. We quit skipping church. My schedule was still busy. I had a lot of responsibilities, but Jesus was by my side.

Busyness can get in the way of spending time with Jesus. He longs for a relationship with us. He wants to lead us, guide us, and flood our lives with His grace and mercy. That only happens when we are in His presence, soaking up His love. —KATIE MINTER JONES

FAITH STEP: *Spend time in Jesus's presence today. Make Him your priority.*

SATURDAY, OCTOBER 3

And he withdrew himself into the wilderness, and prayed. Luke 5:16 (KJV)

TWO BOSTON TERRIER PUPPIES PLAY at my feet as I type this. They wrestle, rolling around before they take off across my great room, toe-nails clicking wildly. When they try to stop, they slide sixteen inches on the hardwood floor. In a moment they'll give out. When they do, they will flop down wherever they are with their little round bellies in the air. And soon they'll be snoring through their adorable bulldog noses.

Their idea is play hard, sleep hard. Our lives are not so simple, but whether we work or play hard, we all need rest. This shouldn't be hard to remember. But it is. I look out at the world and see so much that needs to be done that I'm overwhelmed. It seems like there's no time to rest.

The Talmud says (and I'm paraphrasing): "Do not be daunted by the enormity of the world's grief. Do justly, now. Love mercy, now. Walk humbly, now. You are not obligated to complete the work, but neither are you free to abandon it." So how does one manage?

Jesus did the most important work the world has ever known in His short ministry. And yet Luke tells us He took time to rest. He gave Himself until He was tired. Then He withdrew Himself. And prayed.

I love that Jesus went to the wilderness to get away from people and talk to God. He didn't go to the couch or to see Dr. Luke or even to church. He went to the wilderness. I guess I love that because the wilderness is my happy place too. It's where I feel peaceful and safe and closest to God. But it's not the place that's really important. The important thing is the rest. —GWEN FORD FAULKENBERRY

FAITH STEP: *How long has it been since you withdrew to a quiet place for rest and listened to Jesus in prayer? Fill up your bubble bath, fix yourself some good food, or take a hike. He'll meet you there.*

SUNDAY, OCTOBER 4

He is the radiance of the glory of God and the exact imprint of his nature, and he upholds the universe by the word of his power. Hebrews 1:3 (ESV)

WE FILED THROUGH THE RECEIVING line prior to the funeral, touched by mementos of the young woman's too-short life. Jigsaw puzzles—one of her favorite pastimes during chemo treatments. Photos with her husband and two little boys. Pink ribbons.

I lingered at the plaster casting of the young woman's left forearm, her hand clutching a casting of her older son's forearm, clutching the younger son's forearm, which was clutching the husband's forearm, whose hand was clutching his wife's forearm. A circle of undying love captured in plaster.

Her wedding ring was so distinct in the plaster that it drew my attention. It was realistic to the finest detail, because it was an exact imprint, an exact impression from the real ring.

What a treasure for the family to cherish. So lifelike, but with a permanence the world couldn't offer. As worship music filled the sanctuary, I couldn't stop thinking about that circle of arms and hands holding on to one another and imagining the day when that circle will one day be real for them again in heaven.

The Bible tells us that Jesus is worth following because He's an exact imprint of God's nature. It's Jesus, we're told, who holds the universe together by the Word of His power, not just the power of His Word. Mountains tremble at the mention of His Name. Death itself trembles. Defeated already, it will one day disappear. Praise be to the One who holds us together and shatters death to pieces!
—CYNTHIA RUCHTI

FAITH STEP: *Are you a clear imprint of Jesus's nature? Or do you need sanding or polishing?*

MONDAY, OCTOBER 5

Make them holy in the truth; your word is truth. John 17:17 (CEB)

As MY HUSBAND DROVE THROUGH heavy traffic on the interstate, I turned to look at the cars behind us. When I turned back around, the side-view mirror caught my eye. Then I looked at the vehicles behind us again. "Well, I'll be!" I exclaimed. "The objects in this mirror are closer than they appear." Through decades of driving, I'd seen those exact words on the mirror without ever stopping to think about what it meant—that the mirror did not give an accurate view of the traffic behind my car. I shuddered to think how my lack of understanding could've easily caused a wreck.

Like that side-view mirror, my eyes often don't give an accurate view of what I see around me. My vision can be clouded by many things—preconceived ideas, fear, sinful attitudes, or the enemy. My emotions are changeable and often deceptive, distorting my perception. What the culture presents as truth has often been twisted and molded to fit a particular bias. How can I be sure I'm getting an accurate view of what's going on around me?

When Jesus referred to God's Word, He didn't use an adjective; He didn't say it was "true." He used a noun, "truth," implying that the Word is the only standard of truth against which everything else must be evaluated. Jesus prayed for the Scriptures to purify His followers, to convict, correct, and guide them.

We need the lens of the Bible to interpret the circumstances of our life as well as current events. As we study the life-changing truth it contains, we learn to see things from a true perspective. But if we depend on our own limited vision and human understanding, we can easily make a wreck of our lives. —DIANNE NEAL MATTHEWS

FAITH STEP: *Ask Jesus to reveal truth to help you see things more clearly.*

TUESDAY, OCTOBER 6

Take my yoke upon you and learn from me, for I am gentle and humble in heart, and you will find rest for your souls. Matthew 11:29 (NIV)

MY HUSBAND IS A FOOTBALL coach and his days are devoted to helping young men develop character even as they learn the ins and outs of the game. One of the things he does is meet regularly with members of the team who aspire to be leaders and discuss what makes someone a good leader. They've talked about "grit," courage, and work ethic. The lesson this week was humility. It seemed to be the hardest one for them so far, and yet it's probably the most important.

It's easy to get confused about what humility is. The football guys wanted to associate it with being quiet and shy, not being competitive, lacking self-confidence. While mental toughness, being brave, and working hard all made sense to them as leaders, humility seemed foreign. It's not what they thought of as a leadership skill.

C. S. Lewis said, "Humility is not thinking less of yourself, but thinking of yourself less." My husband told the players that humility is really just keeping your accomplishments and talent in proper perspective. It's confidence without arrogance. It's being strong enough to lift others up.

Our perfect example in this is Jesus. What kind of God issues the invitation in the verse above? The same God who chose to be born in a barn, work as a carpenter, hang out with prostitutes, and die on a cross. For His followers, humility is not optional. It's the essence of being a Christian. —GWEN FORD FAULKENBERRY

FAITH STEP: *Is humility a word most people associate with Christianity in America? With you? Find a humble way to serve. Help at the food bank. Babysit someone's kids. Clean out your neighbor's flower bed. The options aren't glamorous, but they're endless.*

WEDNESDAY, OCTOBER 7

There is a time for everything, and a season for every activity under the heavens. Ecclesiastes 3:1 (NIV)

WHAT AN AWESOME OPPORTUNITY, I thought as I read a magazine announcing a writing contest. Several winners would be chosen to take classes with well-known authors. What a dream! I started writing as a child to escape my difficult childhood. Later, I'd wanted to pursue writing, but between balancing a family and working, I was unable to take writing classes. I debated whether to enter. Thoughts flooded my mind. *I've entered contests before and wasn't selected. But this time I might win, especially since I've been published. Jesus, please let me be chosen.*

I wrote and rewrote my stories. Following the advice of a wise and talented writer, I "slept" on the stories, and then reread them later. I got feedback. Finally I sent them in.

After the deadline passed, I waited and waited. *Please, Jesus, let me win.* Each day seemed like a week. When the results were finally announced, I wasn't chosen. Disappointed, I decided I wouldn't write anymore. I prayed heartbroken prayers. *Jesus, please take the desire to write from me.* Being rejected hurt too much.

Shortly afterward, I underwent a medical procedure. The healing process took several months. I was still having issues when the writing class started. Looking back, I realize that Jesus's timing was perfect. He knew that I wouldn't be able to attend the class. He knew I would need time to heal. He also knew my heart's desire was to write, and I've resumed writing.

We have hopes and dreams, but we need to remember Jesus has plans for us. He guides us and leads us in the way everlasting. His timing is perfect, every time and in every way. —KATIE MINTER JONES

FAITH STEP: *Ask Jesus to show you His will.*

THURSDAY, OCTOBER 8

Even though I walk through the darkest valley, I will fear no evil, for you are with me; your rod and your staff, they comfort me. Psalm 23:4 (NIV)

FOR WEEKS, I'D BEEN PRAYING for my friend. She was far from home, staying near a university hospital where her son was being treated for a complex and devastating disease. One day she emailed and said, "I could've never imagined that I'd experience this."

Another friend with a disabled child expressed this same feeling. There were still blessings to be found, but her new reality shifted her idea of what day-to-day life would be and required daily adjustments.

Have you ever felt the wave of unreality?

My friends never expected the turns their lives would take. As someone with boundless energy and enthusiasm for life, I likewise never could have imagined I'd find myself in the wasteland of chronic illness that steals so much of my daily function. Yet here we are. The good news is that when we find ourselves in strange places—even the darkest valleys—we discover that Jesus is there too.

He doesn't forsake us. He isn't surprised or bewildered by the unexpected turns our lives have taken. He's still working out His purposes. In Luke 17:20–21 (NIV) Jesus said, "The coming of the kingdom of God is not something that can be observed, nor will people say, 'Here it is,' or 'There it is,' because the kingdom of God is in your midst."

In the difficult places, those we feared, dreaded, or never even imagined, Jesus is supporting us with His love and grace. —SHARON HINCK

FAITH STEP: *What are the darkest valleys you've experienced recently? Ask Jesus to reveal His presence to you and reassure you that He is with you.*

FRIDAY, OCTOBER 9

As you know, it was because of an illness that I first preached the gospel to you, and even though my illness was a trial to you, you did not treat me with contempt or scorn. Instead, you welcomed me as if I were an angel of God, as if I were Christ Jesus himself. Galatians 4:13–14 (NIV)

I AM FEELING SPIRITUALLY BROKEN. I have been sick and tired lately, but that is not the broken part of me. It is that I do not seem to remember how to rest. I do not know how to receive as fully as God is asking me to receive.

I love the picture that Paul paints in the Scripture above—it sounds as if he got so sick that a community had to take care of him, and in that relationship they discovered the good news of Jesus Christ. I know that Jesus may be whispering to me, *Follow me into this fatigue.* Christ can work through me just as powerfully in my weakness as in my strength—maybe even more powerfully!

But I resist it. I am in the habit of *working* for Christ, of doing one thing after another as if the kingdom of God were an infinitely long to-do list with my name on it. I feel lost when my body is telling me that today is a to-be day, not a to-do day. It is such a difficult leap of faith for me to rest! I feel a little sad about this brokenness.

For now, all I can do is recognize when part of me says, "Rest!" and another part says, "Earn it!" And I can ask Jesus to help me in that internal tug of war. I can breathe into the parts of me that need rest and imagine an expanded capacity to receive.
—ELIZABETH BERNE DEGEAR

FAITH STEP: *If getting rest is difficult for you, ask Jesus to help you rest in Him. Receive His peace.*

SATURDAY, OCTOBER 10

When Jesus saw Nathanael approaching, he said of him, "Here truly is an Israelite in whom there is no deceit." "How do you know me?" Nathanael asked. Jesus answered, "I saw you while you were still under the fig tree before Philip called you." John 1:47–48 (NIV)

NATHANAEL MUST HAVE BEEN STARTLED that Jesus was aware of his physical location and situation and even more surprised that He knew the state of his heart. Yet the recognition of all that Jesus knew is what led Nathanael to proclaim Jesus as the Son of God and king of Israel. It can be difficult to absorb the all-knowing nature of our Savior. My little brain has trouble keeping track of my handful of family and friends, and even then I'm not truly aware of every need, longing, or dream in their hearts. Can Jesus really know each of us intimately? Does He really hear our every prayer?

One afternoon, my husband and I drove out into the country, enjoying a brilliant sunny day. As we drove past home after home, I wondered about the people living there. That town house with the swing set in the front yard—did it hold a weary mom who had been up late with a sick toddler? Or that huge mansion with perfectly manicured landscaping—was there an executive inside, weary of the pressures of keeping a business afloat? And that cottage with the peeling paint and crooked gutters—was an elderly widow staring out the screen door wishing someone would visit? Every building hinted at a story.

A sense of wonder filled me as I prayed for the unfamiliar people. I was catching a glimpse, but Jesus knows each story completely. He not only knows every detail, He cares. He is actively working to draw all people to Himself, where they will find the comfort, answers, and strength that they need. —SHARON HINCK

FAITH STEP: *Take a walk or a drive today and pray for the people in each home you see.*

SUNDAY, OCTOBER 11

I was glad when they said unto me, Let us go into the house of the LORD.
Psalm 122:1 (KJV)

SUNDAY MORNING CAME, AND I did not rise singing. I grumbled over my bowl of cereal, when I considered my plight. Saturday had been busy and did not leave me time to finish the laundry, clean the house, buy groceries, or write. My mind was fixed. This Sunday, the dirty clothes, messy house, and grocery list would have to wait. I decided to skip church and make writing my priority due to a pressing deadline that was before me.

My mother called as I sat at my desk and powered on the computer. It was her regular Sunday call and during our brief conversation, she asked, "Are you going to church today?" In that instant, the pointed question made me reconsider why I was staying home.

Didn't I need a sermon, a hymn, and prayer to bolster me in my writing and to encourage me in my housework and other duties throughout the week? Sure I did. And as it says in Hebrews 10:25, I needed to assemble myself with believers. After speaking with my mother, I prepared myself for church, and the day that started with a grumble ended in a spirit of gratitude. I heard a meaningful sermon. I completed my writing assignment after church, and that evening my husband washed and folded our clothes.

What do I know for sure? Worshipping the Lord fuels the heart with energy and inspiration. The joy and embrace of the congregation are encouragement for the soul. Therefore, when we feel overwhelmed, worshipping Jesus should be a first response. —ALICE THOMPSON

FAITH STEP: *Take time today to write a letter or poem that expresses your love and gratitude for our Lord and Savior, Jesus.*

MONDAY, OCTOBER 12

I'm a mess. I'm nothing and have nothing; make something of me.
You can do it; you've got what it takes. Psalm 40:17 (MSG)

I LOVE THE WAY THE Message Bible shares Scripture in unvarnished, often very raw, terms. When I ran across this verse in a recent devotional, I nearly jumped for joy. *Yes!* Arm pump, fist bump, and all that. So often, this verse speaks my heart.

Some days I feel like a genuine mess. I clearly see my failings, the persistent defects, large and small, that simply haven't gone away. But with grace, I no longer let these things paralyze or demoralize me with self-condemnation. In Christ, this verse, and a few familiar others, lead to restful joy. Clinically busy, I sometimes rush through a day in a near panic, snappy, and self-righteous. I ignore my child's request to stop and play, or my own body's cry for rest. Then the shame wells up and I finally stop to pray. Moments later, I get a do-over with my family and with myself.

Even my inspirational writing…I'm in awe of the privilege that I have been given. My mess has become my message, only by His grace, molded by His hands.

Psalm 40:17 foreshadows John 15:5, when Jesus Himself said, "Apart from me you can do nothing" (NIV), and Paul's oft-quoted assertion, direct from our Savior's mouth, "My grace is sufficient for you, for my power is made perfect in weakness" (2 Corinthians 12:9, NIV).

Indeed, in my flesh, I'm a mess. In Christ's robe, I can increasingly recognize and rest in both my progress and pesky defects. In Jesus, I have all I will ever need to accomplish His will.
—ISABELLA YOSUICO

FAITH STEP: *When you're feeling especially aware of some personal messiness, remember Christ in you!*

TUESDAY, OCTOBER 13

These people turn toward me with their mouths, and honor me with lip service while their heart is distant from me, and their fear of me is just a human command that has been memorized. Isaiah 29:13 (CEB)

I'M OFTEN PERPLEXED BY POLLS that ask, "Do you consider yourself a Christian?" For many people, that question is different than if asked, "Are you a Christ follower?"

Not that Jesus pays attention to opinion polls or census results (although a census was a key plot point at the time of His birth. See Luke 2:1–2). But if He did, I can imagine His face when reading the percentage of people who checked the box marked "Christian."

"Hmm. News to Me."

Those who "consider themselves" Christians because it seems the most fitting of the options—who see it as a label rather than a lifestyle, an affiliation rather than a life-altering commitment—may be among those referred to in today's verse.

They "turn" to Jesus the Lord, following Him with their lips only, not their body (heart), mind, soul, and strength. Their reverence for Him is human wording they memorize rather than a heartfelt, "Jesus, I'm all in."

Can you imagine Jesus responding, "I didn't give My life to offer you access to a club or a free trial membership. I conquered death to give you real life. I invite you to follow Me on a wild ride of grace, trials, answers, questions, forgiveness, and hope—exposing you to the merciful heart of God. Come walk with Me into an unimaginable future, and after that, an even more unimaginable eternity"?

Pretty much describes what it's like to follow Him, doesn't it?
—CYNTHIA RUCHTI

FAITH STEP: *Thank Jesus for His invitation to follow Him. Get specific.*

WEDNESDAY, OCTOBER 14

So he got up from the table, took off his robe, wrapped a towel around his waist, and poured water into a basin. Then he began to wash the disciples' feet, drying them with the towel he had around him. John 13:4–5 (NLT)

"LET'S EAT OUT," I SAID to my father. There was a new mall nearby, and I thought taking him there would ward off loneliness and boredom. Even though he hadn't said anything, I knew he missed my mother. He rose from his rocking chair to get dressed and when he came out in a shirt and walking shorts, he returned to his rocking chair and gently asked me to clip his toenails.

I can't recall a time when Papa ever asked me to clip his nails. But when I was younger, he would ask me to pluck the white hairs from his scalp, and I would, though impatiently. But now I kneeled, reached out for his feet, and started trimming each of his tough nails. As I did, I imagined what the disciples' feet must have looked like as Jesus washed them before they ate their last supper together. Surely they were surprised by Jesus's act of humility and servanthood.

I am still stunned by Jesus's display of humility in washing the feet of the disciples. Jesus intentionally performed a task assigned to the lowliest of servants. But His ultimate act of humility and servanthood was dying on the cross. He died a criminal's death to pay for my sins. When I think about Jesus, the Son of God, becoming a human being like me, I am humbled and amazed. He poured out His life for me so that I could live. I bow and worship Jesus for His love and grace. —MARLENE LEGASPI-MUNAR

FAITH STEP: *Jesus set us an example of humility and service to others. He also lives in us today and empowers us to serve others. Choose one person in need and consider how you may serve this person.*

THURSDAY, OCTOBER 15

I in them and you in me, that they may become perfectly one,
so that the world may know that you sent me and loved them
even as you loved me. John 17:23 (ESV)

MY HUSBAND TOOK OUR GRANDSONS for a fishing mini-vacation. As always, they returned with tales to tell. This trip included a misadventure that could have become more than merely frustrating.

Hot day. Bugs were bad. Fishing was too. Rain had raised the level of the small lake. When the fishermen finally called it quits and decided to head for the cabin, trouble intensified. The makeshift boat ramp had lost a bit of its integrity, so the tires of the boat trailer sank deep in mud and threatened to take the car with it.

They unhooked the trailer and pulled the car forward, out of danger. But they had to find a way to pull the boat and trailer free. The rope attached to the bow of the boat wasn't long enough for my husband plus grandsons to maintain solid footing on shore. So they tied two lengths of rope, end to end. The rope broke. Twice. They drove to town, bought more rope, and it, too, broke. Eventually, they wrapped one length of rope around the other to make it stronger. Success. Crisis averted.

"A cord of three strands is not quickly broken," Solomon said in Ecclesiastes 4:12 (AMP). Jesus expressed the same thought in John 17:23, when He spoke to His Father about the power of being intertwined with us for His holy purposes. "I in them," He said of us, "and you in Me," He said of His Father, to prove the strength of His love for us. *Jesus, bind our hearts to You.* —CYNTHIA RUCHTI

FAITH STEP: *If anything about this day or your current life circumstances makes you feel too weak to have any "pull," consider the word picture of Jesus wrapping His strength around you to fortify it for whatever you need.*

FRIDAY, OCTOBER 16

These things I have spoken to you, that my joy may be in you, and that your joy may be full. John 15:11 (ESV)

I SMILED AND ASKED THE customer, "How are you today?"

"Fine," she answered curtly. Her face, however, told a different story. You could see her sadness. The woman was frowning and looked heartbroken. *Maybe she's just having a bad day,* I thought.

She continued to come into the pharmacy about twice a week, but I could never get her to smile, no matter how hard I tried.

"Why is she always sad?" I asked a coworker.

"Something happened that broke her heart and she never got over it," she answered. That evening as I read my Bible, I kept thinking about that lady. *Jesus wants us to be joyful, and she's let something steal her joy.* The joy we receive from Jesus is mentioned throughout the Bible, so I read verses about joy and meditated on the life-giving joy that I wanted for this woman. John 16:22 says, "So with you: Now is your time of grief, but I will see you again and you will rejoice, and no one will take away your joy" (NIV). I started praying that Jesus would restore her joy.

Over the months, she slowly began to change. She began to smile and became more talkative. She even started to laugh again. It was beautiful to see Jesus restore her joy.

Heartbreak is a harsh reality in this world, but Jesus has an abiding joy that He wants to share with us. It is not a momentary, flighty kind of happiness. Jesus has unshakable joy that comes when He resides in us. In His presence? There is fullness of joy.
—KATIE MINTER JONES

FAITH STEP: *Embrace the joy that Jesus has given you.*

SATURDAY, OCTOBER 17

Elijah said to her, "Don't be afraid. Go home and do as you have said. But first make a small loaf of bread for me from what you have and bring it to me, and then make something for yourself and your son. For this is what the LORD, the God of Israel, says: 'The jar of flour will not be used up and the jug of oil will not run dry until the day the LORD sends rain on the land.'"
1 Kings 17:13–14 (NIV)

DO YOU EVER FEEL LIKE you're running on empty? Perhaps like the widow at Zarephath, your cupboards are bare and your bank account is empty. Or perhaps you are exhausted from difficult people, conflicts that never resolve, and daily wounds. You may feel like your emotional resources are mere crumbs of flour. Or maybe illness or injury has worn your body down until you stare at the last drops of oil in the jug and wonder how to guard your meager reserves of strength before you collapse.

Throughout the Gospels, Jesus encourages us to trust Him in a radical way. He calls us to put His kingdom first and serve others before ourselves. His call can seem almost cruel when we feel empty. I've often thought Elijah sounded a bit thoughtless in asking the widow to feed him when she was in such need.

Yet as the woman offered her emptiness and meager resources to God, He met her and then supplied enough for her needs and her son's. Not just that day, but every day of the famine.

We don't have to wear a facade of being something we aren't. We can come to Jesus in honesty about our emptiness and ask Him to be the provider. Then we can follow as He guides us to someone we can serve. And in the beautiful economy of the kingdom, as we meet the needs of others, Jesus meets our needs. —SHARON HINCK

FAITH STEP: *Ask Jesus to bring you someone to serve today.*

SUNDAY, OCTOBER 18

But He was wounded for our transgressions, He was bruised for our iniquities; The chastisement for our peace was upon Him, and by His stripes we are healed. Isaiah 53:5 (NKJV)

I AM NOT COMFORTABLE WITH broken things. It's probably a sign of obsessive-compulsive disorder. But if something gets broken in my house and it is not hidden from me first, my tendency is to throw it away. I hate chipped bowls, plates, and cups. I despise broken toys. I am not a gluer. I have no confidence in things that are "fixed." I know it is only a matter of time before they fall apart again.

My husband, Stone, is the opposite. I am forever finding contraptions holding together objects that he has glued for the kids. "Don't touch it!" he'll say. "It just has to set." It's no small wonder I am bypassed when the dog chews a stuffed animal's eye out or the play toaster gets dropped and the door falls off. One parent's trash is another parent's treasure.

But neither approach works for spiritual things. If I'm in a broken relationship or something's broken in me, the easier thing is to scrap it. Or, like Stone does with toys, fix it. We never think of broken things being usable. They have to be scrapped or fixed.

Except that's the opposite of what God did at the cross. God took what was perfect—His Son—and broke Him, in order to make us whole. Our healing was contained in His brokenness. That's what's useful to God. Not what's perfect. Not even what's fixed. The broken thing. And because He lives in us, our brokenness is the thing that brings healing to others. —GWEN FORD FAULKENBERRY

FAITH STEP: *That thing that broke your heart? The thing you keep struggling with that you wish was fixed? Challenge yourself today to think about it differently, to see it as your thing Jesus wants to use to help someone else.*

MONDAY, OCTOBER 19

Do not be anxious about anything, but in every situation, by prayer and petition, with thanksgiving, present your requests to God, And the peace of God, which transcends all understanding, will guard your hearts and your minds in Christ Jesus. Philippians 4:6–7 (NIV)

OIL AND WATER DON'T MIX; neither do faith and worry.

Years ago, my husband's job was in jeopardy. Clay's company was undergoing reorganization. A third of the workforce was being laid off. He was in line to be laid off next. We had three children and had recently purchased a new home. Worry hung like a dark cloud above us, blocking out the sunlight. We didn't want to live in fear, so we decided to turn our worry over to Jesus and have faith in Him. In return, He filled us with peace and the knowledge that He would sustain us.

Our faith was recently tested again when I decided to retire. Clay and I made this difficult decision after months of prayer. A few days after my retirement, our refrigerator broke. The next week, we had to purchase new tires. Then our home's heating and air system died. Our savings have dwindled some, but we have peace knowing Jesus will meet our needs. Things continue to happen, but we refuse to worry. He has come through for us over and over, most recently by providing writing opportunities for me and overtime work for my husband. We continue to pray and make our needs known to Him, and always thank Him for His blessings. —KATIE MINTER JONES

FAITH STEP: *Memorize Philippians 4:6–7 in the translation you prefer.*

TUESDAY, OCTOBER 20

You have heard that it was said, "Love your neighbor and hate your enemy." But I tell you, love your enemies and pray for those who persecute you, that you may be children of your Father in heaven. Matthew 5:43–45 (NIV)

SHE ENTERED THE ROOM, WAVING. Her personality grated on my nerves. I didn't like her and had no plans to love her.

Sitting down beside me, she smiled. "Can we talk? I trust you."

She wanted to talk to *me*?

Jesus's words slammed into my thoughts, hitting as fast and hard as the stone from David's slingshot. *Love your enemy.*

I lowered my eyes to the floor. When had I come to equate "different" with bad? Why had I focused on our differences instead of our similarities? I hurried to beg Jesus's forgiveness.

Taking a deep breath, I returned her gaze. I continued picking logs from my eyes and asked, "How can I help?" I was suddenly surprised to find I truly wanted to help.

"Well, you're a Christian, right? Where do you go to church?"

Her questions surprised me. Wiping sweaty palms on my pants, I shared information about my place of worship, and what it means to follow Jesus. My heart swelled with purpose.

Pastor and speaker Andy Stanley said it well. "Serving people we don't see eye to eye with is the essence of Christianity. Jesus died for a world with which He didn't see eye to eye."

This lady has since joined my church, and I've moved to a new town. I've learned to love people who are different than I am. And they still ask, "Where do you go to church?"

I tell them where I go to church, but the most important thing I tell them is to go to Him. Go to Jesus. —HEIDI GAUL

FAITH STEP: *Ask Jesus to help you to love others the way He loves them . . . and you.*

WEDNESDAY, OCTOBER 21

Even though you planned evil against me, God planned good to come out of it. Genesis 50:20 (GW)

WHENEVER I READ THE STORY of Joseph's early life, I get caught up in the conflict, emotional tension, and turmoil. But then I sigh when I reach chapter 45 and see a beautiful picture of peace and restored relationships. After Joseph revealed his identity, he assured his brothers that what had happened to him was part of God's plan. Joseph released them from their burden of guilt. Once they recovered from their shock that Joseph was alive, they sat down and talked about how things had changed. The formerly despised brother is now a powerful leader. The guilty brothers are not only forgiven but protected and provided for by the one they had wronged. The aging father still grieving the loss of his beloved son learns he is not only alive, but greatly honored; he'll soon see him again. A family struggling to survive the famine is promised the best Egypt has to offer.

When God takes evil and works good out of it, unbelievable things happen. And it's all because of grace. Joseph's story is thrilling, but the New Testament shows how grace took the form of a human being. Amazing things happened after Jesus came to earth. Broken bodies and broken hearts were healed. Weary souls found hope and a way opened to find forgiveness and eternal life.

I'm convinced that Jesus can take all the broken dreams, strained relationships, and past mistakes in my life and use them for good. I want to grow in trust and obedience so that one day I will look back and say, "How things have changed—all because of grace!"
—DIANNE NEAL MATTHEWS

FAITH STEP: *What problem or situation in your life seems senseless? Ask Jesus to infuse it with His grace and bring good and beauty out of those circumstances.*

THURSDAY, OCTOBER 22

And we know that God causes everything to work together for the good of those who love God and are called according to his purpose for them.
Romans 8:28 (NLT)

SOMETIMES WHEN I'M FACING A difficult situation, I think back to when I started using alcohol to help ease my stress. At eighteen, I used it to escape, to help me relax, and to feel more comfortable when I went out with friends. As time passed, my reliance on alcohol grew into an everyday habit. Maybe you've never struggled with alcohol, but we all have different coping mechanisms. Whether it's overeating, shopping sprees, overusing prescription drugs, spending too much time on social media, or binge watching television shows, we're all looking for a way to cope with life's pain.

Twenty years ago, while pregnant, I stopped drinking for a season, so I wouldn't hurt my baby. But after my daughter stopped nursing, I slowly started drinking wine again. As my marriage crumbled around me I found myself reaching back to my familiar coping mechanism, but this time I knew that only Jesus could help me. One day while crying out to Jesus for strength and direction, I realized that I couldn't pray and be under the influence of alcohol at the same time. I needed to be sober, so I could fight the enemy. I went to the kitchen and poured all the liquor down the drain. And that was that.

Even though my marital distress was painful, Jesus used it to show me a better way to cope with stress—prayer. Prayer wasn't just a momentary fix. It ushered in the connection with Jesus that my broken heart was longing for. —TRACY ELDRIDGE

FAITH STEP: *What coping mechanism can be replaced with prayer and faith in Jesus?*

FRIDAY, OCTOBER 23

Jesus, knowing that the Father had given all things into His hands, and that He had come forth from God and was going back to God, got up from supper, and laid aside His garments; and taking a towel, He girded Himself. Then He poured water into the basin, and began to wash the disciples' feet and to wipe them with the towel with which He was girded.
John 13:3—5 (NASB)

BELIEVERS REGARD THIS SCENE AS one of the most beautiful examples of servant-leadership in the Bible. The Son of God got on His hands and knees to wash the dirty, smelly feet of His disciples. He's giving them His theology in a nutshell. The Son of Man came not to be served but to serve. To give His life as a ransom for all.

We get what He did. But do we understand how? Look back at the beginning of the story. Jesus knew who He was. He was secure in His position: *knowing that the Father had given Him all things... and that He had come from God and was going back to God.*

I saw a picture of this at a basketball game once. A little kid vomited in the middle of the court. It was a thing you wanted to forget. But what followed was something you'd want to remember. The superintendent of the school rose from his seat, grabbed paper towels, walked to center court, and cleaned it up. He was the leader of the school. How could he do a janitor's job? Old-fashioned people couldn't believe it. It was women's work, after all. Where was that kid's mama?

I think the guy did what he did because he was secure in who he was. And knowing who you are in Christ enables you to freely serve others as Jesus did. —GWEN FORD FAULKENBERRY

FAITH STEP: *Do you know who you are? Or whose you are? Do a little Bible search. Write down what it means to belong to Jesus. Post those things on your mirror until they sink into your soul, becoming your identity.*

SATURDAY, OCTOBER 24

Let each of you look not only to his own interests,
but also to the interests of others. Philippians 2:4 (ESV)

ONE SATURDAY MORNING, I WOKE with ambitious goals for the day. Unfortunately illness interfered. I chafed at once again having to adjust my plans. Disappointment made me grumpy. I like the illusion of control over my own life.

My daughter-in-law shared that she can relate. As a mom of three little ones, she may start the day planning to take a shower, fold all the laundry, and work on her Bible-study homework. Instead, one child after another needs her, interrupts her, or undoes her work. She does a great job at adapting and shifting direction, accepting that sometimes we have to let go of our own plans. As we talked about how we've been learning to pivot from our own agendas to serving the ever-changing needs around us, I realized that attitude can be useful as a Christ follower.

Our culture applauds those with strong wills who set their own course and avoid distractions. But the kingdom of Jesus works differently. He calls us to put the needs of others above our own. The person who drops by our desk to chat may have a deep need for encouragement. The driver that cuts us off on the freeway may be in need of prayer that we can lift up on his behalf. Even a sick day in bed that stalls my plans can be an opportunity for me to fellowship with Jesus and learn from Him—a chance to offer praise and to intercede for friends.

As we follow Jesus's example and look to the interests of others, we can find joy in releasing our wish for control and trust His purposes. —SHARON HINCK

FAITH STEP: *Be alert to interruptions today. Instead of getting frustrated by them, see if they are signals that you can meet another person's needs.*

SUNDAY, OCTOBER 25

When Jesus saw his mother there, and the disciple whom he loved standing nearby, he said to her, "Woman, here is your son," and to the disciple, "Here is your mother." From that time on, this disciple took her into his home. John 19:26–27 (NIV)

I'M THANKFUL THAT GOD SPEAKS to me in various ways, especially when I need direction or confirmation. Sometimes I read a Bible passage and the Holy Spirit helps me see its connection to my current situation. Or when I listen to an online sermon as I do my chores, I sense Jesus speaking to me personally.

Such was the case when the preacher I was listening to one morning talked about taking care of aging parents. The preacher mentioned the example of one of Jesus's closest disciples, John. During His last hours on the cross, Jesus entrusted His mother Mary to John. Jesus made sure that His beloved disciple would provide for and protect His beloved mother.

The preacher observed that children may take care of their aging parents, but in return, those who take care of their parents are blessed. In the case of John, he was certainly honored and blessed by Jesus asking him to take care of Mary. I could imagine John and Mary exchanging stories about Jesus and encouraging each other to follow His teaching.

As I listened to the sermon, I felt that Jesus was speaking to me that morning—reminding me that while providing care for my father was tiring, in the process I've experienced Jesus's strength. My love for my father has also increased, and I've been able to express my love for him by keeping him company and serving him—and that's a blessing beyond measure. —MARLENE LEGASPI-MUNAR

FAITH STEP: *Write down the blessings you get from caring for others. Be encouraged.*

MONDAY, OCTOBER 26

"*. . . first of all, then, I urge that supplications, prayers, intercessions, and thanksgivings be made for all men.*" *1 Timothy 2:1* (ESV)

"THE PET SCAN WILL TAKE forty-five minutes to an hour," the radiology technician told me. "The table will go inside the tube and you'll have to lay very still. Do you think you can do it?" I'm claustrophobic, and the PET scan tube looked ominous. I inhaled. "I really don't have a choice," I answered. I'd been diagnosed with cancer, and I needed more tests.

As the table moved inside the tube, I started panicking. *Jesus, please, be with me*, I prayed. Instantly I remembered hearing that if you prayed for others in alphabetical order, you could distract yourself. So I began with the A's and prayed for my friend, Alexis, then my daughter-in-law, Ann, and continued praying through the alphabet. Occasionally, I would forget someone and have to go back a few letters. I prayed sincerely to Jesus for the health and circumstances of my loved ones. While I was inside that tube I focused on the needs of the people who I was praying for and not myself.

"Five more minutes," the technician yelled. *I'm still not finished talking to Jesus!* I thought. I had been so deep in my prayers that the time had passed quickly. I thanked Jesus for being with me during the test and for helping me focus on others. A few days later when I received clear test results, I thanked Him for my good results but also for being given the privilege to pray for others.
—KATIE MINTER JONES

FAITH STEP: *Pray for your loved ones in alphabetical order today.*

TUESDAY, OCTOBER 27

A bruised reed he will not break, and a smoldering wick he will not snuff out.
In faithfulness he will bring forth justice. Isaiah 42:3 (NIV)

TEETERING ON THE EDGE OF burnout, I'd lost my way in a drive to build up an arts ministry. Obstacles, questions, and doubts threatened to push me over the edge. I'd become short-tempered with family and friends. Even worse, I'd begun to question the love of Jesus, since He had led me onto this path. One morning as I sat down to pray about the situation, I found myself pulling away from Jesus. I was ashamed to tell Him the ways I was failing or admit how weak I felt. I'd envisioned myself as a bold warrior for His kingdom. Where had my strong faith gone?

When I stopped pretending I could handle everything on my own, I timidly asked Him for help. Instead of the chiding I expected, Jesus's love and grace washed over me. He reminded me that He knew my tendency to take the reins. In my time of exhaustion and despair, He would help me learn to follow instead. He also knew the wounds of the past that shaped me and offered His words of healing. As I poured out my doubts and confusion, He had compassion on my frailty. He kindled the smoldering wick of faith back into flame. He ultimately led me in a new direction, freeing me from burdens I wasn't meant to carry.

I experienced the truth of this verse in Isaiah. We don't need to be ashamed to come to Him in our weakness. He is tender and patient. When we feel bruised by life, His gentle hand will prop us up. When our enthusiasm grows cold, He will breathe life into the embers of our heart. —SHARON HINCK

FAITH STEP: *Write down a few ways you feel you've failed or are floundering. Dare to bring them to Jesus, knowing that He has compassion.*

WEDNESDAY, OCTOBER 28

A man with leprosy came and knelt in front of Jesus, begging to be healed. "If you are willing, you can heal me and make me clean," he said. Moved with compassion, Jesus reached out and touched him. "I am willing," he said. "Be healed!" Instantly the leprosy disappeared, and the man was healed. Mark 1:40–42 (NLT)

I LOVE READING THE NEW Testament stories about Jesus healing people and how their lives changed on the spot. I also like to read testimonies of people today who receive immediate healing after praying for a miracle. But often, healing is a process, sometimes a long one. Besides physical problems, a broken heart takes time to mend, a ruptured relationship takes time to be restored. But just as in the account of the leper, the first step is always a touch from Jesus. His compassion and power can make the impossible happen.

Since Jesus is no longer physically on the earth, He calls us to be His hands to the hurting. He expects us to feel the same compassion that moved Him to respond to the needs of those around Him. A few encouraging words, a kind gesture, or an offer of practical help might be exactly what's needed to set someone on the road to recovery.

It would be easier if others came directly to us and expressed their need, just as the leper did with Jesus. Unfortunately we often have no idea of how people around us are hurting. Many are reluctant to share their needs; others feel like nobody cares. Thank goodness we have the Holy Spirit to teach and direct us. We can depend on Jesus to prompt us when He wants us to reach out to a hurting soul with the same love and compassion He always demonstrated.
—DIANNE NEAL MATTHEWS

FAITH STEP: *Ask Jesus to show you someone who needs a touch of His love.*

THURSDAY, OCTOBER 29

And though a man might prevail against one who is alone, two will withstand him—a threefold cord is not quickly broken. Ecclesiastes 4:12 (ESV)

SOME WOMEN AT CHURCH WERE talking to a young newlywed couple and reminiscing about when they were first married. "We were so broke! We ate a lot of peanut-butter-and-jelly sandwiches and rarely ate out. We learned to rely on Jesus," one lady said. Another said, "Together we worked hard to get where we are now. It definitely takes two to make a marriage work, and it's not fifty-fifty. Each person has to give one hundred percent." They rehashed stories about silly arguments, growing up together, and the struggles of being newlyweds. "We used to argue about whose cooking was worse," one lady laughed. "Neither of us could cook."

Then one lady said, "It takes three to have a good marriage, the husband, the wife, and Jesus. Each person must give one hundred percent to Jesus and one hundred percent to each other. The Bible says that a cord of three strands is not easily broken. Couples have to walk with Jesus to have a strong marriage."

My husband and I married young and struggled through difficult times, but when we started putting Jesus first, we grew closer and our marriage grew stronger. Now I feel the closest to Clay when we hold hands and pray together, following Jesus's will.

Just like Jesus needs to be the first priority in our lives, He also needs to be the first priority in marriage. His guidance knits together our hearts. His sacrificial love is the perfect reminder of how we need to take care of each other. His presence unites us in purpose and surrounds us with peace. One hundred percent.
—KATIE MINTER JONES

FAITH STEP: *Write your spouse a love letter today and include a prayer.*

FRIDAY, OCTOBER 30

I have told you these things, so that in me you may have peace.
In this world you will have trouble. But take heart! I have overcome
the world. John 16:33 (NIV)

MY DISCOMFORT IN LIFE IS magnified when I think that I shouldn't have certain struggles because I'm a Christian. An unexpected household expense sends me reeling with financial anxiety. My husband's grumpiness triggers the martyr in me. I scream at my kids over something trivial. *Won't I ever change?* Even that thought is extreme.

The reality is, Jesus Himself told us we'd have problems (John 16:33), but the sweet luxury we have as Christians is to choose to bring all our feelings to Christ (2 Corinthians 10:5). We Christians have the same problems as everyone else, but the solution is different: Jesus. With Jesus we can focus on the fact that we have His mind (1 Corinthians 2:16) and His power, love, and self-control (2 Timothy 1:7). Through praise, prayer, and gratitude, we can enjoy rest and peace (Philippians 4:6–7).

Sometimes I remain still enough to tune into the reality that in Jesus, I'm safe and secure. I admit that I often find that peace only when I've reached the end of my rope and my way isn't working. In that moment of failure or disappointment, Jesus is there, as He always is. When I'm in Christ, I realize the work has already been done. I don't have to be afraid. Jesus has overcome the world. I can take heart, find rest, and receive all I need from Him. —ISABELLA YOSUICO

FAITH STEP: *Today, choose to focus on Jesus and His completed work. Receive the grace that you so desperately need and want.*

SATURDAY, OCTOBER 31

*So do not fear, for I am with you; do not be dismayed, for
I am your God. I will strengthen you and help you; I will uphold
you with my righteous right hand. Isaiah 41:10 (NIV)*

MY THREE TEENAGE BOYS ARE constantly trying to talk me into watching scary movies. I will have none of it. I get anxious enough watching the news. There are enough things to be scared about in this world without watching terrifying cinema.

The older I get, the easier it is to give in to fear. *Fear.* Such a small word with such an enormous impact. It fills up the fissures of our hearts and the nooks and crannies of our minds. Fear will take up any and all space that we give it in our lives. I know this because I have battled with it for so long. But the truth is? There is one person who has conquered fear. His name is Jesus, and He has an alternative to living scared. He invites us to live out our lives *with Him...surrounded by His love.* When we crack open the door to Jesus and His love? His love shatters fear. *Love.* Such a small word has such an enormous impact. The more that His love occupies the fissures in our hearts and nooks and crannies of our minds, the less scary life seems. This is because we are not alone. Ever. Jesus will take up any and all space that we give Him in our lives. His words calm the chatter of anxiety and regret. His power emboldens the faintest of heart and gives strength to the weary. His voice thunders out across the universe, "Don't be afraid! Do you hear me? *I am right here!*" —SUSANNA FOTH AUGHTMON

FAITH STEP: *Fear can overwhelm you if you let it. Name your fears out loud to Jesus. Ask Him to show you His love at work in your life.*

SUNDAY, NOVEMBER 1

And the God of all grace, who called you to his eternal glory in Christ, after you have suffered a little while, will himself restore you and make you strong, firm and steadfast. 1 Peter 5:10 (NIV)

I TOOK A DEEP BREATH as I walked up to the podium. I was speaking to a group of alumni at the children's home where I grew up. *Jesus, please help me get through this speech without crying.* As I looked at the audience, my mind went totally blank. But despite my fear, Jesus gave me the words to speak: "I never thought I would be standing here speaking. Many of us have different memories of growing up here. Our relationship with Jesus affected who we've become. Some of us are survivors, others are victims."

My childhood was extremely difficult. My parents separated before I was born and gave me up when I was an infant. I was shuffled between relatives, foster homes, and a children's home. When I was grown, I finally realized Jesus had always been with me and He put good people in my life to guide me. Jesus used the obstacles of my childhood to make me stronger. Now I cherish my own family because of the love I missed growing up. Jesus restored me and has transformed me into a determined and compassionate person. He blessed me with the talent of writing to help others. Over time, my walk with Jesus has grown more intimate, and I thank Him for His love and grace.

The tragedies of our past can paralyze us. We're victims of our circumstances, but Jesus wants to take those obstacles and struggles and use them for His glory. Because of the deep, restorative love of Jesus and His grace, we can move beyond painful memories. Jesus brings hope and healing to the deepest wounds of our hearts. —KATIE MINTER JONES

FAITH STEP: *Whatever you've experienced, believe that Jesus loves you and will restore you.*

MONDAY, NOVEMBER 2

Jesus got up and ordered the wind and the waves to be quiet. The wind stopped, and everything was calm. Mark 4:39 (CEV)

IT WAS COLD AND FOGGY that first week of November in Germany. I was visiting my aunt and uncle, and they were eager to give me a tour of the popular spots. They wanted me to experience a Rhine River cruise, but cruises were suspended because of the fog. My aunt and uncle decided we would take the train from Frankfurt to Mainz and then transfer to another train going to Koblenz.

"Let's try our luck and see if the fog vanishes," my uncle said. If it did, there would be a chance for us to get an amazing view of the river from the train. I had seen photos of the wonderful scenes along the Rhine River. I wanted to see the castles and vineyards along the mountain slopes, as well as the legendary rock on the bank of the Middle Rhine called Lorelei.

Silently I prayed, "Lord, visiting this place is a once-in-a-lifetime experience for me. I want to see the river. Please make the fog go away." In a few minutes, the fog disappeared, clearing the area and revealing the castles as we passed by the river. I was even able to take a snapshot of Lorelei!

My uncle kept saying that I was lucky that day. But I said, "I was blessed." When I requested Jesus to allow me to see the river, He dispersed the fog. I felt His love and pleasure in that moment. Oh, how gracious of Him to let me see His beautiful creation!
—MARLENE LEGASPI-MUNAR

FAITH STEP: *Are there forces of nature or man-made situations that are hindering you? Acknowledge that Jesus is sovereign over all things and ask Him to intervene.*

TUESDAY, NOVEMBER 3

A great windstorm arose, and the waves beat into the boat, so that the boat was already being swamped. But [Jesus] was in the stern, asleep on the cushion; and they woke him up and said to him, "Teacher, do you not care that we are perishing?" He woke up and rebuked the wind, and said to the sea, "Peace! Be still!" Mark 4:37–39 (NRSV)

THESE DAYS WE'RE ALL BEING swamped by media storms that threaten to flood us with overstimulation and anxiety.

Friends accuse me of hiding my head in the sand because I avoid these media storms. They say some version of what the disciples squawked to Jesus: "Do you not care that we are perishing?" But I'm not hiding; I'm following Jesus. I'm following Him to the stern—the most protected, most comfortable part of the boat.

Every day I find a place where I'm not bombarded. I say, "Yes!" to simple spiritual comforts that help me ward off the anxiety swirling around me.

How wonderful that Jesus was asleep on a cushion! By choosing to move to the back of the boat and lie down, Jesus positioned himself to minimize the storm's impact on His experience. And by lying on a cushion, He was taking care of Himself even further: adding a layer of comfort at a time when there was chaos surrounding Him.

So what's my proverbial cushion? It may be a ten-minute walk in a local garden or a spontaneous dance party with my family. By following Jesus in this practical way, my reality shifts, and I know that Jesus is with me, saying to the storms of today, "Peace! Be still!"

—ELIZABETH BERNE DEGEAR

FAITH STEP: *Next time you feel your world is in peril, ask Jesus to show you how to find the stern and the cushion in your daily life.*

WEDNESDAY, NOVEMBER 4

The LORD replied, "My Presence will go with you, and I will give you rest."
Exodus 33:14 (NIV)

LATELY I HAVE BEEN HAVING some sleeping issues. I keep waking up during the wee morning hours, long before I need to get up for work. My mind starts racing. I worry. I problem-solve. I toss and turn. And finally, exhausted, I get up. The other morning, I woke up at four o'clock, hearing the garbage truck rumbling down our street. Realizing we had forgotten to take out the recycling, I climbed out of bed, pulling on the first pair of shoes I could find. I headed out the door and grabbed the giant recycling can. Tiptoeing down our path to the street, I misjudged my footing, and rolled my ankle. Badly. One second, I was taking out the garbage...the next I was lying in our wood chips and lavender, gazing up at the stars. I thought, *I should have stayed in bed.* I should have.

Rest can be an elusive thing. The stress of family dynamics can keep us up at night. Financial difficulties and pressures at work can rob us of our peace. But when we let our worries overtake us, it rarely ends well. We end up exhausted...sometimes laid out in the lavender bush. We need rest in order to function and to heal. In those anxious moments, when we can't seem to find peace of mind or rest in body, we can turn to Jesus. When we give Him our worries, we can find rest. Jesus is with us. He cares for us body, mind, and spirit. He makes us lie down in green pastures. He leads us beside still waters. He restores our souls. —SUSANNA FOTH AUGHTMON

FAITH STEP: *Take a moment to close your eyes, knowing Jesus is there with you. Share your worries with Him. Know that He will take care of them and restore your soul.*

THURSDAY, NOVEMBER 5

Christ has freed us so that we may enjoy the benefits of freedom. Therefore, be firm in this freedom, and don't become slaves again. Galatians 5:1 (GW)

I DON'T ALWAYS AGREE WITH the decisions and policies that our government officials enact. I'm not always pleased with the results of our elections. But that doesn't mean I don't appreciate the wonderful privilege of living in the United States. We enjoy liberties that people in many other countries long for but have never known in their lifetime. Despite our nation's shortcomings and problems, we have much to celebrate.

In New Testament times, the nation of Israel was ruled by Rome. The people suffered from tyranny and unfair treatment. As the promised Messiah, Jesus did not set Israel free from oppression, which confused many of His followers. He did, however, set Mary Magdalene free from evil spirits. He freed the woman at the well from guilt over a shameful past. He freed a man roaming a graveyard from mental illness. He set countless people free from blindness, paralysis, and all sorts of infirmities. He even set Lazarus and a few others free from the grave. But He didn't stop there.

Most importantly, Jesus died on the cross and rose again to set us free from the penalty of our sins. We no longer have to live under the tyranny of harmful habits and destructive behaviors. We don't have to be in bondage to ungodly temptations.

Our human nature will keep fighting to drag us back into slavery to sin. But with help from Jesus, we can choose to draw from His divine power to live a life that pleases Him and brings us joy and purpose. And that is certainly worth celebrating every single day.
—DIANNE NEAL MATTHEWS

FAITH STEP: *Take a few moments to prayerfully examine your life. What is it that you need Jesus to set you free from?*

FRIDAY, NOVEMBER 6

The LORD our God said to us at Horeb, "You have stayed long enough at this mountain." Deuteronomy 1:6 (NIV)

WE MOVED INTO OUR HOUSE and lived in it for three years without painting a room or replacing the worn carpet. My husband, Mick, was busy selling real estate, and I was busy writing and promoting books. One day while a friend visited our home, she glanced at the floor and blurted out, "You need new carpet!"

My friend was right, but I was taken aback by her remark.

When she left my home, I studied the worn carpet and our walls that needed new paint. I made note of our bathrooms that needed new countertops and updated light fixtures. How many more months or years would we go on procrastinating and accepting this drab "landscape," which was not Jesus's best for us? Within a week, I purchased new carpet and called a painter. A carpenter installed new countertops for the kitchen and bathrooms. Within the year, we purchased new furniture and original artwork and the house was transformed into a refreshing oasis for living, loving, and communing with the Lord.

Sometimes we grow so content in a situation that Jesus has to send something analogous to a thunderbolt to rattle us. The Gospel of John says that the truth will set us free (John 8:32). My friend shone light on a truth that moved me to rise and make change for the better. Take note and don't be offended when someone speaks a true word that pricks your heart. Heed their message and leave your wilderness. Walk gladly into your promised land. —ALICE THOMPSON

FAITH STEP: *Is Jesus urging you to address something? Do it today.*

SATURDAY, NOVEMBER 7

A man's mind plans his way [as he journeys through life], But the LORD directs his steps and establishes them. Proverbs 16:9 (AMP)

RECENTLY I HAD TO MAKE a difficult career decision. I wanted to make sure I wasn't stepping out of the will of God by trying to escape an arduous assignment for something easier. I prayed, asking Jesus to make the decision for me. Shortly after praying that prayer, I found out that is not how Jesus operates. The choice was mine. But I wanted to make sure I was making the right choice. I didn't want be thrown into chaos all over again. I was also comfortable in my current position. Was I afraid to leave my familiar surroundings?

After much prayer, I decided to stay in my current position. Again I sought the guidance of Jesus, asking Him to close the door on the other option if I was making the right decision. But Jesus kept the other door open, and I continued to vacillate between the two choices. I wanted to choose correctly.

Midprocess, I began to realize that I can make plans, but ultimately Jesus is the One who will direct my path if I trust in Him. Regardless of our decisions in some areas of our lives, Jesus will have His way. When we seek His guidance, He will determine the direction of our steps and authenticate our decisions, assuring us that we are on the right course. After much back and forth, I chose to make the career move. I know I will miss the familiar surroundings, but I am confident that Jesus is directing my steps. Even though I am uncertain about what I will face, I believe it'll be a good career decision. I know that Jesus is leading the way.—TRACY ELDRIDGE

FAITH STEP: *When making potentially life-changing decisions, go to Jesus in prayer for guidance. "Lean not on your own understanding; In all your ways acknowledge Him, And He shall direct your paths" (Proverbs 3:5–6, NKJV).*

SUNDAY, NOVEMBER 8

By the seventh day God had finished the work he had been doing; so on the seventh day he rested from all his work. Then God blessed the seventh day and made it holy, because on it he rested from all the work of creating that he had done. Genesis 2:2–3 (NIV)

YESTERDAY, AT THE FUNERAL OF a member of our church, I heard these verses from our Bible in an entirely new way. Kathy—whose funeral it was—was known to all of us because every Easter she would read the story of the seven days of creation. Kathy was blind, and for close to two decades she would proclaim this story on Holy Saturday. She read it in braille, as the congregation sat listening in semidarkness from the pews.

At her funeral, we had a bit of a shock: as we settled in to hear the first reading, we were greeted by Kathy's voice, clear as day, proclaiming to us, "In the beginning God created the heavens and the earth…" (Genesis 1:1, NIV). Apparently the pastor had recorded Kathy last Easter, so we got to hear this story in her voice one last, beautiful, memorable time.

As we listened, teary-eyed, the end of the story opened up a new understanding in my heart. God's "resting from all the work of creating" was death—in this case Kathy's death. She had come to the end of her days, and now she could rest in God. This rest was something blessed, something holy. I experienced Kathy's death as a space in which all the holy creativity of her life could come to fruition and be celebrated. I felt Jesus embrace Kathy in the arms of His resurrection, once again changing my perception of death into holy victory. —ELIZABETH BERNE DEGEAR

FAITH STEP: *Is there a loss you are mourning? Ask Jesus to show you the ways in which this loss is a necessary rest from the work of creation. Ask Jesus to bless you in your loss.*

MONDAY, NOVEMBER 9

And Jesus stopped and said, "Call him." And they called the blind man, saying to him, "Take heart. Get up; he is calling you." And throwing off his cloak, he sprang up and came to Jesus. Mark 10:49–50 (ESV)

AT MY DESK, I JOTTED down a list to organize my work. Scenes waited to be critiqued for my writing group. Chapter fifteen of my work-in-progress novel languished as I figured out the next twist in the story. I needed to write a summary letter for a client whose manuscript I'd edited. And a slew of new emails clamored for a response.

When Jesus led me into these various projects, I'd had a clear sense of His calling. But surveying the pending work, my shoulders sagged under the weight. I wanted to hand my list back to Him. Have you ever lost sight of the value or purpose in your efforts?

Work can sometimes cloud our vision. As we tackle each task before us, we may lose sight of Jesus in the midst. We may stagger under yet another sink of dirty dishes, a volunteer session reading to squirming children at a local library, or a committee meeting at church. An office job may trigger headaches and stress. A cashier job can make our feet throb. Yet we are in these places because we've heard Jesus call us to follow Him and serve Him. Each new day, He calls us anew. Like blind Bartimaeus in today's Scripture, we can respond with fresh enthusiasm. He threw off his cloak, sprang up, and came to Jesus. What if we remembered to hear Jesus's voice as we tackle our work today? We can recall the joy we felt when He first invited us to serve Him in this way. We can ask Him to lift the scales from our eyes, so we can see the value and purpose again. — SHARON HINCK

FAITH STEP: *Today, let's ask Jesus to open our eyes so that we can see Him in the midst of even the most tedious work. Let's respond to Him with joy.*

TUESDAY, NOVEMBER 10

Who, though he was in the form of God, did not count equality with God a thing to be grasped, but emptied himself, by taking the form of a servant, being born in the likeness of men. Philippians 2:6–7 (ESV)

MARINES, NAVY SEALs, GREEN BERETS…when I think of them, I see heroic, ultrafit freedom fighters. They're parachuting into the dark to rescue captives and conquer enemies, working as a finely tuned unit as comrades in arms. I'm not an aggressive, physical sort myself, but I love the idea. Recruiting commercials promote this image with rousing music and compelling narration. Inspiring imaginings aside, these elite forces are in fact at the front lines of any battle or mission.

To be in this select group, men and women must endure a grueling initiation that weeds out all but the most committed. The soldier is torn down and learns to submit to authority, growing stronger in the process. The result is a soldier who's fearless, fierce, focused, dedicated to the brethren, and ready to serve.

You see where I'm headed. I don't want to be sheared and seared like these elite fighters, but I can testify that it's the Lord's spiritual surgery and fire that refines me for maximum usefulness. I don't like it, but I can't argue with results. Failure has led to greater humility. Fear has given way to deeper faith. Hard-heartedness has been transformed into tender love.

Just as Jesus became nothing to be glorified, so we too are being transformed from glory to glory (2 Corinthians 3:18) by His loving hand—through the fire, in the fire, and by the fire.
—ISABELLA YOSUICO

FAITH STEP: *Take a moment to mindfully reflect on what characteristics Jesus is cultivating in you to conform you to His likeness (Romans 8:29).*

VETERANS DAY, WEDNESDAY, NOVEMBER 11

When my father and my mother forsake me, then the LORD will take me up.
Psalm 27:10 (KJV)

MY FATHER ABANDONED OUR FAMILY when I was in grade school. Mother and I returned home from church one Sunday to find his clothes gone. As a child, I was angry with my father. As an adult, I offered him compassion and forgiveness. He was a Vietnam War veteran who had witnessed death on the battlefield. He had returned from war with ripped limbs and a body riddled with shrapnel wounds.

Church folks sing "Nobody Knows the Trouble I've Seen." I don't know what my father saw in war or just how deeply the experience left him broken. In his absence, I know that my mother and I lived a quiet life filled with love. And without my father's salary, the two of us learned to lean on Jesus as our provider. As a child, I understood completely when Mother and I prayed, "Our Father which art in heaven..." (Matthew 6:9, KJV). When my biological father did not provide for us, our heavenly Father stretched my mother's earnings in miraculous ways. She paid our bills on time, managed our suburban home, and paid my way through college.

The Bible says, "I was young and now I am old, yet I have never seen the righteous forsaken or their children begging bread" (Psalm 37:25, NIV). This is a true word that still applies to us today. When you have no mother, father, or friend to be your provision or help, Jesus can be trusted to keep you. He will be your water in a desert. He will be your light in the dark. I know this from experience. Jesus kept my mother and me in the middle of our trying times. —ALICE THOMPSON

FAITH STEP: *Ask Jesus to help you release and forgive those relatives and friends who have hurt you in the past.*

THURSDAY, NOVEMBER 12

But Peter and John replied, "Which is right in God's eyes: to listen to you, or to him? You be the judges! As for us, we cannot help speaking about what we have seen and heard." Acts 4:19–20 (NIV)

I LOVE THIS VERSE BECAUSE Peter and John are essentially saying, "We can't help ourselves. You'll just have to excuse us. Or kill us or put us in prison or whatever. But we're not going to hush about Jesus; we can't."

I can see them holding up their arms. They don't really understand it either. Just yesterday, they were selling fish. Now they're running around preaching and proclaiming a revolution—a religion no one's ever heard of before—the idea that love plus nothing saves you. You don't have to be Jewish. You don't have to be a good person. You don't have to go to church or sacrifice your lambs or offer your firstfruits. Just let yourself be loved.

That's what happened to them. They let Jesus love them. When Peter doubted, sinking under the waves...loved. When he had to be rebuked for his pride and ignorance...loved. Even when he denied he knew Jesus, Peter was still loved, still given more chances. He was still a valuable part of the team. Always.

This is an irresistible message. When we have an encounter with Jesus—really see and hear Him—we are changed, because love like this changes things. Truth like this sets us free. May we never deny it, never back down, never give up. May we never be able to help ourselves but keep on sharing Him with others.
—GWEN FORD FAULKENBERRY

FAITH STEP: *Think about what a difference having a relationship with Jesus has made in your life. Write a letter thanking Him for all He means to you.*

FRIDAY, NOVEMBER 13

By this all will know that you are My disciples, if you have love for one another. John 13:35 (NKJV)

IT'S TEMPTING TO THINK THERE'S more to the Christian life than loving people. That there's more advanced theology in it than that. It's difficult to understand. More complicated. More confusing. That it's something we have to study more and argue about and defend. A set of rules to follow. I think all of this is because really, deep down, we'd like to get around it. Love is fun when it's easy, but the rest of the time, it's hard, and it's the hard kind of love Jesus is talking about here. If people are going to recognize us as His disciples by our love, that means they'll see that we love as He loves. That's how they'll know we belong to Him.

The most obvious picture of Jesus's love is the cross—where He gave up His rights and willingly laid down His life to save the world. It cost Him everything. Love doesn't get any harder than that.

Other times we see His love in the form of compassion, guiding and caring for people and meeting every need, like sheep. When crowds are hungry He feeds them. When people come to Him for healing, he never turns anyone away.

Sometimes Jesus loves people by telling truths they don't want to hear. As He did with the Pharisees, Peter, and Nicodemus. One time Jesus showed His love by crying. He wept with those who wept.

There's no one formula for love, just an example for us to follow. And we can only do that by keeping our eyes on Him.
—GWEN FORD FAULKENBERRY

FAITH STEP: *Write a thank-you note to someone who's shown you true love—the love of Jesus.*

SATURDAY, NOVEMBER 14

Jesus answered: "Watch out that no one deceives you. For many will come in my name, claiming, 'I am the Messiah,' and will deceive many."
Matthew 24:4–5 *(NIV)*

LAST WEEKEND, MY HUSBAND AND I hiked a small section of the Superior Hiking Trail in northern Minnesota. It was late autumn, so the maple forests had already shed their leaves, which added a new challenge to our hike. The underbrush had died, and the surrounding land was coated with the same carpet of leaves, so everything looked like a path.

When we live in a culture where so many claim to have answers for us, it can be difficult to discern the true path. The deceptions come not only from false religions or obvious cult leaders who claim to be a messiah. Many systems of thought can "come in His name," claiming to be compatible with the way of Jesus, even when they are not. Pursuing material wealth, chasing fame, elevating human wisdom as god—all are common temptations, even within our own churches.

Just as the volunteers who maintain the trail system have provided signs to guide us, Jesus has provided us with His Word in Scripture, so we can test each message we hear. He's also placed us within His body, the church, so we can practice discernment in community. He also nudges us in the right direction through His indwelling Holy Spirit.

Because of these gifts, we can journey without fear. Psalm 16:11 tells us, "You make known to me the path of life; you will fill me with joy in your presence, with eternal pleasures at your right hand" (NIV). As we seek His guidance, Jesus will steer us away from deceit and pitfalls. He will lead us forward on the path of serving Him with our lives. —SHARON HINCK

FAITH STEP: *Take a walk or hike and thank Jesus for how He guides you away from dangers in your journey through life.*

SUNDAY, NOVEMBER 15

After six days Jesus took with him Peter, James and John the brother of James, and led them up a high mountain by themselves. Matthew 17:1 (NIV)

GOOD FRIENDS ARE LIKE YOUR favorite pairs of shoes. You love them all. However, some friends are suited to walk through hailstorms and rain, while other friends are only suited for sunshine and clear skies.

Dee, Lynn, Katrina, and Yvette are good friends who stand with me at all times. Dee stood by me as I grieved my father's death. Lynn gifted me with a collection of writing books to help hone my writing when I could not land a publishing contract. Katrina called me every day to tell corny jokes and speak positive words when I suffered a grim season of depression. Yvette is my childhood friend who never disconnected as we both traversed rocky terrains from elementary school to our adult lives. Yvette is also my friend who studies the Bible voraciously. In her company, when I call the names Obadiah, Zephaniah, or Haggai, no amplification is needed.

Jesus had twelve friends—the disciples. Of the twelve, Peter, James, and John were in His inner circle, and as they proved their devotion during persecution and peril, Jesus gave His three friends a foretaste of heaven. He revealed His shining glory to them on the Mount of Transfiguration.

Jesus now calls us "friends" in John 15:15. Our personal relationship with Him gives us access to His glory, peace, and eternal life. As for our earthly friends, while they supply us with support until heaven is our permanent home, we can be sure that our friends are heaven-sent. Jesus has given us earthly friends so that we never walk alone. —ALICE THOMPSON

FAITH STEP: *Share your care and appreciation for a beloved friend. Write her a thank-you note expressing your gratitude for her friendship.*

MONDAY, NOVEMBER 16

So do not worry, saying, "What shall we eat?" or "What shall we drink?" or "What shall we wear?" For the pagans run after all these things, and your heavenly Father knows that you need them. But seek first his kingdom and his righteousness, and all these things will be given to you as well. Therefore do not worry about tomorrow, for tomorrow will worry about itself. Each day has enough trouble of its own. Matthew 6:31–34 (NIV)

AS I WRITE THIS, MY treasured business's future is uncertain, my freelance writing jobs are intermittent, and we're struggling to make ends meet. Why wouldn't I worry? Yet Jesus said simply, "Don't." In this verse, Jesus pointed out a long list of commonsense reasons not to worry.

I'm putting this to the test in a very practical way as I seek Jesus's direction on my vocation. I'm struggling to keep an open mind and follow where He leads. I'm taking one day at a time, trying hard to ignore my bank balance. Circumstances are forcing me to lean on Jesus more than ever.

Having faith doesn't mean doing nothing, but rather *prayerfully* doing what I can today and recognizing what I cannot do. When I let go, trust God, and am obedient, life becomes far more serene.

Jesus has used this situation to teach me priceless lessons about Him, His provision, His sufficiency, and His faithfulness. I'm learning to stay in the present day, entrusting uncertainties to Christ.

Even with some fine examples of God's care, Jesus is really pointing to blind faith. Underlying all the reasons we shouldn't worry...is simple trust. —ISABELLA YOSUICO

FAITH STEP: *If you're facing a big challenge of any kind, bring it to Jesus and ask what you can do today. Then ask Him to help you let it go until tomorrow.*

TUESDAY, NOVEMBER 17

Who Himself bore our sins in His own body on the tree, that we, having died to sins, might live for righteousness—by whose stripes you were healed.
1 Peter 2:24 (NKJV)

JESUS'S HEALING POWER IS REAL! I'm reminded of that every time I see commercials for fibromyalgia medication. Years ago, I was diagnosed with that disorder which causes pain in the muscles and bones. Fibromyalgia also caused me to have insomnia, irritable bowel syndrome, and extreme fatigue. The pain was so debilitating I was forced to leave my job where I was required to lift heavy packages.

While waiting in the doctor's office one day, I picked up a Christian magazine. Some of the articles were written by people with various illnesses who were thanking Jesus for entrusting them with the burden of chronic pain. I shared what I read with my ex-mother-in-law and she encouraged me instead to find healing Scriptures and pray them back to God, asking Him to heal me. I began quoting healing Scriptures every day. The worse the pain, the louder I cried out, "I am healed by the stripes of Jesus!"

About six months later, I drove several hours to see my terminally ill uncle. Normally a trip of that sort would leave me in crippling pain, but I didn't have any pain. The next day, I was still pain free. I rejoiced, realizing that Jesus had healed me! Almost thirty years later, I'm still walking in that healing. Although God does not answer every prayer for healing with a yes, His healing power is still at work today—I'm a living testimony. —TRACY ELDRIDGE

FAITH STEP: *Identify healing Scriptures in the Bible. Quote them daily and pray to the Great Physician for healing from your pain or illness.*

WEDNESDAY, NOVEMBER 18

While Jesus was here on earth, he offered prayers and pleadings, with a loud cry and tears, to the one who could deliver him out of death. And God heard his prayers because of his reverence for God. Even though Jesus was God's Son, he learned obedience from the things he suffered.
Hebrews 5:7–8 (NLT)

MY DAD HAD ALREADY BEEN diagnosed with congestive heart failure and had suffered two massive strokes when his doctor diagnosed him with advanced prostate cancer and lung fibrosis.

I lived nearly a thousand miles from my parents for most of my adulthood. I visited them whenever possible, but it never seemed enough, especially when Dad was so sick. As the end approached, I prayed and pleaded for the privilege of sitting with him when he entered Jesus's presence.

God said *no*.

I was teaching at a string of women's conferences in Eastern Europe when Dad died. I wasn't able to attend his funeral. I felt like my prayers and pleadings had gone unheard—until I remembered Jesus's situation.

Jesus prayed and pleaded to avoid the cross, but God said *no*. He accepted God's answer even though He knew it meant suffering.

I chose to follow Jesus's example. I hurt deeply, but He comforted me because He'd walked a similar path.

Have you been praying and crying for God to change your circumstances? How will you respond if He says *no*? I encourage you to follow Jesus's example. Accept His answer and your circumstances. You won't avoid pain, but you'll certainly avoid regrets. —GRACE FOX

FAITH STEP: *Write a description of a circumstance you'd like Jesus to change, then add a prayer of surrender.*

THURSDAY, NOVEMBER 19

And as Elijah stood there, the LORD passed by, and a mighty windstorm hit the mountain. It was such a terrible blast that the rocks were torn loose, but the LORD was not in the wind. After the wind there was an earthquake, but the LORD was not in the earthquake. And after the earthquake there was a fire, but the LORD was not in the fire. And after the fire there was the sound of a gentle whisper. 1 Kings 19:11–12 (NLT)

MY HEART SANK AS I neared the bridge that would take me to my medical appointment in the city. Hundreds of cars were backed up as traffic inched along. On top of that, the steady rain had turned into a downpour; I could barely see the lights of the car in front of me. Finally I reached the base of the one-and-a-half mile long bridge that rose a hundred and forty feet in the air. Frequent lightning flashed in my eyes, and thunder assaulted my ears.

It took me a few minutes to realize that the oldies radio station was playing a classic Bob Dylan song, *Like a Rolling Stone*. I hit the power button and said out loud, "I am not on my own and I am not unknown." Then I began to pray to Jesus, the One who had seen me safely across every bridge I've ever encountered. While the thunder and lightning didn't ease up, I noticed them less as I concentrated on the gentle assurance of Christ's presence and the peace it brought to my spirit.

Later, I wondered how often I choose to listen to the negative voices blaring in my ears from the culture around me just because they're the loudest. I promised to become more sensitive to the gentle whisper of Jesus, which I would much rather hear.
—DIANNE NEAL MATTHEWS

FAITH STEP: *Whose voice will you listen to today? When you feel fearful or troubled, ask Jesus to whisper reassurance to your spirit.*

FRIDAY, NOVEMBER 20

Come to me, all you who are weary and burdened, and I will give you rest.
Matthew 11:28 (NIV)

ALONG WITH BEING STILL, REST is a theme Jesus has brought to my attention this past year. (Have you found Jesus is always seeking to teach you something?) The way Jesus's loving intent has come to light is the intersection of my desperate need for rest and a bevy of messengers repeatedly urging me to "rest."

Stillness and rest, I'm finding, are not the same thing but are close cousins. In my case, the call to stillness came first. I had to carve out time to be still to hear and fully understand the invitation to rest.

In my case, rest is not about spending more time relaxing or having fun. It's a state of mind that informs my very being. Rest means that no matter what's going on, I'm trusting Jesus is ordering my steps, solving my problems, providing, refining me—lovingly, completely, and right on time. It mostly feels like going with the flow, enjoying my life.

Yet neither stillness nor rest is passive. They both depend entirely on the intimacy of my relationship with Jesus—a level of intimacy that, as with any relationship, comes only with time, nearness, and attention to Him.

This idea of rest is gradually revolutionizing my life as I lean into it more and more. *Could it have always been this simple? Could I have skipped some of my striving and anxious analyzing and gone straight to rest?* I don't know. Maybe everything has led me here, right on time. —ISABELLA YOSUICO

FAITH STEP: *Consider Christ's invitation to rest in Him. Seek to learn how you can receive Jesus's rest in your current situation.*

SATURDAY, NOVEMBER 21

I have given them the glory that you gave me, that they may be one as we are one—I in them and you in me—so that they may be brought to complete unity. John 17:22–23 (NIV)

I LOVE TO MAKE "KITCHEN SINK" soup. It's made from whatever veggies I find in the refrigerator and some chicken broth. Two things are true about it: it's always delicious, and it never comes out the same.

My world as a believer is like that pot of soup. Most of the time I'm scrambling from one errand to another, and I don't always know what Jesus has planned for me. Just as unexpected ingredients meld together into a delicious meal, I can be surprised at the "who" and "what" He adds into my day. When peace and joy flood those unscheduled moments, I stand in awe of His grace.

My faith life isn't made up solely of church and Bible studies. Though those activities add flavor to my time just as veggies build a tasty broth, they alone don't define me as a Christian. Instead, my trust in Jesus grows stronger as I meet the challenges He's chosen for me.

Jesus is with me every minute, helping me add spice to the lives of others. He knows what ingredients are missing, both in theirs and mine. As I reach out in obedience, He nourishes my soul.
—HEIDI GAUL

FAITH STEP: *Volunteer to serve at a soup kitchen, keeping watch for what and who Jesus adds into your time there. Notice how He feeds your faith as you act in obedience to Him.*

SUNDAY, NOVEMBER 22

Come to me, all you who are weary and burdened, and I will give you rest. Take my yoke upon you and learn from me, for I am gentle and humble in heart, and you will find rest for your souls. Matthew 11:28–29 (NIV)

MANY NIGHTS I'VE HAD TROUBLE sleeping. Even when I'm exhausted and desperate for sleep. When I can't sleep at night, I start tossing and turning, and there's nothing worse than looking at the clock and seeing the hours roll by. Then I start worrying about how I'm going to feel the next day without having had enough sleep. But this isn't how Jesus means for us to live. He longs to give us rest. Jesus doesn't want us to worry. He wants us to talk to Him about our worries. When we pray, we transfer our doubts and fears and worries to the One who can take care of them. Jesus is our endless source of peace and strength.

We need rest physically, emotionally, mentally, and spiritually. Sleep deprivation can lead to various problems. Psalm 4:8 (NIV) encourages us, saying, "In peace I will lie down and sleep, for you alone, LORD, make me dwell in safety." Jesus offers us hope, encouragement, peace, and safety if we reach out to Him and depend on Him. Jesus will give us complete rest for our bodies, minds, and souls. Psalms 23:1–2 (KJV) reminds us that, "The LORD is my shepherd; I shall not want. He maketh me to lie down in green pastures: he leadeth me beside the still waters."

Now when I lie down each night, I pray. Sometimes I am so relaxed when talking to Jesus I fall asleep. But what better way to fall asleep than talking to the One who loves you? —KATIE MINTER JONES

FAITH STEP: *Pray when you climb into bed tonight, giving Jesus your burdens. He will give you peace and rest.*

MONDAY, NOVEMBER 23

*For our dying bodies must be transformed into bodies that will
never die; our mortal bodies must be transformed into immortal bodies.*
1 Corinthians 15:53 *(NLT)*

I SHRIEKED AT THE SIGHT of my first white hair. But mirrors don't lie—there it was, a single strand of white amid my dark hair! At first, I was in a state of denial, because for several years prior people kept telling me I looked younger than my age. But lately the reality checks keep coming in different ways. Along with more gray hair and crow's-feet, I now have to wear reading glasses.

I've accepted the fact that I'm growing old, but I still want to grow old gracefully. I dye my hair, apply moisturizer to my face, and take multivitamins. But I don't spend money on expensive products and procedures that promise a youthful look. Sometimes I make homemade beauty products with ingredients from my kitchen, like coffee body scrub, raw honey facials, or a coconut oil mixture for my hair. But the best beauty secret I have is prayer. I often pray that Jesus will let His glory shine on me and make me radiant. I think it's working!

But I realize that as I advance in years, my body will get more wrinkled and grow weaker. My comfort is in knowing that one day my physical body will be transformed by Jesus into a spiritual body, a glorious body fit for heaven. I cannot imagine what that body is going to look like, but I sure hope it's going to be dye and wrinkle free. —MARLENE LEGASPI-MUNAR

FAITH STEP: *Pay attention to your body's need for healthy food, sleep, rest, prayer, and exercise. Focus on Jesus's promise to renew and sustain you in your old age.*

TUESDAY, NOVEMBER 24

Count it all joy. . . . James 1:2 (ESV)

MY HUSBAND AND I OFTEN create a pro/con list when making an important decision. Is it time to purchase a truck? Should we replace the limping furnace or wait another year? Is it wise to fit a vacation into our schedule and budget?

As it is for many others, the pro/con list helps guide decision-making. Seeing the options laid out visually often makes the choice obvious. One or the other column is more heavily weighted. We pray over the list and come to an informed conclusion.

The pro/con list even helped me understand a Bible verse that can seem like an impossibility. "Count it all joy, my brothers, when you meet trials of various kinds" (James 1:2, ESV). Count a *trial* as a *joy*? I know I'm not the only one who's wrestled with that.

Jesus both mastered and modeled the principle. "Because of the joy awaiting him, he endured the cross, disregarding its shame. Now he is seated in the place of honor beside God's throne" (Hebrews 12:2, NLT). That's how we too can *count* it all joy. We don't ignore how hard it is or pretend it isn't difficult or deny the trial's true nature. It's all there—real and raw and painful. But we mark it in the joy column of the joy/misery, pro/con list. Because by comparison, our "light and momentary troubles are achieving for us an eternal glory that far outweighs them all" (2 Corinthians 4:17, NIV). Pretend it's not pain? No. Do the math. Tally it in the joy column. —CYNTHIA RUCHTI

FAITH STEP: *Take a few moments today to create a joy/misery tally sheet. Intentionally mark what you consider trials in the joy column. Then lay your hand over the list and ask Jesus to help you see it that way every day.*

WEDNESDAY, NOVEMBER 25

*For whosoever shall do the will of my Father which is in heaven,
the same is my brother, and sister, and mother. Matthew 12:50 (KJV)*

MY MATERNAL FAMILY CELEBRATES MOST holidays in my mother's cozy home. When we gather there, her crowded kitchen bustles with twenty guests or more. They go back and forth, passing plates and clinking serving dishes as everyone engages in lively chatter or family stories that never grow old.

Throughout my mother's home, there are happy faces in the crowd who are not kinfolk. Georgie, Carol, Verna, David, and Maxine attend my mother's church. By the world's standards, they are merely our "good friends."

These five friends have gathered in my mother's home for more than thirty years. Their faces are featured prominently in our family photographs. We enjoy their company completely. They vacation with our family and attend our family reunion. They attend our family birthday parties, school graduations, weddings, and funerals. When they are sick, we, like a loving family, come to their aid. When we are sick, they, like a loving family, come to our aid. While they are not blood relatives, we are deeply connected. Our friends love the Lord, and it is the blood of Jesus that makes us kin.

Jesus said in Matthew 12:50 that His family was anybody who lived to do the will of God.

These encouraging words help us know that wherever we travel or reside, we are not alone. Like with Jesus, who found companionship with Mary, Martha, and Lazarus, it is possible for us to share a family connection with friends who live to serve the Lord.
—ALICE THOMPSON

FAITH STEP: *This morning, pray for the friends who are like family.*

THANKSGIVING, THURSDAY, NOVEMBER 26

Give thanks in all circumstances; for this is God's will for you in Christ Jesus. 1 Thessalonians 5:18 (NIV)

I LEFT HOME FOR A college that was three hundred miles away. For a student who never learned to write research papers, that first semester was a disaster. My college composition teacher littered my papers in red ink and gave me failing grades. I wanted to improve, but the professor did not offer me proper writing instructions. Over Thanksgiving break, I packed my dorm room, returned home, and told my mother that I was transferring. I was going to complete my education at the state college in town. Returning home made me feel like a failure—especially when I considered the time and cost of tuition I wasted.

Today, I don't regret that experience. Romans 8:28 says, "All things work together for good to them that love God" (KJV). I understand now that my initial failure in college led me to a local university where the professors took time to teach writing. My new professors paved the way to my publishing career. And upon my graduation, many of them wrote me letters of recommendation for graduate school.

I understand now that the Lord uses our detours and missteps to teach us wisdom. He uses these things to teach us lessons that will help us fulfill the calling on our lives. Nothing trivial or tragic in life is wasted. Each personal foible and feat is a stepping-stone to the Savior's victorious plan. You are reading my words today because failing my first college composition class inspired me to transfer to a school that gave me the tools to write well. I thank Jesus for that. I am grateful indeed. —ALICE THOMPSON

FAITH STEP: *Sit down today and make a list of thirty people and/or events that have blessed your life. Watch your heart bubble over in a spirit of gratitude and praise toward Jesus.*

FRIDAY, NOVEMBER 27

*My God will meet your every need out of his riches in the glory
that is found in Christ Jesus. Philippians 4:19 (CEB)*

JESUS COMPLETELY PROVIDES FOR OUR needs. All of them.

I stumbled over a reminder of that when rushing across campus
during a conference. The terrain made the trek a challenge for my
heart, lungs, legs, and the blister forming on my toe.

As I pulled my wheeled briefcase to the workshop I was about to
teach, I said aloud, "Jesus, I could really use a Band-Aid."

On the sidewalk not three feet in front of me lay a pink Band-Aid.
"Wow. That was quick. But I should have been a little more specific,
I suppose." The Band-Aid—used—was stuck to the concrete.

I told my class the story as an example both of divine provision
and the need to be specific when we pray. From the back of the
room, attendees flung Band-Aids my way like paper airplanes. I
wound up with more than enough to last the week. Jesus had provided in a way that gave me a story to tell and more than a handful
of people to thank.

As the conference drew to a close, I hiked up the last hill to my
room to pack. Guess what I found plastered to the asphalt? Yet
another used Band-Aid. I pictured Jesus winking at me. I could have
chosen half a dozen routes to get back to my room. But that route
held the reminder that He meets all of my needs. In abundance.

The joy of that reminder will "stick" with me for a long time.
And I'm a little more careful about how I word my prayers too.
—CYNTHIA RUCHTI

FAITH STEP: *Have you lost sight of the abundant ways Jesus provides for your
needs? Stick a Band-Aid as a bookmark in your Bible, perhaps at this verse. You
never know when it'll come in handy.*

SATURDAY, NOVEMBER 28

But let patience have its perfect work, that you may be perfect and complete, lacking nothing. James 1:4 (NKJV)

I AM NOT A PATIENT person, but I know that Jesus is working in me every day. Last night, Jesus showed me a single powerful lesson about how patience and excellence are related. My aunt Shirley, who is my fellow church member and the church secretary, is extremely detail-oriented. Last night after our church leadership meeting, Aunt Shirley and I were driving off when she told me to stop the car. She wasn't sure if anyone was left in the building. If no one else was there, she would have to go back and turn on the alarm. I told my aunt that more than likely the hospitality workers were still in the church kitchen on the other side of the building, but my aunt wanted to be sure. Impatiently I screamed in my mind, *Can we just go?*

Aunt Shirley called them and found out they had gone to the store. They were not in the church as I kept trying to make my aunt believe. Instantly Jesus spoke to me, *This is why she has a spirit of excellence.* Sheepishly I exhaled and waited patiently while she went back into the church to turn on the alarm.

It's in everyday moments such as these that Jesus works patience in our lives. He shows us the fruit that can be borne from patience. Jesus is always patient with us as we go through our growing stages in Him. He realizes that we are works in progress. Jesus said in John 15:5 that if we abide in Him, we will bear much fruit. Patience is a fruit that leads to excellence in all things. —TRACY ELDRIDGE

FAITH STEP: *"Let patience have its perfect work."* The word *"perfect"* is synonymous with *"excellent."* When tempted to be impatient in any situation today, remember that excellence is the other side of patience.

SUNDAY, NOVEMBER 29

Jude, a servant of Jesus Christ and brother of James, to those who are called, beloved in God the Father and kept for Jesus Christ: May mercy, peace, and love be multiplied to you. Jude 1:1–2 (ESV)

MY SON AND HIS WIFE were expecting their third child close to Christmas. Big sister and brother seemed excited about the coming baby but a little uneasy about the change the birth would bring. Our five-year-old granddaughter asked her parents if they would love her less once the new baby arrived.

As we gathered around the Advent wreath in the living room, our son helped his daughter with an object lesson. He lit the first candle. "Your mommy and I love each other. This flame is like that love. Then we had you." He lit the second candle. "That didn't take away the light from the first candle, it added more. Then we had your brother." He lit another candle. "Did that take away any love from you? Of course not. Love keeps growing. Now when the new baby comes, we'll all have love for her too, but it will never take away the love we have for you."

My heart swelled as I listened, and memories swirled of my own wedding day, each of our children's births, and now our grandchildren's lives. Yet her question wasn't a silly one. Love is difficult. In our own power, we sometimes do feel depleted, unable to love each person Jesus brings across our path. Our own desires get in the way, our limitations exhaust us, and we need supernatural wisdom to figure out the best way to offer love to each unique person. Only our holy Savior is able to give us unselfish, unfailing, and perceptive relationships with family, friends, and even enemies. As we follow Jesus, He truly multiplies our love. —SHARON HINCK

FAITH STEP: *Light a candle. Ask Jesus to kindle His love in your heart, so that you can share it with others and watch it grow.*

MONDAY, NOVEMBER 30

When he had finished speaking, he said to Simon, "Put out into deep water, and let down the nets for a catch." Simon answered, "Master, we've worked hard all night and haven't caught anything. But because you say so, I will let down the nets." When they had done so, they caught such a large number of fish that their nets began to break. Luke 5:4—6 (NIV)

AFTER TOILING ALL NIGHT WITH nothing to show for it, Peter and his partners had to wash their nets and stretch them out so they wouldn't rot. But after Jesus used Peter's boat as a pulpit while teaching the crowds, He told the experienced fisherman to row out to deep water and lower the nets. This instruction went against Peter's knowledge and training. In the Sea of Galilee, fishermen went out at night in the shallow water.

Peter respectfully expressed doubts about the wisdom of this action, but he did obey Jesus's command. The nets filled with so many fish they began to tear. Peter called his partners for help. The men loaded both boats so full of fish they almost sank (v. 7).

Jesus often asks His followers to do something that flies in the face of logic. He may ask us to change our vocation, end a relationship, move to a new area, make friends with an enemy, or any number of things. We choose between following our natural instincts or human understanding and obeying our Master's words. There are also times when our life events don't seem to make sense at all. We wonder why we should keep on praying, going to church, and studying His Word. We may not see our acts of obedience bring an immediate miracle as Peter did, but it's always the better choice to tell Jesus, "…but because you say so…" —DIANNE NEAL MATTHEWS

FAITH STEP: *Is Jesus prompting you to do something that seems illogical? Ponder all the miracles He performed. Obey whatever He asks of you.*

TUESDAY, DECEMBER 1

To them God has chosen to make known among the Gentiles the glorious riches of this mystery, which is Christ in you, the hope of glory.
Colossians 1:27 (NIV)

I LOVE DECORATING WITH WORDS. Each time I walk by a plaque stamped with an encouraging thought, it gives me a boost. My kitchen wall shouts, Chill…God's Got This. My hallway, hung with a beautiful print of two sparrows perched on either side of a deep red heart, states, We Have Everything We Need. My living room bookcase is topped by four tin letters lit with mini lightbulbs reading…hope. H-O-P-E. It is my favorite word because, mid-chaos, it reminds me that Jesus always brings hope to the table. *Hope.* In Him. And Him alone. The hope of kindness and joy and generosity and miracles. The hope of salvation. For you and me. We are made with the great capacity for hope. Because we are like Jesus, made in His image and tethered in His love. And the craziest part of hope is that Jesus is leaving it up to us to share it with the world.

Christ in you…the hope of glory. He doesn't have another plan. You and me? We are supposed to be getting the job done. In the midst of our own struggles and craziness, with families and work and heartache and bills…we can reach out with…hope. His hope. We are charged to share hope with those around us. Echoing the richness of Jesus's love. Speaking truth and light. Putting an arm around frazzled neighbors. Taking coffee to our mom friends. The hope of Jesus shines out in our actions and words. Let's spread some hope today. —SUSANNA FOTH AUGHTMON

FAITH STEP: *Make a plan to be a hope spreader today…take a cup of coffee to a discouraged coworker, hug your children and tell them how much you love them, or help an elderly neighbor with his or her overgrown yard.*

WEDNESDAY, DECEMBER 2

In the beginning was the Word, and the Word was with God, and the Word was God.... And the Word became flesh and dwelt among us.
John 1:1, 14 (ESV)

ONE THING ABOUT CHRISTIANITY THAT keeps me coming back for more: God with us. It's even what Jesus's name means: "Emmanuel." Who can resist a God who became human to be with us?

What a mind-blowing concept. In my World Literature class, we read all kinds of sacred texts. Some texts use descriptive words about God that are similar to those found in the Bible. There is a plethora of images of a majestic being, a creator, a powerful authority figure. But the similarities end when we get to the idea of Jesus—the Almighty One—who chooses to laugh and cry, feel pain, and get dirt under His fingernails.

Louisa May Alcott said, "I don't want a religion that I put away with my Sunday clothes. I want something to see and feel and live day by day." Jesus also wanted to see and feel and live—to dwell—with us.

What did that look like? It looked like an unwed mother. A family who became refugees. A king on a donkey. It meant that those whom religion rejected could join the party. That no one was unclean. It meant women were special—bringing baby God into the world, being with Him at the cross, the first to see His resurrected body.

And now Jesus dwells in us. We are His body. He uses our ears to listen, our eyes to see, our mouths to speak. He touches and heals with our hands. He walks through the world on our feet.
—GWEN FORD FAULKENBERRY

FAITH STEP: *Today spend extra time abiding in Jesus.*

THURSDAY, DECEMBER 3

Then Jesus went around teaching from village to village. Calling the Twelve to him, he began to send them out two by two. Mark 6:6–7 (NIV)

TWO COUPLES I KNOW RECENTLY went on a cruise. It was the first time the four of them had traveled together. My girlfriends, one of whom turns eighty this year, were laughing when they told me about it. Their favorite part of the trip was that they each had someone to go with them to explore the various ports of call. The guys laughed too when they told me *their* favorite part: having a buddy to back them up in their decision to hang around on the boat and do nothing for a few hours.

My husband and I have a similar dynamic: my idea of wasted time is his idea of a good time. And my urge for adventure often sounds to him a little too much like work. I've been wondering, is Jesus saying to Tony, *Follow me to the couch so we can watch some football*? When I try to drag him away from his man cave, am I pulling him away from an experience that may be his way of recharging his batteries?

As I continue to grow in faith and experience, I believe I am better able to discern when Jesus says to me, *Follow me*. And it rarely, if ever, means sitting around watching TV. But I'm not sure I can apply that wisdom when it comes to understanding my husband's relationship with Jesus. I guess that's where I need to trust Jesus *and* trust Tony. I need to trust the "personal" part of the phrase "my personal Savior." Jesus's relationship with each one of us is as unique as we are. He sends us forth two by two but honors how we each find Him through different experiences. —ELIZABETH BERNE DEGEAR

FAITH STEP: *Is there some activity that is sacred or meaningful to you that your spouse or best friend does not enjoy? Ask Jesus to connect you with someone who will enjoy it with you.*

FRIDAY, DECEMBER 4

One day Jesus told his disciples a story to show that they should always pray and never give up. Luke 18:1 (NLT)

I'VE ALWAYS BEEN A STORYTELLER. As a child, I would make up stories to tell my friends, sometimes cobbling together a makeshift costume with dramatic flair. As a mom, I've told and retold my kids tales reflecting their interests at the time: trains, dinosaurs, basketball. I even immortalized one by typing it up and may someday publish it. I'm sure my storytelling skills are partly inspired by the many outstanding books I've read, but as with everything, I recognize my ability as a gift from the best Storyteller ever. Jesus.

Sometimes, before I tell a story, the outline is delivered to my mind in a flash, start to finish. Other times, I'll begin with a simple prompt and am as curious as my kids are about where the story will lead as I tell it. It's unfathomable to ponder that the Alpha and Omega knows every little bit of *every* story from before time and sees precisely where it's heading. Every character, every plot twist, every single scene. He's the third-person Narrator who sees it all. What's more, He is present in every scene, the hovering Director, ready to offer guidance if I ask.

As I look at my life, I can see a spiritual narrative, how Jesus took my garbled, imperfect words and with the loving, blood-red pen of grace, folds every detail into the rich adventure my life has been. I don't know what the next chapter holds, and though I earnestly seek His will to write my story, only He knows where it's headed. He's trustworthy. —ISABELLA YOSUICO

FAITH STEP: *Draft an outline of your life story on a single sheet of paper. What has happened according to your plan? How has Jesus shaped your story?*

SATURDAY, DECEMBER 5

*She will give birth to a son, and you are to give him the name Jesus,
because he will save his people from their sins. Matthew 1:21 (NIV)*

WE'D SPENT THE MORNING UNPACKING holiday decorations and hanging them on the tree. As I stepped back to view the finished product, memories warmed me from the inside out. My husband and I exchanged smiles. It was time to set up the crèche—our favorite way to welcome Christmas. Our nativity is extensive, made up of close to thirty pieces. One by one, we unwrapped the white porcelain forms, placing them in a rough arrangement. We had more than half of the boxes emptied when I began to worry.

I didn't see the container holding baby Jesus anywhere. I pushed the collector's boxes back and forth, searching. "Where's the Holy Child?" Panic tinged my voice. My husband pointed to a coffee table where he'd set the piece aside. I blinked and took a deep breath. It was as if I'd been jostled awake, thoughts crowding my mind and emotions.

What if God hadn't decided to redeem us? What if an obedient virgin hadn't accepted the terrible and marvelous honor of motherhood? And most important, what if there hadn't been a baby Jesus? I shuddered.

But Jesus was with God in the beginning and will be with us forever, to the end of the age. My soul finds peace in that promise. For today, I gaze at this tiny figurine that represents our Lord's humble entry into the chaos of our world. Once again, I experience the wonder of a second chance, the vast and eternal hope represented in His birth. And I sigh.

I know how the story ends—happily ever after—for every believer. And I offer a prayer of thanks. —HEIDI GAUL

FAITH STEP: *Spend a few minutes today thinking about what your life would be like if Jesus had never been born. Invite someone over for coffee and give thanks in celebration.*

SUNDAY, DECEMBER 6

---

*For to us a child is born, to us a son is given, and the government will be
on his shoulders. And he will be called Wonderful Counselor, Mighty God,
Everlasting Father, Prince of Peace. Isaiah 9:6 (NIV)*

THE CHRISTMAS TREE IS DECORATED, and stockings are hung. Carols
waft through the air, joining the scent of holiday baking to create a
sense of home and love. And giving.

Every year, I look forward to this season. I enjoy selecting presents
that speak to the loved ones in my life, letting them know how
much they mean to me. The gratitude I see in their eyes is priceless.
And when I give something that's especially dear to me, it makes the
moment even more precious.

This Christmas, hidden among the pile of boxes and bags beneath
the tree is a tiny package for my daughter. It's a gold ring set with
a semiprecious stone I gave my mother long ago. Mom wore it for
special occasions until she went to be with Jesus. It's time for me to
invite my daughter into the circle of love this bit of jewelry represents. I know she'll cry. I will too.

Long ago, God considered me and my hopeless situation. He
saw past my sin and knew exactly what I needed. Surrendering this
baby, His Son, would hurt Him more than I can imagine. But He
did it, so I could enter their circle of love.

Through Jesus, He gave us eternal life and life abundant. It's a
gift. Open it. And try not to cry. —HEIDI GAUL

FAITH STEP: *Remember the Gift you were given. What special item can you let
go of to welcome someone into your circle of love? If it's a gift, wrap it. If they're
words, speak them.*

MONDAY, DECEMBER 7

And there were shepherds living out in the fields nearby,
keeping watch over their flocks at night. Luke 2:8 (NIV)

THE STORY OF THE SHEPHERDS leaving their sheep to go see Jesus fascinates me. Who were these men that an angel of the Lord spoke the Good News to them? They were poor, dirty, and probably unremarkable, at least to society. But they knew how to watch and listen and protect—they were sheepherders, after all.

Yet these simple men possessed a powerful sense of discernment. When those triumphant words announcing Jesus's birth rang out, they knew to trust in that truth. They were terrified but didn't run or hide. They listened, accepted the responsibility of the knowledge, and then acted on their beliefs. They departed so quickly they left their flocks, their livelihood, behind. And when they'd seen our infant Lord, they spread the word (Luke 2:17).

Sometimes, when Jesus speaks to me, I'm only half listening. Or I convince myself that He asked something different of me, something convenient or more in line with my will. And when at last I submit to His choices, the dawdling begins. I conclude He isn't the type of Lord who'd want me to serve impulsively. And He'd never demand me to abandon my other projects.

But He is and He does. He knows what's best for me, even if I'm slow to admit it. I pray to be more like those shepherds. When God honored them with His sacred announcement, they stepped past their fears and believed. And in living out their obedience, they were rewarded with witnessing the glory of Christ.

The next time Jesus calls, may I be ready, watching, and listening.
—HEIDI GAUL

FAITH STEP: *How is Jesus calling you to move beyond your fears?*

Tuesday, December 8

Study to shew thyself approved unto God, a workman that needeth not to be ashamed, rightly dividing the word of truth. 2 Timothy 2:15 (KJV)

I READ THE BIBLE EACH morning. God's Word supplies me with wisdom and encouragement throughout my day. For a time, I understood Bible reading as a ritual that only fortified my spiritual growth; a personal pursuit that benefited only me. But I learned otherwise when a friend called me in a panic: her daughter, a recent college graduate, wanted to travel around the world for a year.

I asked Jesus to give me a Scripture of encouragement. Proverbs 22:6 bubbled up in my soul, and I shared it. The Message Bible translation says, "Point your kids in the right direction—when they're old they won't be lost."

I reminded my friend that she had raised her child under the banner of Christ and in the admonition of the Lord. As a new college graduate, the young woman was surely prone to making immature choices. However, the Word promised that in due season, the child would return to her parents' wise instruction.

"Be encouraged!" I reminded my friend that her daughter loved Jesus and in Him, the future was secure. My friend thanked me for the gift of Proverbs 22:6. And in that moment, I thanked Jesus for saturating my heart with His right Word at the right time. I have come to understand that the Bible is refreshing like "living water." While it quenches my spiritual thirst, it helps me offer refreshment to others too. —ALICE THOMPSON

FAITH STEP: *Today during your morning devotion time, memorize a Bible verse to share with friends in their time of need.*

WEDNESDAY, DECEMBER 9

... that Christ may dwell in your hearts through faith; that you, being rooted and grounded in love, may be able to comprehend with all the saints what is the width and length and depth and height—to know the love of Christ which passes knowledge; that you may be filled with all the fullness of God. Ephesians 3:17–19 (NKJV)

IN THE 1980S, I WAS a FedEx courier, and I would listen to cassettes in my truck as I drove. One of my favorite groups is Take 6, and during the Christmas season I would play their *He is Christmas* cassette. I didn't have a relationship with Jesus at the time.

One day while I was driving my van and listening to the cassette, "Sweet Little Jesus Boy" started to play. I sang along to the lyrics as I always did, but this time, as I sang the words about Jesus being born to save me, tears started streaming down my cheeks. I felt a rush of love that I never knew existed. I was driving in the middle of nowhere, delivering packages, and a song that I'd sung so many times before suddenly affected me in the most wonderful and unexpected way.

That day was the beginning of the greatest love relationship of my life—my relationship with Jesus Christ, my Lord and Savior. My blinded eyes were opened to the true miracle and reason for the birth of the sweet Little Jesus Boy. Whenever I think back on that thrilling life-changing event, I am reminded of the amazing "width and length and depth and height" of love that Jesus has for all of us. He wants to draw us to His love and let us know He is our loving Savior who gave His life to save me and you! —TRACY ELDRIDGE

FAITH STEP: *This season think back to the time Jesus opened your eyes and heart to the realization of who He is and the love He has for you. Then remember the reason for the season—Jesus was born to save us!*

THURSDAY, DECEMBER 10

When Jesus saw her weeping, and the Jews who had come along with her also weeping, he was deeply moved in spirit and troubled. "Where have you laid him?" he asked. "Come and see, Lord," they replied. Jesus wept. John 11:33–35 (NIV)

MY FRIEND CALLED ME WITH terrible news. Her husband's test results were back, and he had cancer. After I found my voice, I told her how sorry I was. I struggled to find words of encouragement and comfort, feeling useless in the face of the frightening issues she was facing. I could reaffirm what she already knew—that Jesus loved her and would walk this hard road with her. But I longed to offer more. I wanted to be the "hero friend" who had the perfect thing to say to make things better.

When we aren't sure how to support our friends who are hurting, we can follow Jesus's lead. He always responded to pain with profound love and compassion. As He arrived at Lazarus's funeral, He manifested that compassion in several ways. He gave the gift of His presence. He showed interest and involvement. And He joined in the pain, weeping with those who wept. Jesus, the all-knowing God of the universe, knew that He was about to call Lazarus forth from the grave. Yet first He cried with the mourners, sharing their sorrow.

A sense of helplessness can tempt us to avoid reaching out, avoid engaging with those who need support. But if we follow Jesus's lead, we're emboldened. We're tenderhearted and enter in to the pain of our friends. We listen and let our friends know we care. We stand alongside them so they aren't alone. And the best support we have to offer is approaching our Savior, asking Him to see the need and trusting Him to respond. —SHARON HINCK

FAITH STEP: *Choose a friend who is hurting. Find a way to be present for her and show her the compassion of Jesus.*

FRIDAY, DECEMBER 11

When he has brought out all his own, he goes on ahead of them,
and his sheep follow him because they know his voice. John 10:4 (NIV)

SINCE MOVING TO FLORIDA, I'VE relied on my phone's navigation app more than ever. Yet even with a watchful satellite and Siri's smooth-toned guidance, I can get really turned around. Throw in a detour or side trip and getting where I'm headed becomes even more complicated. Thank God for...um...grace? Stay with me.

Visiting a new friend's house for coffee recently, I was distracted by my own thoughts and took a wrong turn. Siri patiently redirected. A few turns later there was a detour, so I took another uncharted turn. Again, Siri quickly and calmly rerouted me. No shaming tone. No exasperated correction. Just a gentle course correction. Moments later, I pulled into my friend's driveway safe and sound, right on time. Jesus immediately came to mind.

I've taken a few wrong turns in my life, made some misguided choices. Sometimes I relied on my own feelings and desires rather than trusting Jesus and the navigation offered in the Bible. Had I checked the "road map" of Scripture and Jesus's Spirit before taking off or even when I first got disoriented, I might have gone the right way sooner, saving myself time and grief. Other times, I've found myself off track because of someone else's poor "directions" or choices or even just a random, unforeseen event.

Still, my gracious Navigator lovingly seeks even one wandering sheep and patiently reroutes, gently guiding me where He intended all along, without condemnation. —ISABELLA YOSUICO

FAITH STEP: *Think of the life events or choices that seemed like detours at the time. Consider how Jesus actually used your detours to get you someplace better than you'd planned yourself.*

SATURDAY, DECEMBER 12

The King will reply, "Truly I tell you, whatever you did for one of the least of these brothers and sisters of mine, you did for me." Matthew 25:40 (NIV)

A FEW YEARS AGO, I was invited to a Christmas party with a group of women who were in a Bible study together. The women were mostly young married professionals, mothers, and all friends except for one new person. Her husband was disabled, and she didn't work outside the home. She'd shared some of their troubles—financial, physical, and emotional—with the group. We were surprised she made it to the party. And although it was meant for adults only, she had brought along her toddler because she didn't have a sitter.

At the gift exchange, I cringed at the woman's gift. It seemed naked and exposed in a discount store shopping bag, knotted at the top, and placed among extravagant, glittered boxes and bags with giant bows from specialty stores. In my angsty way, I began to feel sick about how the "Santa" game might play out.

But I needn't have worried. As the gifts were selected, a striking woman in heels and skinny jeans stepped forward to claim the newcomer's sack. She picked it—out of all the other gifts. I held my breath as she pulled out a fuzzy blanket imprinted with the head of a tiger. I thought it was the most hideous blanket I'd ever seen. But this elegant lady wrapped it around herself like a shawl. "I love animal prints! This is so perfect!"

I caught the other woman beaming, and I had to blink back tears. The woman at the well, the blind beggar, and the children in the Bible all must have beamed the same way. What else can you do when you experience Jesus's love? —GWEN FORD FAULKENBERRY

FAITH STEP: *Today, show love to someone others may overlook or ignore.*

SUNDAY, DECEMBER 13

For we are God's masterpiece. He has created us anew in Christ Jesus, so we can do the good things he planned for us long ago. Ephesians 2:10 (NLT)

IT'S A HUMBLING REALIZATION TO know that I'm God's masterpiece made new in Jesus. Ephesians 2:10 also makes me think about the good things He planned for me long ago. Am I doing those good things? Does it mean "good things" in my career, or "good things" in my relationships, or "good things" in the works that I do? After wrestling with these questions I'm pretty sure it means "good things" in all areas of my life.

Years ago, after watching news story after news story about young people committing crimes almost on a daily basis, I fell to my knees and asked Jesus how I could make a difference in our community. The answer came to me in a dream—teach. I was surprised. I never wanted to teach because I'd have to be with children all day!

But Jesus walked me through the process of becoming a teacher, and now I am a teacher. But there are days when I feel ineffective, and many times I still pray, asking Jesus if teaching is the "good thing" that He planned for me. But my mother, with her educator wisdom, assures me that even if just one child is helped, a teacher has made a difference. So I continue doing good things.

As God's masterpieces made anew in Christ, we have an assurance that Jesus will help us do those good things that He planned for us long ago even when we face challenges along the way. He will continue to shape us into the masterpieces that He created us to be. —TRACY ELDRIDGE

FAITH STEP: *Ask yourself if you are doing the "good things" that God planned for you long ago. If you're not, ask Jesus to show you what you need to do to start doing those "good things."*

MONDAY, DECEMBER 14

You call me "Teacher" and "Lord," and you are right, because that's what I am. And since I, the Lord and Teacher, have washed your feet, you ought to wash each other's feet. I have given you an example to follow. Do as I have done to you. John 13:13—15 (NLT)

THE DOORBELL RANG AT 10:00 a.m. Monday. I'd been busy for four hours already, unpacking boxes after moving over the weekend, and I knew many hours of work lay ahead. The thought of entertaining an unexpected guest held no appeal.

My lack of enthusiasm for company changed to delight when I opened the door and saw Larry, my Sunday school teacher, standing there. He grinned. "I'm at your service," he said. "I read your Facebook post about unpacking, and I thought you could use some help. Put me to work."

Besides his willingness to lend a hand, Larry brought gifts—a pair of rubber gloves for cleaning, and a roasted chicken. "I figured you might be able to use this for dinner tonight," he said as he handed me the bird.

Larry spent two hours washing dusty light fixtures that day. Then he assembled a set of storage drawers before other duties called him away. "I see you have another set of drawers to assemble," he said before he left. "Let me take those with me. I'll work on them tonight and bring them over tomorrow."

Jesus stooped before His disciples and washed their feet. Larry stooped and washed my light fixtures, assembled drawers, and brought me a roasted chicken. He modeled Jesus and taught me what true servant leadership looks like. —GRACE FOX

FAITH STEP: *Ask Jesus to show you who needs a foot washing, so to speak. Resolve to bless that person with an enthusiastic servant's heart and a practical act of kindness.*

TUESDAY, DECEMBER 15

For by one sacrifice he has made perfect forever those who are being made holy. Hebrews 10:14 (NIV)

SINCE I AM ALWAYS CHASING perfection, I key in on verses like this one that we're discussing in Sunday school. I begin to imagine myself with no blemishes, no cellulite, and good hair. In my magazine-cover daydream, I am a Pulitzer Prize–winner/supermodel/world-class pianist who never yells at her kids and never fights with her husband. I always make my parents happy. Students beg to be in my classes. I'm not afraid of anything, and I have no regrets.

Of course, this is not what the writer was talking about, the Sunday school teacher reminds us. *What a buzzkill.* The Hebrew word for perfect is more like "complete." We are made *complete* in Him. So, whatever is lacking in us is provided in Jesus. We live in wholeness, not scarcity, not living a partial life. I begin to wrap my head around this when I notice the last part of the verse. We're being made holy.

My goal is perfection. It's how we're graded in school; the goal is 100 percent. Doctors and charts tell us our optimum weight. Judges at music competitions give us "superior" ratings when we get everything right. There's only one winner in a spelling bee—the one who never misses a word. One team gets the state-championship trophy. It's the way the world works.

But it's not how Jesus works. His goal for us is not perfection. It's growth. First, He makes us complete; that's a onetime thing that happened on the cross and is good forever. Then our life is a process of being made holy. Not working for holiness, not reaching perfection. *Being made.* By the work He does in us day by day.
—GWEN FORD FAULKENBERRY

FAITH STEP: *Commit Colossians 2:9–10 to memory. It's light for your every step.*

WEDNESDAY, DECEMBER 16

There is salvation in no one else! Under all heaven there is no other name for men to call upon to save them. Acts 4:12 (TLB)

AFTER SEVENTEEN YEARS AS A Christian, I'm still looking for a savior. No, not a savior of the spiritual variety. Someone to bail me out, clean up my mess, tell me what to do. Not mere help. Rescue. At times, I've cast my husband, a friend, or a family member in this role, straining our bonds. Other times, I've sought someone else—for pay or for pity. Or some codependent fixer finds me. Over and over, my spirits are buoyed with the false hope of salvation from whatever or whomever. I think, *Finally a rescuer! Now I can let go!* Inevitably the miscast messiah disappoints. I bail. They bail. The problem remains.

In John 16:7, Jesus tells us He's sending the Holy Spirit, an advocate or helper, among other roles. Isaiah 9:6 (NLT) tells us God was graciously giving us His Son, a "Wonderful Counselor, Mighty God, Everlasting Father, Prince of Peace." Read that again. In other words, the ultimate "life" management consultant: A perfect, all-knowing, loving, and stable Dad, all-powerful yet serene. Wow. While Jesus urges us to seek wise counsel, we were never meant to seek substitute saviors. Indeed, it's the number-one sin in the Ten Commandments.

Even while I seek the caring counsel of loving friends, there is One who ultimately has all the answers and comfort I want. Jesus: the Savior who forgives even my misguided idolatries. When I seek Him, I find the One that I have always been looking for. He is the One who holds the universe in His hands and placed the stars in the sky. Jesus alone is able to bring the hope and salvation we all truly need. —ISABELLA YOSUICO

FAITH STEP: *Today, carry all your cares to your perfect personal Advocate and Counselor, the only Savior you will ever need. Jesus.*

THURSDAY, DECEMBER 17

For I can do everything God asks me to with the help of Christ who gives me the strength and power. Philippians 4:13 (TLB)

WHENEVER I VISIT MY MOM, I love it when I can attend Sunday services with her. The minute I walk into the small country church, memories flood my mind. On the last visit, I remembered the time I sang a special duet with the only other girl my age in the congregation. Elaine and I both wore homemade white summer dresses with sky-blue sashes around our waists.

I don't recall what we sang, but I clearly remember what happened after service. When I walked by, the pastor bent down and said, "Why, Dianne, I didn't know you could sing like that!" I hesitated a moment, and as usual, said the first thing that popped into my head: "I didn't either." Everyone burst out laughing as though I'd told a joke. I never did figure out what was so funny.

I've made similar comments to myself over the years after I've followed the Holy Spirit's nudging to take on something that seemed impossible. *I didn't know I could plan our church's Christmas dinner and program... help my husband work on our roof despite my fear of heights... teach a workshop at the women's conference... come up with enough ideas for a one-year devotional book—four times.* And yet I accomplished those things through Christ's power working in me.

Lately I've seen a popular saying on plaques, shirts, and jewelry: "She believed she could, so she did." Personally, I'd like a shirt that reads, "She believed Jesus would help her, so she did."
—DIANNE NEAL MATTHEWS

FAITH STEP: *Do you feel called to do something that seems impossible? Memorize Philippians 4:13 so you can recite it each time doubts arise.*

FRIDAY, DECEMBER 18

Brothers and sisters, we want you to know about those who have died. We don't want you to be sad like other people—those who have no hope. We believe that Jesus died, but we also believe that he rose again. So we believe that God will raise to life through Jesus any who have died and bring them together with him when he comes. 1 Thessalonians 4:13–14 (ERV)

THERE WAS A SPIRIT OF Christmas cheer in the air but one of my friends felt melancholy. It was her first holiday season without her father. She said, "There was traffic everywhere, so I decided to pass the time in Rockwell last night." Rockwell is one of the newest malls in the business district.

"As I walked through the parking lot, I felt a bit sad as I remembered Father and his harmonica." The first shop at the mall entrance was a music store which fed her wistful thinking. "I used to frequent that store in search of a Hohner harmonica for Father. Had he been around, I might have gotten him a harmonica for Christmas."

Anyone who has had a loved one pass away knows what my dear friend felt. I know I do. I miss my aunt and frequently dreamed about her the year following her death. The longing for those we've lost can be so painful that sometimes only a promise of a reunion in heaven can bring comfort. Jesus promised that He will come back for us and reunite us with our departed loved ones who believed in Him. Until then, we will keep cherishing our memories of them and keep holding on to His promise which He will surely soon fulfill. —MARLENE LEGASPI-MUNAR

FAITH STEP: *Turn to God for comfort as you overcome grief. Give yourself time and space to mourn the passing of a loved one, accepting the comfort that Jesus gives.*

354 | Mornings with Jesus 2020

SATURDAY, DECEMBER 19

A virgin shall be with child, and shall bring forth a son, and they shall call his name Emmanuel . . . God with us. Matthew 1:23 (KJV)

MY SISTER, WHO LIVES NEXT door, is a bit of an alarmist. I can't tell you the times she's called me, panicked she's poisoned our children because she found them munching toothpaste, afraid they've been kidnapped only to find them hiding in the closet, or worried because I let them play with balloons or eat hard candy or didn't cut up their grapes tiny enough—all of which, according to her, constitute high-risk choking hazards. The problem is you never know when it could be something serious. What if, for example, one out of the ten times she calls, there actually is an emergency? This question plagued me one Christmas when I was home with two babies in the bathtub.

"Get over here!" Rene was literally crying. "It's Madeline! There's a gash on her head gushing blood! She may need stitches!" I wrapped my kids in a towel and sped the three hundred feet to their house. Madeline, her toddler, answered the door. Brushing back blond bangs from her forehead, she revealed a small bump with an even smaller cut. There was hardly any blood.

"Baby Jesus fell off the shelf and hit Madeline's head!" Rene yelled. I quickly assessed that no stitches were needed, but I asked her why the nativity set was on a high shelf. "She's been playing with the baby Jesus. Chewing on him, banging him on the table. I was afraid he was going to break."

Later I thought about the metaphor this is for our lives. We tend to keep Jesus on a shelf, neat and tidy, a symbol. But He wants to be present with us, accessible. He is never out of reach.
—GWEN FORD FAULKENBERRY

FAITH STEP: *Tell the story of Jesus—God with us—to someone who needs to hear it.*

SUNDAY, DECEMBER 20

Then Jesus said to them, "So wherever you go in the world, tell everyone the Good News." Mark 16:15 (GW)

ONE DECEMBER OUR YOUTH PASTOR paid a visit to a church member who'd been hospitalized. As James neared the patient's room, another door at the far end of the hallway opened and a man rushed out. This man ran down the hall, shouting at the top of his lungs, "She's all right! She's all right!" He stopped in front of James, grabbed his shoulders, and repeated his message. Then he continued shouting.

Pastor James never learned the details of this stranger's situation. But it was obvious the man had good news that he wanted to share with everyone. How appropriate that this scenario played out in December, a season when we celebrate the words of an angel to shepherds announcing that the Savior of the world had been born: "I have good news for you, a message that will fill everyone with joy" (Luke 2:10, GW).

As Jesus ascended back to heaven after His resurrection, He instructed His followers to tell everyone the good news about God's kingdom wherever they went (Mark 16:15). While I often fall short in this area, I've decided that December is the perfect time to improve. I will resist the pressure to try to craft the picture-perfect holiday. Instead I will plan activities, choose gifts, and engage in conversations that point toward Jesus and what His life and death made possible: forgiveness of sins, unconditional love, and eternal life. What better time to share the most wonderful news than the most wonderful time of the year? —DIANNE NEAL MATTHEWS

FAITH STEP: *Why not read the book of Luke over the next couple of weeks and ask Jesus to help you share the Good News?*

MONDAY, DECEMBER 21

Then he said to them, "The Sabbath was made for man,
not man for the Sabbath. Mark 2:27 (NIV)

WE MOVED TO FLORIDA JUST two years ago and it's been impossible to travel to celebrate Christmas with our family up north. Sure, we've had lots of family visits throughout the year, but not at Christmas. It's been kind of hard. And weird. And... unexpectedly liberating.

We used to make the universal (and exhausting) pilgrimage to various loved ones' homes in the days around Christmas, celebrating over and over. These past two years, we've fumbled to create new traditions and have discovered new joy.

Both years, we've visited a nearby nursing home to sing Christmas carols and bring treats. We've spent time with new friends, including those far from family themselves. We've also enjoyed the luxury of not having to do anything at all. Last Christmas Day, we got dressed up for the buffet feast at a local resort, then hung around the pool and watched football. As an avid cook, I thought this seemed especially radical, yet it freed me from the burden of too-high expectations that sometimes overshadow holiday cheer.

While we still miss family, I can't help noticing the unexpected freedom we've discovered. Christmas is the day we celebrate the arrival of our Savior, who liberated us from the bondage of sin and death (Romans 8:2). Christmas, like the Sabbath, is more a state of being than a particular day or activity. In Christ, I do have a radical freedom. I can enjoy that freedom, wherever and whenever.
—ISABELLA YOSUICO

FAITH STEP: *Is this Christmas season different than usual? Or would you like it to be different? Look for the freedom, and enjoy it in Jesus's name.*

TUESDAY, DECEMBER 22

The King will reply, "Truly I tell you, whatever you did for one of the least of these brothers and sisters of mine, you did for me." Matthew 25:40 (NIV)

LIFE WAS FINANCIALLY DIFFICULT FOR our family when we were growing up. My youngest sister remembers a time when she arrived home from school, starving, but found no food anywhere in the house. With nothing to satisfy her hunger, she decided to sleep. She was wakened by a visit from our eldest sister who lived in another part of town. Much to our youngest sibling's delight, our older sister invited her to eat at a nearby noodle house.

Our youngest sister is now working and earning on her own. She often has extra money to treat our parents, nieces, and nephews to lunch or dinner. She remembers how hard it was to be hungry and how her hunger was satisfied through the kindness of a sister. Now she's paying it forward.

During His earthly ministry, Jesus was sensitive to people's physical needs. When His disciples suggested sending away the crowd to buy their own food after listening to Him, Jesus insisted on feeding the weary crowd. On two occasions, Jesus miraculously fed the multitudes by multiplying a few fish and loaves of bread (Matthew 14:13–21; 15:32–39). It's worth noting that although it was Jesus who performed the miracle, He entrusted the task of feeding the hungry to His disciples. Today, we can be that sister, friend, or neighbor through whom Jesus can satisfy someone's hunger.
—MARLENE LEGASPI-MUNAR

FAITH STEP: *Consider donating food to an organization that helps the under-privileged. Volunteer at a soup kitchen or prepare a meal for a sick person. Each time you give people food, you also give them a good reason to thank the Lord.*

WEDNESDAY, DECEMBER 23

But Jesus called the children to him and said, "Let the little children come to me, and do not hinder them, for the kingdom of God belongs to such as these. Truly I tell you, anyone who will not receive the kingdom of God like a little child will never enter it." Luke 18:16–18 (NIV)

EVERY YEAR, JUST FOR FUN, my daughter and son-in-law give me a new toy. I've received water pistols, kaleidoscopes, and paints. These small gifts keep the wonder inside me alive. This year my present was a bottle of bubbles—the kind with a wand you blow through. As I watch those translucent orbs float through the air, I'm able to see my surroundings through the fresh eyes of a child. For a few moments, I regain the ability to look at everything as if for the first time. The thrill of Jesus's creation fills me with a bright perspective.

Jesus loved children. As the creator of all things (John 1:3), He understood their spark of excitement as they encountered new experiences in daily life. The innocence and exuberance kids show over the simplest of pleasures must have delighted Him.

Bringing—and maintaining—this sense of awe in my faith is important to both Jesus and me. To receive His kingdom, I must enter with the trust, hope, and humility of a small child. Revisiting familiar Bible stories with the curiosity of my youth, I find the characters and circumstances coming alive as if I'd never heard them before. New insights bless me.

On days when I feel empty and lost, I run to Jesus and climb into His lap. There's no place safer, nothing more comforting than resting in His care as I pray. I can trust in His love and acceptance today, tomorrow, and always. —HEIDI GAUL

FAITH STEP: *Buy yourself a toy and let it reawaken the child in you. Apply that fresh perspective to your relationship with Jesus. His lap is empty and waiting.*

CHRISTMAS EVE, THURSDAY, DECEMBER 24

Whoever is generous to the poor lends to the LORD,
and he will repay him for his deed. Proverbs 19:17 (ESV)

I WAS VERY POOR GROWING up. I lived in a children's home and also was in foster care. One important lesson I learned from that struggle was to be generous to the less fortunate. Jesus placed compassion in my heart for others who suffer...especially children.

When I was a child I received used and broken toys for Christmas. In the unique way that Jesus does things, I am now in charge of a program that provides underprivileged children with new gifts at Christmas. My husband, Clay and I organize volunteers, set up toy drives, and purchase toys. One lady in our community provides Bibles for the children. High school students have gift drives. Firemen, deputies, and a jolly Santa help deliver the toys, and it's such a blessing to see our community come together to help these beautiful children. Every year before Christmas the other volunteers and I pray Jesus will meet our needs, and He always provides.

Some of the kids' parents feel hopeless when they meet with us, but we minister to them and give them hope. We let them know that we care for them and their children. They are so thankful. And I am so thankful to be able to usher in the joy that I didn't have as a child. The joy I receive from helping these children completely overshadows the bad memories from my childhood.

Acts 20:35 reminds us that it is more blessed to give than receive. Jesus wants us to take care of His kids, both big and little. We can never out-give Jesus, but when we let His generosity pour through us, everyone ends up blessed. —KATIE MINTER JONES

FAITH STEP: *Think of ways you can share your blessings with those who are less fortunate.*

CHRISTMAS DAY, FRIDAY, DECEMBER 25

Just as the Son of Man did not come to be served, but to serve,
and to give his life as a ransom for many. Matthew 20:28 (NIV)

MY AUNT DOT LIVES TO help others. She volunteers her time in nursing homes, supplies toiletries to homeless shelters, and decorates the church for Sunday services. She seldom recruits others to help her. But one Christmas, Aunt Dot decided that our family should band together and use the holiday to feed senior citizens in a local Meals on Wheels program. She contacted all her nieces and nephews via email. And while it was the coldest winter *ever*—everyone participated. We bundled up and hit the road.

My husband and I had just purchased a new sports utility vehicle. It was perfect for transporting the large coolers and insulated bags filled with food. As he drove to several homes, it was my task to hop from the car, knock on the door, and deliver the meals to the seniors on our route.

The December sky was sunny and blue as our family caravan of five cars crisscrossed the city delivering food. When the deliveries were complete, my husband and I reflected on our day as we drove home. With joy in his eyes, he said, "That was so much fun!"

People say often, "It is more blessed to give than receive." After delivering meals to the sick and shut-in, I know this to be a true word. Sharing with others during the holiday filled my heart with joy and goodwill. Diamond rings, fur coats, and exotic flowers did not compare with the gift of serving others. And Aunt Dot's encouragement to join her holiday caravan was the greatest Christmas present I have ever received. Like Jesus during His ministry, my aunt provided an opportunity to serve. —ALICE THOMPSON

FAITH STEP: *In the spirit of Jesus, seek ways to share your abundance of time and resources with others today.*

SATURDAY, DECEMBER 26

. . . Give me an undivided heart, that I may fear your name.
Psalm 86:11 (NIV)

RESTAURANTS ARE SUCH GOOD ENVIRONMENTS for book research . . . and for unintentional eavesdropping, which are sometimes one and the same. My sisters and I enjoyed a rare "all three of us" lunch not long ago.

That day, as we looked at our menus, I overheard the woman at the table behind us tell the waitress, "I'll have a piece of Dutch apple pie . . . and a diet cola."

Decadent dessert . . . and a diet drink. It struck me as funny. And then it didn't.

My heart was quickened by how often I choose a similar combo. I couple my prayer with a complaint. I finish off my expression of gratitude to Jesus with a chaser of a request. I'm in the middle of a serving of worship and find it laced with thoughts of myself, or the music, or the lighting, or something other than Jesus. I take a big bite of peace . . . with a side of worry. I dish up a big ladle of kindness to a friend and an impatient retort to my husband.

The Bible has a lot to say about the double-minded (James 1:8), the waffler (James 1:6), and the mouth that speaks both blessing and cursing (James 3:10). It's making me look more intentionally at the combos I "order" as I follow Jesus. —CYNTHIA RUCHTI

FAITH STEP: *In your efforts to follow Jesus more closely today, stay alert for the incompatibles. Ask for His help in making the best choice.*

SUNDAY, DECEMBER 27

And let us not neglect our meeting together, as some people do, but encourage one another, especially now that the day of his return is drawing near. Hebrews 10:25 (NLT)

NOW, I CAN SEE MORE clearly how my church journey reflects the seasons of my life.

As a new Christian, I found a Bible church with a scholarly pastor who taught Scripture verse by verse, and I faithfully took notes. My husband worked most Sundays, so I immersed myself in Bible-study classes, growing significantly in my Bible knowledge.

Soon after, my first son was born, and my husband stopped working weekends. We were led to a small, local, community-oriented, family-friendly mainline church. The intellectual preacher had a varied spiritual background. The Bible studies were less formal. I taught Sunday school. The Bible lessons were simple but instructive.

Two years ago, we moved to a more populated area offering many good churches. After praying, visiting, waiting, and sensing an unmistakable prompt from the Holy Spirit, we found a new church home. The friendly pastor inspires us with lots of biblical motivational insights for daily life. The church is engaged in our community. Our small group is very intimate and relevant.

In each of these churches, Jesus provided just the right place for us, once again demonstrating His loving attention to needs we could not even fully define. When we obeyed the prompt to assemble, Jesus showed up, just as He promised. —ISABELLA YOSUICO

FAITH STEP: *How does your current faith family reflect your wants and needs? Who has Jesus placed in your life right now to encourage you?*

MONDAY, DECEMBER 28

*Therefore, you also should be prepared, because the Human
One will come at a time you don't know. Matthew 24:44 (CEB)*

IT WASN'T ON MY NUTRITION list for the day, but I ordered a s'mores cappuccino after my fasting blood work. S'mores. I mean, the word on the sign was enough to convince me.

It's been said that the average millennial spends more on coffee annually than he or she puts away for retirement. Sounds shocking, until you stop to think about twentysomethings fifty years ago. They weren't investing in s'mores cappuccinos, but many probably weren't planning for retirement. Those who reached the future without a solid retirement income now live with daily regret.

Jesus often asked His followers to consider the days to come. Matthew 24 and 25 record one long message from Jesus about preparing for the future. He repeatedly encourages us to plan ahead, to stay alert, to ready our hearts, to closely adhere to His teaching, because—in His words—"you don't know the day or the hour" of His return (Matthew 25:13, CEB). Being ready for His return has nothing to do with financial planning or long-range career goals. But it does mean "a long obedience in the same direction" (Friedrich Nietzsche). Or as Solomon put it, "Let us hear the conclusion of the whole matter: Fear God, and keep his commandments: for this is the whole duty of man" (Ecclesiastes 12:13, KJV). Long obedience. Same direction. Unwavering. Intentional. Until. —CYNTHIA RUCHTI

FAITH STEP: *How are you investing in your spiritual bank account for eternity? Not performance, but deposits.*

TUESDAY, DECEMBER 29

But the one who hears and does not do them is like a man who built a house on the ground without a foundation. When the stream broke against it, immediately it fell, and the ruin of that house was great. Luke 6:49 (ESV)

DO YOU EVER HAVE DAYS where life feels like a rollercoaster? Today my granddaughter drew me a picture, and my heart soared. Later someone said something unkind and my spirits slumped. A reader emailed me to tell me they appreciated one of my novels, and I felt joyous fulfillment. Then projects came up, and I felt hassled and stressed. Shifting sand is a good description for my emotions on any given day.

A beloved hymn says, "On Christ, the solid Rock, I stand; all other ground is sinking sand." In Jesus's parable, He compares a man who builds a house on rock to one who builds with no strong foundation. When I build my life on the approval of others or even my own self-esteem, I can structure a fine edifice for a while. But eventually, when rivers of adversity roll against me, that foundation collapses.

What a blessing that Jesus invites us to hear Him, follow Him, and put into practice the things He teaches us. He promises that when the torrent hits us, we will be safe on the solid Rock. Today when moment-by-moment circumstances make the ground feel shaky, instead of trusting in my fluctuating emotions, I want to stand squarely on His love for me. When Jesus told this parable, I wonder if He also reminded the listeners of a psalm that He fulfills. "God is our refuge and strength, a very present help in trouble. Therefore we will not fear though the earth gives way, though the mountains be moved into the heart of the sea" (Psalm 46:1–2, ESV).
—SHARON HINCK

FAITH STEP: *Notice different surfaces today. Bogs, sand, or slippery ice. Thank Jesus for being a solid foundation for our lives.*

WEDNESDAY, DECEMBER 30

And why do you worry about clothes? See how the flowers of the field grow. They do not labor or spin. Yet I tell you that not even Solomon in all his splendor was dressed like one of these. Matthew 6:28–29 (NIV)

I LOVE FASHION. I TEND to overdress for most occasions, and friends tease me that I even like to be coordinated when I run. I think this is a combination of my Italian heritage, my mom's example, a creative temperament, and yes, garden-variety vanity.

If my bankroll permitted, I might just be one of those celebrities with a giant dressing-room closet with neatly, color-coded shelves and racks, and an ever-changing wardrobe. Alas, I don't have that kind of cash but am grateful that my heavenly Daddy loves me and allows me to be richly satisfied with thrift-store finds and discount bargains and dresses I've had for twenty years.

Usually I can indulge my inner fashionista without fretting. I can pull together a fine outfit quickly, accessories and all. Sometimes, though, because of an extra-special occasion or just plain lack of inspiration, I do worry about what to wear. I'll stand in my closet bewildered. I'll try on three outfits and nothing will look right. This is more discouraging than maybe it ought to be, which highlights my unhealthy preoccupation.

Thankfully I have this verse, which I hear with a note of Jesus's loving laughter. "Don't worry about what to wear, honey." He gently chuckles. "Come to me, beautiful. You're perfect!" Jesus isn't checking my makeup or outfit, He's seeing the flawless creation He is fashioning with each passing day. I am robed in Him. —ISABELLA YOSUICO

FAITH STEP: *Next time you can't figure out what to wear, ask Jesus for help to clothe you like the lilies of the field.*

NEW YEAR'S EVE, THURSDAY, DECEMBER 31

And the one who was seated on the throne said, "See, I am making all things new." Revelation 21:5 (NRSV)

MY FAVORITE MOVIE, *ANNE OF Green Gables,* has a great line: "Tomorrow is fresh with no mistakes in it!" Sometimes I share that with my students at the beginning of a new semester. It's a great feeling to start with a clean slate.

Making us new is what Jesus is all about. This is the theme of the Christian story—redemption. Rising from ashes. Over and over again. From His perspective, it doesn't matter what happened in the past year, what mistakes we made or problems we faced. Those things don't define us in His eyes. What matters is the new thing He's doing today.

I'm sure you've seen the caricatures of the old and new year. The year that is ending is always pictured as an old man, stooped, haggard, and tired. On his way out. And the new year comes in like a perfect, shiny baby, with light in his eyes. It's a marvelous metaphor for how Jesus makes us new. He takes the tired, the worn out, the hopeless and defeated, and He breathes new life into us. New strength, new energy, new hope. New life.

Jesus came to give us life to the fullest. That starts the moment we accept Him and begin to share His perspective. He's not looking for perfection. He's looking for someone to grow in Him, becoming more like Him, moment by moment, year by passing year.
—GWEN FORD FAULKENBERRY

FAITH STEP: *Write down and commit to Jesus three areas in which you'd like to grow. Ask Him to make them new.*

ABOUT THE AUTHORS

 SUSANNA FOTH AUGHTMON is an author and humor writer who recently moved to Idaho. She is the mother of three fantastic teenage boys, Jack, Will, and Addison. Susanna is also wife to pastor-writer Scott, who makes her laugh every day. Susanna's books include *Hope Sings* and *Queen of the Universe*. She loves to use Scripture and personal stories as a way of embracing God's grace and truth every day. Susanna often connects with her readers and fellow Christ followers through her blog, Facebook page, and speaking engagements. Find out more about Susanna on her website, www.tiredsupergirl.com.

 DR. ELIZABETH BERNE DEGEAR, BCC, is a chaplain, teacher, and Bible scholar. She has been teaching Bible studies at her local church for many years and also teaches psychology and religion courses to pastoral professionals. As a chaplain, Lizzie offers pastoral care to people in church and hospital settings and provides memorial services for people who have known homelessness during their lives. Lizzie is the author of *For She Has Heard* about the standing stone in the book of Joshua. She has lived in Rhode Island, New Mexico, Alaska, and France, and now makes her home in New York City with her husband and two children.

 TRACY ELDRIDGE is a middle school librarian in Memphis, Tennessee. She graduated from the University of Memphis with a BA in English and an MA Ed from Union University in Jackson, Tennessee. Tracy is an artist who handcrafts prayer journals, wall calendars, and planners with inscriptions from the Holy Word. She has a favorite saying: "When God opens a door of opportunity, believers must open that door and seize the

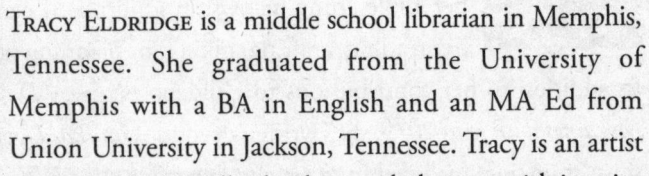

moment, even in the face of fear." Serving God makes way for seasons of miracles and unexpected opportunities.

GWEN FORD FAULKENBERRY is an Ozark hillbilly. Really. That's the mascot of her hometown in the Arkansas mountains where she lives, teaches, writes, runs, plays music, bakes bread, and makes mischief of one kind or another. She's becoming quite a famous author. But you can call her Grace, Harper, Adelaide, and Stella's mom. Or Coach Faulkenberry's wife. That's what she's best known for. And she likes that just fine.

GRACE FOX lives on a forty-eight-foot sailboat moored in Vancouver, British Columbia. She says, "Contrary to popular belief, this is not the fulfillment of a dream. It's a calling that requires perseverance, flexibility, and a sense of humor." Grace and her husband, Gene, celebrate their thirty-eighth anniversary in February 2020. Together they direct International Messengers Canada, a mission organization that serves in twenty-seven countries, including Nepal, Lebanon, Peru, Uganda, Egypt, and Eastern Europe. Grace is the author of nine books and is a contributor to P31's online Bible studies. She enjoys speaking at international women's events, reading, exercising, and spending time with her family—husband, Gene, three grown kids, and nine grandchildren.

HEIDI GAUL lives in Oregon's beautiful Willamette Valley with her husband and furry family. When she's not leading her Bible study fellowship group, you can probably find her reading, crafting, hiking, or planning her next getaway. In addition to her contributions to Guideposts' *Every Day with Jesus* and *Mornings with Jesus 2019*, she's written devotions for *The Upper Room*. Heidi's short stories are included in *Short and Sweet Takes the Fifth* and ten *Chicken Soup for the Soul* anthologies. Connect with her at her Facebook author page or www.heidigaul.com.

 SHARON HINCK has been a youth worker, a choreographer, a church organist, a craft teacher, a speaker, and a teacher. One day she'll figure out what to be when she grows up. Meanwhile she treasures her roles as a wife, mom, grandmother, daughter, and friend. In addition to contributing to *Mornings with Jesus* for many years and doing freelance editing, she is busy writing novels, especially a new fantasy series, The Dancing Realms. She also loves interacting with visitors on her website, www.sharonhinck.com.

 MARLENE LEGASPI-MUNAR is from the Philippines, where she writes, translates, and edits books. Her published books cover marriage, motherhood, and midlife. Marlene enjoys traveling, which led her to write *Traveler's Notebook: Insights from Life's Journey*. She has also contributed to various devotionals, including *Light for the Writer's Soul: 100 Devotions by Global Christian Writers*. Marlene volunteers at a local church where her husband serves as the pastor. She and her husband have two grown-up children whom they love dearly. Visit Marlene's author page at www.facebook.com/Author-MarleneLegaspiMunar.

 KATIE MINTER JONES began writing as a small child. Her stories have been published in *Guideposts*, *Angels on Earth*, *Soul Matters*, *Rainy Day Book*, and several newspapers. She has published a children's book, *Oak Trees and Flowers in Heaven*. Her poetry has been in several publications. Childhood experiences taught her the value of family, the power of forgiveness, and the importance of a relationship with Jesus. Two bouts with cancer awakened Katie to the importance of following one's dreams and cherishing life. Katie lives in Georgia in a town so small it has no red light. She enjoys spending time with her husband, Clay, their three children, their two amazing grandchildren, and several pets. Katie and Clay are active in their community and church.

DIANNE NEAL MATTHEWS has been privileged to share her everyday life and faith journey with *Mornings with Jesus* readers since the 2013 edition. She is the author of four daily devotional books, including *The One Year Women of the Bible* and *Designed for Devotion: A 365-Day Journey from Genesis to Revelation* (a Selah Award winner). Dianne recently collaborated with Ron L. Deal on *Daily Encouragement for the Smart Stepfamily*, and has published hundreds of articles, guest blog posts, and stories for compilation books. She and her husband of forty-five years currently live in southwest Louisiana and have three children and four grandchildren. She loves to connect with readers through her Facebook author page or website, www.diannenealmatthews.com.

CYNTHIA RUCHTI considers her connections with *Mornings with Jesus* readers one of life's great joys. She is the author of more than thirty-two books and compilations, both fiction and nonfiction, and is a literary agent with Books & Such Literary Management. Cynthia is a frequent speaker for women's retreats and events and writers' conferences, and serves on her church's worship team. Her tagline is "I can't unravel. I'm hemmed in Hope." It serves as an overarching theme in her books, in speaking opportunities, and in conversations with those who cross her path. Although she has been known to hike in desert heat, climb rocky trails, ice fish on the Mississippi River, canoe and backpack in the Canadian wilderness, and go rafting on the Colorado River, she is most comfortable with a cup of tea in her hand, a good book by her side, and the quiet of the Wisconsin countryside beyond her window. If only winter were warmer. Last year, she reported having five grandchildren. She's pleased to update that number to six!

ALICE THOMPSON is a teacher and librarian. She writes mostly for young readers under the name Alice Faye Duncan. Her celebrated books include *Memphis, Martin, and the Mountaintop*, *A Song for Gwendolyn Brooks*, and

Honey Baby Sugar Child. Beyond the workday, her time is dedicated to writing. Summer vacations are devoted to art museums, research, and more writing. She lives in the Volunteer State of Tennessee. Jesus is her Lord and Savior. Her mother is her best friend. Her husband is a resounding voice of encouragement. Readers can visit her website, www.alicefayeduncan.com.

 ISABELLA YOSUICO sees the Proverbs 31 woman of the Bible as complex and dynamic, defying common religious stereotypes of Christian womanhood, leaving many of us feeling guilty and inadequate. She longs for us all to live authentically and gracefully as God made us, abiding in His loving acceptance that affirms we are *different by design.* Isabella enjoys frolicking with her family, writing, reading, running, arts and culture, random adventures, deep conversation, the beach, music, and singing. *Mornings with Jesus 2020* is the fourth Guideposts book for which she has written. She's also the author of *Embracing Life: Letting God Determine Your Destiny*, a Bible study aimed at helping women navigate challenging life events. With an MS in public relations and management, Isabella is also an inspirational writer and founding president of MightyTykes, a special-needs-product company inspired by her youngest son, who has Down syndrome. Isabella, her husband, Ray (an artist and addictions counselor), and their two sons, Pierce (the athlete) and Isaac (the minister/musician), live life fully on Florida's suncoast. Connect with Isabella at www.isabellayosuico.com, Instagram, Twitter, www.mightytykes.com, or on Facebook.

SCRIPTURE REFERENCE INDEX

TOPICAL INDEX

A NOTE FROM THE EDITORS

WE HOPE YOU ENJOYED *Mornings with Jesus 2020*, published by the Books and Inspirational Media Division of Guideposts, a nonprofit organization that touches millions of lives every day through products and services that inspire, encourage, help you grow in your faith, and celebrate God's love.

Thank you for making a difference with your purchase of this book, which helps fund our many outreach programs to military personnel, prisons, hospitals, nursing homes, and educational institutions.

We also create many useful and uplifting online resources. Visit Guideposts.org to read true stories of hope and inspiration, access OurPrayer network, sign up for free newsletters, download free e-books, join our Facebook community, and follow our stimulating blogs. To delve more deeply into *Mornings with Jesus,* visit MorningswithJesus.org.

You may purchase the 2021 edition of *Mornings with Jesus* anytime after July 2020. To order, visit Guideposts.org/MorningswithJesus, call (1-800) 932-2145, or write to Guideposts, PO Box 5815, Harlan, Iowa 51593.